Thalaba the Destroyer by F

Robert Southey was born on the 12th of August 1774 in Bristol. A poet of the Romantic school and one of the "Lake Poets".

Although his fame has been eclipsed by that of his friends William Wordsworth and Samuel Taylor Coleridge, Southey's verse was highly influential and he wrote movingly against the horrors and injustice of the slave trade. Among his other classics are Inchcape Rock as well as a number of plays including Wat Tyler.

He was great friends with Coleridge, indeed in 1795, in a plan they soon abandoned, they thought to found a utopian commune-like society, called Pantisocracy, in the wilds of Pennsylvania.

However, that same year, the two friends married sisters Sarah and Edith Fricker. Southey's marriage was successful but Coleridge's was not. In 1810 he abandoned his wife and three children to Southey's care in the Lake District. Although his income was small and those dependent upon him growing in number he continued to write and burnish his reputation with a wider public.

In 1813 on the refusal of Walter Scott he was offered by George II the post of Poet Laureate, a post Southey accepted and kept till his death 30 years later.

Southey was also a prolific letter writer, literary scholar, essay writer, historian and biographer. His biographies included those of John Bunyan, John Wesley, William Cowper, Oliver Cromwell and Horatio Nelson.

He was a renowned scholar of Portuguese and Spanish literature and history, and translated works from those two languages into English and wrote a History of Brazil (part of his planned but un-completed History of Portugal) and a History of the Peninsular War.

Perhaps his most enduring contribution is the children's classic The Story of the Three Bears, the original Goldilocks story, first published in Southey's prose collection The Doctor.

In 1838, Edith died and Southey married Caroline Anne Bowles, also a poet, on 4 June 1839

Robert Southey died on the 21st of March, 1843 and is buried in Crosthwaite Church in Keswick,

Index of Contents

PREFACE

In the continuation of the Arabian Tales, the Domdaniel is mentioned; a Seminary for evil Magicians under the Roots of the Sea. From this seed the present Romance has grown. Let me not be supposed to prefer the metre in which it is written, abstractedly considered, to the regular blank verse; the noblest measure, in my judgement, of which our admirable language is capable. For the following Poem I have preferred it, because it suits the varied subject; it is the Arabesque ornament of an Arabian tale.

The dramatic sketches of Dr. Sayer, a volume which no lover of poetry will recollect without pleasure, induced me when a young versifier, to practise in this metre. I felt that while it gave the poet a wider range of expression, it satisfied the ear of the reader. It were easy to make a parade of learning by enumerating the various feet which it admits; it is only needful to observe that no two lines are employed in sequence which can be read into one. Two six-syllable lines (it will perhaps be answered) compose an Alexandrine: the truth is that the Alexandrine, when harmonious, is composed of two six-syllable lines.

One advantage this metre assuredly possesses; the dullest reader cannot distort it into discord: he may read it with a prose mouth, but its flow and fall will still be perceptible. Verse is not enough favoured by the English reader: perhaps this is owing to the obtrusiveness, the regular Jews-harp twing-twang, of what has been foolishly called heroic measure. I do not wish the improvisatorè tune, but something that denotes the sense of harmony, something like the accent of feeling; like the tone which every Poet necessarily gives to Poetry.

THALABA THE DESTROYER

THE FIRST BOOK

How beautiful is night!
A dewy freshness fills the silent air,
No mist obscures, no little cloud
Breaks the whole serene of heaven:
In full-orbed glory the majestic moon
Rolls thro the dark blue depths.
Beneath her steady ray
The desert circle spreads,
Like the round ocean, girdled with the sky.
How beautiful is night!

Who at this untimely hour

Wanders o'er the desert sands?
No station is in view,
No palm-grove islanded amid the waste.
The mother and her child,
The widow and the orphan at this hour
Wander o'er the desert sands.

Alas! the setting sun
Saw Zeinab in her bliss,
Hodeirah's wife beloved.
Alas! the wife beloved,
The fruitful mother late,
Whom when the daughters of Arabia named
They wished their lot like her's;
She wanders o'er the desert sands
A wretched widow now,
The fruitful mother of so fair a race,
With only one preserved,
She wanders o'er the wilderness.

No tear relieved the burthen of her heart;
Stunned with the heavy woe she felt like one
Half-wakened from a midnight dream of blood.
But sometimes when her boy
Would wet her hand with tears,
And looking up to her fixed countenance,
Amid his bursting sobs
Say the dear name of MOTHER, then would she
Utter a feeble groan.
At length collecting, Zeinab turned her eyes
To heaven, exclaiming, "praised be the Lord!
"He gave,[1] he takes away,
"The Lord our God is good!"

"Good is he?" cried the boy,
"Why are my brethren and my sisters slain?
"Why is my father killed?
"Did ever we neglect our prayers,
"Or ever lift a hand unclean to heaven?
"Did ever stranger from our tent
"Unwelcomed turn away?
"Mother, he is not good!"

Then Zeinab beat her breast in agony,
"O God forgive my child!
"He knows not what he says!
"Thou know'st I did not teach him thoughts like these,
"O Prophet, pardon him!"

She had not wept till that assuaging prayer....
The fountains of her eyes were opened then,

And tears relieved her heart.
She raised her swimming eyes to Heaven,
"Allah, thy will be done!
"Beneath the dispensation of thy wrath
"I groan, but murmur not.
"The Day of the Trial will come,
"When I shall understand how profitable
"It is to suffer now."

Young Thalaba in silence heard reproof,
His brow in manly frowns was knit,
With manly thoughts his heart was full.
"Tell me who slew my father?" cried the boy.
Zeinab replied and said,
"I knew not that there lived thy father's foe.
"The blessings of the poor for him
"Went daily up to Heaven,
"In distant lands the traveller told his praise.
"I did not think there lived
"Hodeirah's enemy."

"But I will hunt him thro' the earth!"
Young Thalaba exclaimed.
"Already I can bend my father's bow,
"Soon will my arm have strength
"To drive the arrow-feathers to his heart."

Zeinab replied, "O Thalaba, my child,
"Thou lookest on to distant days,
"And we are in the desert far from men!"

Not till that moment her afflicted heart
Had leisure for the thought.
She cast her eyes around,
Alas! no tents were there
Beside the bending sands;
No palm tree rose to spot the wilderness.
The dark blue sky closed round
And rested[2] like a dome
Upon the circling waste.
She cast her eyes around,
Famine and Thirst were there.
Then the mother bowed her head,
And wept upon her child.

... Sudden a cry of wonder
From Thalaba aroused her,
She raised her head, and saw
Where high in air a stately palace rose.
Amid a grove embowered
Stood the prodigious pile,

Trees of such ancient majesty
Towered not on Yemen's happy hills,
Nor crowned the stately brow of Lebanon.
Fabric so vast, so lavishly enriched,
For Idol, or for Tyrant, never yet
Raised the slave race of men
In Rome, nor in the elder Babylon,
Nor old Persepolis,
Nor where the family of Greece
Hymned Eleutherian Jove.
Here studding azure[3] tablatures
And rayed with feeble light,
Star-like the ruby and the diamond shone:
Here on the golden towers
The yellow moon-beam lay;
Here with white splendour floods the silver wall.
Less wonderous pile and less magnificent
Sennamar[4] built at Hirah, tho' his art
Sealed with one stone the ample edifice
And made its colours, like the serpents skin
Play with a changeful beauty: him, its Lord
Jealous lest after-effort might surpass
The now unequalled palace, from its height
Dashed on the pavement down.

They entered, and through aromatic paths
Wondering they went along.
At length upon a mossy bank
Beneath a tall mimosa's shade
That o'er him bent its living canopy,
They saw a man reclined.
Young he appeared, for on his cheek there shone
The morning glow of health,
And the brown beard curled close around his chin.
He slept, but at the sound
Of coming feet awakening, fixed his eyes
In wonder, on the wanderer and her child.
"Forgive us," Zeinab cried,
"Distress hath made us bold.
"Relieve the widow and the fatherless.
"Blessed are they who succour the distrest
"For them hath God appointed Paradise."

He heard, and he looked up to heaven,
And tears ran down his cheeks:
"It is a human voice!
"I thank thee, O my God!
"How many an age has past
"Since the sweet sounds have visited mine ear!
"I thank thee, O my God,
"It is a human voice!"

To Zeinab turning then he cried
"O mortal who art thou
"Whose gifted eyes have pierced
"The shadow of concealment that hath wrapt
"These bowers, so many an age,
"From eye of mortal man?
"For countless years have past
"And never foot of man
"The bowers of Irem trod.
"Save only I, a miserable wretch
"From Heaven and Earth shut out!"

Fearless, and scarce surprized,
For grief in Zeinab's soul
All other feebler feelings overpowered,
She answered, "Yesterday
"I was a wife beloved,
"The fruitful mother of a numerous race.
"I am a widow now,
"Of all my offspring this alone is left.
"Praise to the Lord our God,
"He gave, he takes away!"

Then said the stranger, "Not by Heaven unseen
"Nor with unguided feet
"Thy steps have reached this secret place
"Nor for light purpose is the Veil,
"That from the Universe hath long shut out
"These ancient bowers, withdrawn.
"Hear thou my words, O mortal, in thy heart
"Treasure the wonders I shall tell;
"And when amid the world
"Thou shall emerge again
"Repeat the warning tale.
"Why have the Fathers suffered, but to make
"The Children wisely safe?"

"The Paradise of Irem[5] this,
"And that the palace pile
"Which Shedad built, the King.
"Alas! in the days of my youth
"The hum of the populous world
"Was heard in yon wilderness waste!
"O'er all the winding sands[6]
"The tents of Ad were pitch'd;
"Happy Al-Ahkaf then,
"For many and brave were her sons,
"Her daughters were many and fair.

"My name was Aswad then.

"Alas! alas! how strange
"The sound so long unheard!
"Of noble race I came,
"One of the wealthy of the earth my Sire,
"An hundred horses in my father's stalls
"Stood ready for his will;
"Numerous his robes of silk,
"The number of his camels was not known.
"These were my heritance,
"O God! thy gifts were these;
"But better had it been for Aswad's soul
"To have asked alms on earth,
"And begged the crumbs that from his table fell,
"So he had known thy word.

"Boy who hast reached this solitude,
"Fear the Lord in the days of thy youth!
"My knee was never taught
"To bend before my God,
"My voice was never taught
"To shape one holy prayer.
"We worshipped Idols, wood and stone,
"The work of our own foolish hands
"We worshipped in our foolishness.
"Vainly the Prophet's voice
"Its frequent warning raised,
"REPENT, AND BE FORGIVEN!"—
"We mocked the messenger of God,
"We mocked the Lord, long-suffering, slow to wrath.

"A mighty work the pride of Shedad planned,
"Here in the wilderness to form
"A garden more surpassing fair
"Than that before whose gate,
"The lightning of the Cherub's fiery sword
"Waves wide to bar access
"Since Adam, the transgressor, thence was driven.
"Here too would Shedad build
"A kingly pile sublime,
"The palace of his pride.
"For this exhausted mines
"Supplied their golden store,
"For this the central caverns gave their gems;
"For this the woodman's axe
"Opened the cedar forest to the sun;
"The silkworm of the East
"Spun her sepulchral egg;
"The hunter African
"Provoked the danger of the elephant's wrath;
"The Ethiop, keen of scent
"Detects the ebony,[7]

"That deep-inearthed, and hating light,
"A leafless tree and barren of all fruit,
"With darkness feeds her boughs of raven grain....
"Such were the treasures lavished in yon pile;
"Ages have past away
"And never mortal eye
"Gazed on their vanity.

"The garden's copious springs
"Blest that delightful spot,
"And every flower was planted here
"That makes the gale of evening sweet.
"He spake, and bade the full-grown forest rise
"His own creation; should the King
"Wait for slow Nature's work?
"All trees that bend with luscious fruit,
"Or wave with feathery boughs,
"Or point their spiring heads to heaven,
"Or spreading wide their shadowy arms
"Invite the traveller to repose at noon,
"Hither, uprooted with their native soil,
"The labour and the pain of multitudes,
"Mature in beauty, bore them.
"Here, frequent in the walks
"The marble statue stood
"Of heroes and of chiefs.
"The trees and flowers remain
"By Nature's care perpetuate and self-sown.
"The marble statues long have lost all trace
"Of heroes and of chiefs,
"Huge shapeless stones they lie
"O'er-grown with many a flower.

"The work of pride went on....
"Often the Prophet's voice
"Denounced impending woe....
"We mocked at the words of the Seer.
"We mocked at the wrath of the Lord.
"A long continued drought first troubled us,
"Three years no cloud had formed,
"Three years no rain had fallen.
"The wholesome herb was dry,
"The corn matured not for the food of man,
"The wells and fountains failed.
"O hard of heart, in whom the punishment
"Awoke no sense of guilt!
"Headstrong to ruin, obstinately blind,
"To Idols[8] we applied for aid;
"Sakia we invoked for rain,
"We called on Razeka for food....
"They did not hear our prayers, they could not hear!

"No cloud appeared in Heaven,
"No nightly dews came down.

"Then to the place of concourse,[9] messengers
"Were sent to Mecca, where the nations came,
"Round the Red Hillock, kneeling, to implore
"God in his favoured place,
"We sent to call on God;
"Ah fools! unthinking that from all the earth
"The heart ascends to him.
"We sent to call on God;
"Ah fools! to think the Lord
"Would hear their prayers abroad
"Who made no prayers at home!

"Meantime the work of pride went on,
"And still before our Idols, wood and stone,
"We bowed the impious knee.
"Turn men of Ad, and call upon the Lord,"
"The Prophet Houd exclaimed.
"Turn men of Ad and look to Heaven,
"And fly the wrath to come.
"We mocked the Prophet's words;
"Now dost thou dream old man.
"Or art thou drunk with wine?
"Future woe and wrath to come,
"Still thy prudent voice forebodes;
"When it comes will we believe,
"Till it comes will we go on
"In the way our fathers went.
"Now are thy words from God?
"Or dost thou dream, old man,
"Or art thou drunk with wine?"

"So spake the stubborn race
"The unbelieving ones,
"I too of stubborn unbelieving heart
"Heard him and heeded not.
"It chanced my father went the way of man,
"He perished in his sins.
"The funeral rites were duly paid,
"We bound a camel to his grave
"And left it there to die,
"So if the resurrection[10] came
"Together they might rise.
"I past my father's grave,
"I heard the Camel moan.
"She was his favourite beast,
"One that carried me in infancy,
"The first that by myself I learnt to mount.
"Her limbs were lean with famine, and her eyes

"Looked ghastlily with want.
"She knew me as I past,
"She stared[11] me in the face,
"My heart was touched, had it been human else?
"I thought no eye was near, and broke her bonds,
"And drove her forth to liberty and life.
"The Prophet Houd beheld,
"He lifted up his voice,
"Blessed art thou, young man,
"Blessed art thou, O Aswad, for the deed!
"In the day of visitation,
"In the fearful hour of judgment,
"God will remember thee!"

"The day of visitation was at hand,
"The fearful hour of judgment hastened on.
"Lo Shedad's mighty pile complete,
"The palace of his pride.
"Would ye behold its wonders, enter in!
"I have no heart to visit it!
"Time hath not harmed the eternal monument,
"Time is not here, nor days, nor months, nor years,
"An everlasting NOW of misery!...
"Ye must have heard their fame,
"Or likely ye have seen
"The mighty Pyramids,
"For sure those mighty piles shall overlive
"The feeble generations of mankind.
"What tho' unmoved they bore[12] the deluge weight,
"Survivors of the ruined world?
"What tho' their founder filled with miracles
"And wealth miraculous their ample vaults?
"Compared with yonder fabric, and they shrink
"The baby wonders of a woman's work!
"Her emerald columns o'er the marble courts
"Fling their green rays, as when amid a shower
"The sun shines loveliest on the vernal corn.
"Here Shedad bade the sapphire floor be laid,
"As tho' with feet divine
"To trample azure light,
"Like the blue pavement of the firmament.
"Here self-suspended hangs in air,
"As its pure substance loathed material touch,
"The living[13] carbuncle;
"Sun of the lofty dome
"Darkness has no dominion o'er its beams;
"Intense it glows, an ever-flowing tide
"Of glory, like the day-flood in its source.
"Impious! the Trees of vegetable gold,
"Such as in Eden's groves
"Yet innocent it[14] grew,

"Impious! he made his boast, tho' heaven had hidden
"So deep the baneful ore,
"That they should branch and bud for him,
"That art should force their blossoms and their fruit,
"And re-create for him,
"Whate'er was lost in Paradise.
"Therefore at Shedad's voice
"Here towered the palm, a silver trunk,
"The fine gold net-work[15] growing out
"Loose from its rugged boughs.
"Tall as the Cedar of the mountain, here
"Rose the gold branches, hung with emerald leaves,
"Blossomed with pearls, and rich with ruby fruit,
"O Ad! my country! evil was the day
"That thy unhappy sons
"Crouched at this Nimrod's throne,[16]
"And placed him on the pedestal of power,
"And laid their liberties beneath his feet,
"Robbing their children of the heritance
"Their fathers handed down.
"What was to him the squandered wealth?
"What was to him the burthen of the land,
"The lavished misery?
"He did but speak his will,
"And like the blasting Siroc of the East,
"The ruin of the royal voice
"Found its way every-where.
"I marvel not that he, whose power
"No earthly law, no human feeling curbed,
"Mocked at the living God!

"And now the King's command went forth
"Among the people, bidding old and young,
"Husband and wife, the master and the slave,
"All the collected multitudes of Ad,
"Here to repair, and hold high festival,
"That he might see his people, they behold
"Their King's magnificence and power.
"The day of festival arrived,
"Hither they came, the old man and the boy,
"Husband and wife, the master and the slave,
"Hither they came. From yonder high tower top,
"The loftiest of the Palace, Shedad looked
"Down on his tribe: their tents on yonder sands
"Rose like the countless billows of the sea.
"Their tread and voices like the ocean roar,
"One deep confusion of tumultuous sounds.
"They saw their King's magnificence; beheld
"His Palace sparkling like the Angel domes
"Of Paradise; his garden like the bowers
"Of early Eden, and they shouted out

"Great is the King, a God upon the earth!

"Intoxicate with joy and pride
"He heard their blasphemies,
"And in his wantonness of heart he bade
"The Prophet Houd be brought,
"And o'er the marble courts,
"And o'er the gorgeous rooms
"Glittering with gems and gold,
"He led the Man of God.
"Is not this a stately pile?"
"Cried the Monarch in his joy.
"Hath ever eye beheld,
"Hath ever thought conceived,
"Place more magnificent?
"Houd, they saw that Heaven imparted
"To thy lips the words of wisdom!
"Look at the riches round
"And value them aright,
"If so thy wisdom can."

"The Prophet heard his vaunt
"And answered with an aweful smile,
"Costly thy palace King!
"But only in the hour[17] of death
"Man learns to value things like these aright.

"Hast thou a fault to find
"In all thine eyes have seen?
"Again the King exclaimed.
"Yes!" said the man of God;
"The walls are weak, the building ill secured.
"Azrael can enter in!
"The Sarsar can pierce thro',
"The Icy Wind of Death.

"I was beside the Monarch when he spake....
"Gentle the Prophet spake,
"But in his eye there dwelt
"A sorrow that disturbed me while I gazed,
"The countenance of Shedad fell,
"And anger sate upon his paler lips.
"He to the high tower top the Prophet led,
"And pointed to the multitude,
"And as again they shouted out
"Great is the King! a God upon the Earth!"
"Turned with a threatful smile to Houd,
"Say they aright, O Prophet? is the King
"Great upon earth, a God among mankind?"
"The Prophet answered not,
"His eye rolled round the infinite multitude,

"And into tears he burst.

"Sudden an uproar rose,
"A cry of joy below,
"The Messenger is come!
"Kail from Mecca comes,
"He brings the boon obtained!"

"Forth as we went we saw where overhead
"There hung a deep black cloud,
"On which the multitude
"With joyful eyes looked up
"And blest the coming rain.
"The Messenger addrest the King
"And told his tale of joy.

"To Mecca I repaired,
"By the Red Hillock knelt
"And called on God for rain.
"My prayer ascended and was heard;
"Three clouds appeared in heaven.
"One white, and like the flying cloud of noon,
"One red as it had drunk the evening beams,
"One black and heavy with its load of rain.
"A voice went forth from heaven
"Chuse Kail of the three!"
"I thanked the gracious Power,
"And chose the black cloud, heavy with its wealth."
"Right! right! a thousand tongues exclaimed,
"And all was merriment and joy.

"Then stood the Prophet up and cried aloud,
"Woe, woe, to Irem! woe to Ad!
"DEATH is gone up into her palaces!
"Woe! woe! a day of guilt and punishment,
"A day of desolation!"
"As he spake
"His large eye rolled in horror, and so deep
"His tone, it seemed some Spirit from within
"Breathed thro' his moveless lips[18] the unearthly voice.
"All looks were turned to him. "O Ad!" he cried,
"Dear native land, by all rememberances
"Of childhood, by all joys of manhood dear;
"O Vale of many Waters! morn and night
"My age must groan for you, and to the grave
"Go down in sorrow. Thou wilt give thy fruits,
"But who shall gather them? thy grapes will ripen,
"But who shall tread the wine-press? Fly the wrath,
"Ye who would live and save your souls alive!
"For strong is his right hand that bends the Bow,
"The Arrows that he shoots are sharp,

"And err not from their aim!"[19]

"With that, a faithful few
"Prest thro' the throng to join him. Then arose
"Mockery and mirth; "go bald head!" and they mixed
"Curses with laughter. He set forth, yet once
"Looked back,—his eye fell on me, and he called
"Aswad!"... it startled me,... it terrified,...
"Aswad!" again he called,... and I almost
"Had followed him. O moment fled too soon!
"O moment irrecoverably lost!
"The shouts of mockery made a coward of me;
"He went, and I remained, in fear of MAN!"

"He went, and darker grew
"The deepening cloud above.
"At length it opened, and.... O God! O God!
"There were no waters there!
"There fell no kindly rain!
"The Sarsar from its womb went forth,
"The Icy Wind of Death."

"They fell around me, thousands fell around,
"The King and all his People fell.
"All! all! they perished all!
"I ... only I ... was left.
"There came a Voice to me and said,
"In the Day of Visitation,
"In the fearful Hour of Judgement,
"God hath remembered thee."

"When from an agony of prayer I rose
"And from the scene of death
"Attempted to go forth,
"The way was open, I beheld
"No barrier to my steps.
"But round these bowers the Arm of God
"Had drawn a mighty chain,
"A barrier that no human force might break.
"Twice I essayed to pass.
"With that the voice was heard,
"O Aswad be content, and bless the Lord!

"One righteous deed hath saved
"Thy soul from utter death.
"O Aswad, sinful man!
"When by long penitence
"Thou feelest thy soul prepared,
"Breathe up the wish to die,
"And Azrael comes, obedient to the prayer."

"A miserable man
"From Earth and Heaven shut out,
"I heard the dreadful voice.
"I looked around my prison place,
"The bodies of the dead were there,
"Where'er I looked they lay.
"They mouldered, mouldered here,...
"Their very bones have crumbled into dust,
"So many years have past!
"So many weary ages have gone by!
"And still I linger here!
"Still groaning with the burthen of my sins
"Have never dared to breathe
"The prayer to be released."

"Oh! who can tell the unspeakable misery
"Of solitude like this!
"No sound hath ever reached my ear
"Save of the passing wind....
"The fountain's everlasting flow;
"The forest in the gale,
"The pattering of the shower,
"Sounds dead and mournful all.
"No bird hath ever closed her wing
"Upon these solitary bowers,
"No insect sweetly buzzed amid these groves,
"From all things that have life,
"Save only me, concealed.
"This Tree alone that o'er my head
"Hangs, down its hospitable boughs,
"And bends its whispering leaves
"As tho' to welcome me,
"Seems to partake[20] of life;
"I love it as my friend, my only friend!

"I know not for what ages I have dragged
"This miserable life,
"How often I have seen
"These antient trees renewed,
"What countless generations of mankind
"Have risen and fallen asleep,
"And I remain the same!
"My garment hath not waxed old,
"Nor the sole of my shoe hath worn.

"I dare not breathe the prayer to die,
"O merciful Lord God!...
"But when it is thy will,
"But when I have atoned
"For mine iniquities,
"And sufferings have made pure

"My soul with sin defiled,
"Release me in thine own good time,...
"I will not cease to praise thee, O my God!"

Silence ensued awhile,
Then Zeinab answered him.
"Blessed art thou, O Aswad! for the Lord
"Who saved thy soul from Hell,
"Will call thee to him in his own good time.
"And would that when my heart
"Breathed up the wish to die,
"Azrael might visit me!
"Then would I follow where my babes are gone,
"And join Hodeirah now!"

She ceased, and the rushing of wings
Was heard in the stillness of night,
And Azrael, the Death-Angel stood before them.
His countenance was dark,
Solemn, but not severe,
It awed but struck no terror to the heart.
"Zeinab, thy wish is heard!
"Aswad, thy hour is come!"
They fell upon the ground and blest the voice,
And Azrael from his sword
Let drop[21] the drops of bitterness and death.

"Me too! me too!" young Thalaba exclaimed:
As wild with grief he kissed
His Mother's livid hand,
His Mother's quivering lips,
"O Angel! take me too!

"Son of Hodeirah!" the Death-Angel cried,
"It is not yet the hour.
"Son of Hodeirah, thou art chosen forth
"To do the will of Heaven;
"To avenge thy Father's death,
"The murder of thy race,
"To work the mightiest enterprise
"That mortal man hath wrought.
"Live! and remember Destiny
"Hath marked thee from mankind!"

He ceased, and he was gone.
Young Thalaba looked round,...
The Palace and the groves were seen no more,
He stood amid the Wilderness, alone.

THE SECOND BOOK

Not in the desert
Son of Hodeirah
Wert thou abandoned!
The coexistent fire,
That in the Dens of Darkness burnt for thee,
Burns yet, and yet shall burn.

In the Domdaniel caverns
Under the Roots of the Ocean,
Met the Masters of the Spell.
Before them in the vault,
Blazing unfuelled from the floor of rock,
Ten magic flames arose.
"Burn mystic fires!" Abdaldar cried,
"Burn whilst Hodeirah's dreaded race exist.
"This is the appointed hour,
"The hour that shall secure these dens of night."

"Dim they burn," exclaimed Lobaba,
"Dim they burn, and now they waver!
"Okba lifts the arm of death,
"They waver,... they go out!

"Curse on his hasty hand!"
Khawla exclaimed in wrath,
The woman-fiend exclaimed,
"Curse on his hasty hand, the fool hath failed!
"Eight only are gone out."

A Teraph[22] stood against the cavern side,
A new-born infant's head,
That Khawla at his hour of birth had seized
And from the shoulders wrung.
It stood upon a plate of gold,
An unclean Spirit's name inscribed beneath.
The cheeks were deathy dark,
Dark the dead skin upon the hairless skull;
The lips were bluey pale;
Only the eyes had life,
They gleamed with demon light.

"Tell me!" quoth Khawla, "is the Fire gone out
"That threats the Masters of the Spell?"
The dead lips moved and spake,
"The Fire still burns that threats
"The Masters of the Spell."

"Curse on thee, Okba!" Khawla cried,
As to the den the Sorcerer came,
He bore the dagger in his hand
Hot from the murder of Hodeirah's race.
"Behold those unextinguished flames!
"The fire still burns that threats
"The Masters of the Spell!
"Okba, wert thou weak of heart?
"Okba, wert thou blind of eye?
"Thy fate and ours were on the lot,
"And we believed the lying stars
"That said thy hand might seize the auspicious hour!
"Thou hast let slip the reins of Destiny,...
"Curse thee, curse thee, Okba!"

The Murderer answering said,
"O versed in all enchanted lore,
"Thou better knowest Okba's soul.
"Eight blows I struck, eight home-driven blows,
"Needed no second stroke
"From this envenomed blade.
"Ye frown at me as if the will had failed,
"As if ye did not know
"My double danger from Hodeirah's race,
"The deeper hate I feel,
"The stronger motive that inspired my arm!
"Ye frown as if my hasty fault,
"My ill-directed blow
"Had spared the enemy,
"And not the stars that would not give,
"And not your feeble spells
"That could not force, the sign
"Which of the whole was he!
"Did ye not bid me strike them all?
"Said ye not root and branch should be destroyed?
"I heard Hodeirah's dying groan,
"I heard his Children's shriek of death,
"And sought to consummate the work,
"But o'er the two remaining lives
"A cloud unpierceable had risen,
"A cloud that mocked my searching eyes.
"I would have probed it with the dagger-point,
"The dagger was repelled,
"A Voice came forth and cried
"Son of Perdition, cease! thou canst not change
"What in the Book of Destiny is written."

Khawla to the Teraph turned,
"Tell me where the Prophet's hand
"Hides our destined enemy?"

The dead lips spake again,
"I view the seas, I view the land,
"I search the ocean and the earth!
"Not on Ocean is the Boy,
"Not on Earth his steps are seen."

"A mightier power than we," Lobaba cried,
"Protects our destined foe!
"Look! look! one fire burns dim!
"It quivers! it goes out!"

It quivered, it was quenched.
One flame alone was left,
A pale blue flame that trembled on the earth,
A hovering light upon whose shrinking edge
The darkness seemed to press.
Stronger it grew, and spread
Its lucid swell around,
Extending now where all the ten had stood,
With lustre more than all.
At that protentous sight,
The children of Evil trembled
And Terror smote their souls.
Over the den the fire
Its fearful splendour cast,
The broad base rolling up in wavy streams,
Bright as the summer lightning when it spreads
Its glory o'er the midnight heaven.
The Teraphs eyes were dimmed,
That like two twinkling stars
Shone in the darkness late.
The Sorcerers on each other gazed,
And every face all pale with fear,
And ghastly in that light was seen
Like a dead man's by the sepulchral lamp.

Even Khawla fiercest of the enchanter brood
Not without effort drew
Her fear suspended breath.
Anon a deeper rage
Inflamed her reddening eye.
"Mighty is thy power, Mohammed!"
Loud in blasphemy she cried,
"But Eblis[23] would not stoop to man
"When Man fair statured as the stately palm,
"From his Creator's hand
"Was undefiled and pure.
"Thou art mighty, O Son of Abdallah!
"But who is he of woman born
"That shall vie with the might of Eblis?
"That shall rival the Prince of the Morning?"

She said, and raised her skinny hand
As in defiance to high Heaven,
And stretched her long lean finger forth
And spake aloud the words of power.
The Spirits heard her call,
And lo! before her stands
Her Demon Minister.
"Spirit!" the Enchantress cried,
"Where lives the Boy coeval with whose life
"Yon magic fire must burn?"
DEMON.
Mistress of the mighty Spell,
Not on Ocean, not on Earth.
Only eyes that view
Allah's glory throne,
See his hiding-place.
From some believing Spirit, ask and learn.

"Bring the dead Hodeirah here,"
Khawla cried, "and he shall tell."
The Demon heard her bidding, and was gone.
A moment passed, and at her feet
Hodeirah's corpse was laid.
His hand still held the sword he grasped in death,
The blood not yet had clotted on his wound.

The Sorceress looked and with a smile
That kindled to more fiendishness
Her hideous features, cried,
"Where Hodeirah is thy soul?
"Is it in the [24]Zemzem well?
"Is it in the Eden groves?
"Waits it for the judgement-blast
"In the trump of Israfil?
"Is it plumed with silver wings
"Underneath the throne of God?
"Even if beneath his throne
"Hodeirah, thou shalt hear,
"Thou shalt obey my voice!"

She said, and muttered charms that Hell in fear
And Heaven in horror heard.
Soon the stiff eye-balls rolled,
The muscles with convulsive motion shook,
The white lips quivered. Khawla saw, her soul
Exulted, and she cried,
"Prophet! behold my power!
"Not even death secures
"Thy slaves from Khawla's Spell!
"Where Hodeirah is thy child?"

Hodeirah groaned and closed his eyes,
As if in the night and the blindness of death
He would have hid himself.

"Speak to my question!" she exclaimed,
"Or in that mangled body thou shall live
"Ages of torture! answer me!
"Where can we find the Boy?"

"God! God! Hodeirah cried,
"Release me from this life,
"From this intolerable agony!"

"Speak!" cried the Sorceress; and she snatched
A Viper from the floor,
And with the living reptile lashed[25] his neck.
Wreathed, round him with the blow,
The Reptile tighter drew her folds
And raised her wrathful head,
And fixed into his face
Her deadly teeth, and shed
Poison in every wound.
In vain! for Allah heard Hodeirah's prayer,
And Khawla on a corpse
Had wrecked her baffled rage.
The fated fire moved on
And round the Body wrapt its funeral flames.
The flesh and bones in that portentous pile
Consumed; the Sword alone,
Circled with fire was left.

Where is the Boy for whose hand it is destined?
Where the Destroyer who one day shall wield
The Sword that is circled with fire?
Race accursed, try your charms!
Masters of the mighty Spell,
Mutter o'er your words of power!
Ye can shatter the dwellings of man,
Ye can open the womb of the rock,
Ye can shake the foundations of earth,
But not the Word of God:
But not one letter can ye change
Of what his Will hath written!

Who shall seek thro' Araby
Hodeirah's dreaded son?
They mingle the Arrows[26] of Chance
The lot of Abdaldar is drawn.
Thirteen moons must wax and wane
Ere the Sorcerer quit his quest.

He must visit every tribe
That roam the desert wilderness,
Or dwell beside perennial streams;
Nor leave a solitary tent unsearched
Till he has found the Boy,
The hated Boy whose blood alone
Can quench that dreaded fire.

A crystal ring Abdaldar bore,
The powerful gem[27] condensed
Primeval dews that upon Caucasus
Felt the first winter's frost.
Ripening there it lay beneath
Rock above rock, and mountain ice up-piled
On mountain, till the incumbent mass assumed,
So huge its bulk, the Ocean's azure hue.

With this he sought the inner den
Where burnt the eternal flame.
Like waters gushing from some channelled rock
Full thro' a narrow opening, from a chasm
The eternal flame streamed up.
No eye beheld the fount
Of that up-flowing flame,
That blazed self-nurtured, and for ever, there.
It was no mortal element: the Abyss
Supplied it, from the fountains at the first
Prepared. In the heart of earth it lives and glows
Her vital heat, till at the day decreed,
The voice of God shall let its billows loose,
To deluge o'er with no abating flood
The consummated World;
That thenceforth thro' the air must roll,
The penal Orb of Fire.

Unturbaned and unsandalled there,
Abdaldar stood before the flame,
And held the Ring beside, and spake
The language that the Elements obey.
The obedient flame detatched a portion forth,
That, in the crystal entering, was condensed,
Gem of the gem, its living Eye of fire.
When the hand that wears the spell
Shall touch the destined Boy,
Then shall that Eye be quenched,
And the freed Element
Fly to its sacred and remembered Spring.

Now go thy way Abdaldar!
Servant of Eblis,
Over Arabia

Seek the Destroyer!
Over the sands of the scorching Tchama,
Over the waterless mountains of Naïd,
In Arud pursue him; and Yemen the happy,
And Hejaz, the country beloved by believers.
Over Arabia
Servant of Eblis,
Seek the Destroyer.

From tribe to tribe, from town to town,
From tent to tent, Abdaldar past.
Him every morn the all-beholding Eye
Saw from his couch, unhallowed by a prayer,
Rise to the scent of blood,
And every night lie down.
That rankling hope within him, that by day
Goaded his steps, still stinging him in sleep,
And startling him with vain accomplishment
From visions still the same.
Many a time his wary hand
To many a youth applied the Ring,
And still the dagger in his mantle hid
Was ready for the deed.

At length to the cords of a tent
That were stretched by an Island of Palms
In the desolate sea of the sands,
The weary traveller came.
Under a shapely palm,
Herself as shapely, there a Damsel stood.
She held her ready robe
And looked towards a Boy,
Who from the tree above
With one hand clinging to its trunk,
Cast with the other down the clustered dates.

The Wizard approached the Tree,
He leaned on his staff, like a way-faring man,
And the sweat of his travel was seen on his brow.
He asks for food, and lo!
The Damsel proffers him her lap of dates.
And the Stripling descends, and runs into the tent
And brings him forth water, the draught of delight.

Anon the Master of the tent,
The Father of the family
Came forth, a man in years, of aspect mild.
To the stranger approaching he gave
The friendly saluting of peace,
And bade the skin be spread.
Before the tent they spread the[28] skin,

Under a Tamarind's shade,
That bending forward, stretched
Its boughs of beauty far.
They brought the Traveller rice,
With no false colours[29] tinged to tempt the eye,
But white as the new-fallen snow,
When never yet the sullying Sun
Hath seen its purity,
Nor the warm Zephyr touched and tainted it.
The dates of the grove before their guest
They laid, and the luscious fig,
And water from the well.
The Damsel from the Tamarind tree
Had plucked its acid fruit
And steeped it in water long;
And whoso drank of the cooling[30] draught
He would not wish for wine.
This to the guest the Damsel brought,
And a modest pleasure kindled her cheek,
When raising from the cup his moistened lips
The Stranger smiled, and praised, and drank again.

Whither is gone the Boy?
He had pierced the Melon's pulp
And closed with wax the wound,
And he had duly gone at morn
And watched its ripening rind,
And now all joyfully he brings
The treasure now matured.
His dark eyes sparkle with a boy's delight.
As he pours out its liquid[31] lusciousness
And proffers to the guest.

Abdaldar ate, and he was satisfied:
And now his tongue discoursed
Of regions far remote,
As one whose busy feet had travelled long.
The Father of the family,
With a calm eye and quiet smile,
Sate pleased to hearken him.
The Damsel who removed the meal,
She loitered on the way
And listened with full [32]hands
A moment motionless.
All eagerly the Boy
Watches the Traveller's lips,
And still the wily man
With seemly kindness to the eager Boy
Directs his winning tale.
Ah, cursed man! if this be he,
If thou hast found the object of thy search,

Thy hate, thy bloody aim,
Into what deep damnation wilt thou plunge
Thy miserable soul!
Look! how his eye delighted watches thine!
Look! how his open lips
Gasp at the winning tale!
And nearer now he comes
To lose no word of that delightful talk.
Then, as in familiar mood,
Upon the Stripling's arm
The Sorcerer laid his hand,
And the fire of the Crystal fled.

Whilst the sudden shoot of joy
Made pale Abdaldar's cheek,
The Master's voice was heard:
"It is the hour[33] of prayer,...
"My children, let us purify ourselves
"And praise the Lord our God!"
The Boy the water brought,
After the law[34] they purified themselves,
And bent their faces to the earth in prayer.

All, save Abdaldar; over Thalaba
He stands, and lifts the dagger to destroy.
Before his lifted arm received
Its impulse to descend,
The Blast of the Desert came.
Prostrate in prayer, the pious family
Felt not the Simoom[35] pass.
They rose, and lo! the Sorcerer lying dead,
Holding the dagger in his blasted hand.

THALABA.
Oneiza, look! the dead man has a ring,...
Should it be buried with him?

ONEIZA.
Oh yes ... yes!
A wicked man! all that he has must needs
Be wicked too!

THALABA.

But see,... the sparkling stone!
How it has caught the glory of the Sun,
And streams it back again in lines of light!

ONEIZA.
Why do you take it from him Thalaba?...
And look at it so near?... it may have charms
To blind, or poison ... throw it in the grave!...
I would not touch it!

THALABA.
And around its rim
Strange letters,...

ONEIZA.
Bury it.... Oh! bury it!

THALABA.
It is not written as the Koran is;
Some other tongue perchance ... the accursed man
Said he had been a traveller.

MOATH. coming from the tent.
Thalaba,
What hast thou there?

THALABA.
A ring the dead man wore,
Perhaps my father, you can read its meaning.

MOATH.
No Boy,... the letters are not such as ours.
Heap the sand over it! a wicked man
Wears nothing holy.

THALABA.
Nay! not bury it!
It may be that some traveller who shall enter
Our tent, may read them: or if we approach
Cities where strangers dwell and learned men,
They may interpret.

MOATH.
It were better hid
Under the desert sands. This wretched man,
Whom God hath smitten in the very purpose
And impulse of his unpermitted crime,
Belike was some Magician, and these lines
Are of the language that the Demons use.

ONEIZA.

Bury it! bury it ... dear Thalaba!

MOATH.
Such cursed men there are upon the earth,
In league and treaty with the Evil powers,
The covenanted enemies of God
And of all good, dear purchase have they made
Of rule, and riches, and their life-long sway,
Masters, yet slaves of Hell. Beneath the Roots
Of Ocean, the Domdaniel caverns lie:
Their impious meeting; there they learn the words
Unutterable by man who holds his hope
Of Heaven, there brood the Pestilence, and let
The Earthquake loose.

THALABA.
And he who would have killed me
Was one of these?

MOATH.
I know not, but it may be
That on the Table of Destiny, thy name
Is written their Destroyer, and for this
Thy life by yonder miserable man
So sought; so saved by interfering Heaven.

THALABA.
His ring has some strange power then?

MOATH.
Every gem,[36]
So sages say, has virtue; but the science
Of difficult attainment, some grow pale
Conscious of poison,[37] or with sudden shade
Of darkness, warn the wearer; same preserve
From spells, or blunt the hostile weapon's[38] edge.
Some open rocks and mountains, and lay bare
Their buried treasures; others make the sight
Strong to perceive the presence of all Beings
Thro' whose pure substance the unaided eye
Passes, like empty air ... and in yon stone
I deem some such misterious quality.

THALABA.
My father, I will wear it.

MOATH.
Thalaba!

THALABA.
In God's name, and the Prophet's! be its power

Good, let it serve the righteous: if for evil,
God and my trust in him shall hallow it.

So Thalaba drew on
The written ring of gold.
Then in the hollow grave
They laid Abdaldar's corpse,
And levelled over him the desert dust.

The Sun arose, ascending from beneath
The horizon's circling line.
As Thalaba to his ablutions went,
Lo! the grave open, and the corpse exposed!
It was not that the winds of night
Had swept away the sands that covered it,
For heavy with the undried dew
The desert dust was dark and close around;
And the night air had been so moveless calm,
It had not from the grove
Shaken a ripe date down.

Amazed to hear the tale
Forth from the tent came Moath and his child.
Awhile the thoughtful man surveyed the corpse
Silent with downward eyes,
Then turning spake to Thalaba and said,
"I have heard that there are places by the abode
"Of holy men, so holily possessed,
"That if a corpse be buried there, the ground
"With a convulsive effort shakes it out,[39]
"Impatient of pollution. Have the feet
"Of Prophet or Apostle blest this place?
"Ishmael, or Houd, or Saleh, or than all,
"Mohammed, holier name? or is the man
"So foul with magic and all blasphemy,
"That Earth[40] like Heaven rejects him? it is best
"Forsake the station. Let us strike our tent.
"The place is tainted ... and behold
"The Vulture[41] hovers yonder, and his scream
"Chides us that we still we scare him from his banquet.
"So let the accursed one
"Find fitting sepulchre."

Then from the pollution of death
With water they made themselves pure,
And Thalaba drew up
The fastening of the cords,
And Moath furled the tent,
And from the grove of palms Oneiza led
The Camels, ready to receive their load.

The dews had ceased to steam
Towards the climbing Sun,
When from the Isle of Palms they went their way.
And when the Sun had reached his southern height,
As back they turned their eyes,
The distant Palms arose
Like to the top-sails of some far-off fleet
Distinctly seen, where else
The Ocean bounds had blended with the sky.
And when the eve came on
The sight returning reached the grove no more.
They planted the pole of their tent,
And they laid them down to repose.

At midnight Thalaba started up,
For he felt that the ring on his finger was moved.
He called on Allah aloud,
And he called on the Prophet's name.
Moath arose in alarm,
"What ails thee Thalaba?" he cried,
"Is the Robber of night at hand?"
"Dost thou not see," the youth exclaimed,
"A Spirit in the Tent?"
Moath looked round and said,
"The moon beam shines in the Tent,
"I see thee stand in the light,
"And thy shadow is black on the ground."

Thalaba answered not.
"Spirit!" he cried, "what brings thee here?
"In the name of the Prophet, speak,
"In the name of Allah, obey!"

He ceased, and there was silence in the Tent.
"Dost thou not hear?" quoth Thalaba.
The listening man replied,
"I hear the wind, that flaps
"The curtain of the Tent.

"The Ring! the Ring!" the youth exclaimed.
"For that the Spirit of Evil comes,
"By that I see, by that I hear.
"In the name of God, I ask thee
"Who was he that slew my Father?"

DEMON.
Master of the powerful Ring!
Okba, the wise Magician, did the deed.

THALABA.
Where does the Murderer dwell?

DEMON.
In the Domdaniel caverns
Under the Roots of the Ocean.

THALABA.
Why were my Father and my brethren slain?

DEMON.
We knew from the race of Hodeirah
The destined destroyer would come.

THALABA.
Bring me my father's sword.

DEMON.
A fire surrounds the fated-sword,
No Spirit or Magician's hand
Can pierce that guardian flame.

THALABA.
Bring me his bow and his arrows.

Distinctly Moath heard his voice, and She
Who thro' the Veil of Separation, watched
All sounds in listening terror, whose suspense
Forbade the aid of prayer.
They heard the voice of Thalaba;
But when the Spirit spake, the motionless air
Felt not the subtle sounds,
Too fine for mortal sense.

On a sudden the rattle of arrows was heard,
And the quiver was laid at the feet of the youth,
And in his hand they saw Hodeirah's Bow.
He eyed the Bow, he twanged the string,
And his heart bounded to the joyous tone.
Anon he raised his voice, and cried
"Go thy way, and never more,
"Evil Spirit, haunt our tent!
"By the virtue of the Ring,
"By Mohammed's holier might,
"By the holiest name of God,
"Thee and all the Powers of Hell
"I adjure and I command
"Never more to trouble us!"

Nor ever from that hour
Did rebel Spirit on the Tent intrude,
Such virtue had the Spell.

And peacefully the vernal years
Of Thalaba past on.
Till now without an effort he could bend
Hodeirah's stubborn Bow.
Black were his eyes and bright,
The sunny hue of health
Glowed on his tawny cheek,
His lip was darkened by maturing life;
Strong were his shapely limbs, his stature tall;
He was a comely youth.

Compassion for the child
Had first old Moath's kindly heart possessed,
An orphan, wailing in the wilderness.
But when he heard his tale, his wonderous tale,
Told by the Boy with such eye-speaking truth,
Now with sudden bursts of anger,
Now in the agony of tears,
And now in flashes of prophetic joy.
What had been pity became reverence,
And like a sacred trust from Heaven
The old man cherished him.
Now with a father's love,
Child of his choice, he loved the Boy,
And like a father to the Boy was dear.
Oneiza called him brother, and the youth,
More fondly than a brother, loved the maid,
The loveliest of Arabian maidens she.
How happily the years
Of Thalaba went by!

It was the wisdom and the will of Heaven
That in a lonely tent had cast
The lot of Thalaba.
There might his soul develope best
Its strengthening energies;
There might he from the world
Keep his heart pure and uncontaminate,
Till at the written hour he should be found
Fit servant of the Lord, without a spot.

Years of his youth, how rapidly ye fled
In that beloved solitude!
Is the morn fair, and does the freshening breeze
Flow with cool current o'er his cheek?
Lo! underneath the broad-leaved sycamore
With lids half closed he lies,
Dreaming of days to come.
His dog[42] beside him, in mute blandishment,
Now licks his listless hand,
Now lifts an anxious and expectant eye

Courting the wonted caress.

Or comes the Father[43] of the Rains
From his Caves in the uttermost West,
Comes he in darkness and storms?
When the blast is loud,
When the waters fill
The Travellers tread in the sands,
When the pouring shower
Streams adown the roof,
When the door-curtain hangs in heavier folds,
When the outstrained tent flags loosely,
Comfort is within,
The embers chearful glow,
The sound of the familiar voice,
The song that lightens toil.
Under the common shelter on dry sand
The quiet Camels ruminate their food;
From Moath falls the lengthening cord,
As patiently the old Man
Intwines the strong palm-fibers;[44] by the hearth
The Damsel shakes the coffee-grains,
That with warm fragrance fill the tent;
And while with dextrous fingers, Thalaba
Shapes the green basket,[45] haply at his feet
Her favourite kidling gnaws the twig,
Forgiven plunderer, for Oneiza's sake!

Or when the winter torrent rolls
Down the deep-channelled rain-course, foamingly,
Dark with its mountain spoils,
With bare feet pressing the wet sand
There wanders Thalaba,
The rushing flow, the flowing roar,
Filling his yielded faculties;
A vague, a dizzy, a tumultuous joy.
... Or lingers it a vernal brook[46]
Gleaming o'er yellow sands?
Beneath the lofty bank reclined,
With idle eye he views its little waves,
Quietly listening to the quiet flow;
While in the breathings of the stirring gale
The tall canes bend above,
Floating like streamers on the wind
Their lank uplifted leaves.

Nor rich,[47] nor poor, was Moath; God had given
Enough, and blest him with a mind content.
No hoarded[48] gold disquieted his dreams;
But ever round his station he beheld
Camels that knew his voice,

And home-birds, grouping at Oneiza's call,
And goats that, morn and eve,
Came with full udders to the Damsel's hand.
Dear child! the Tent beneath whose shade they dwelt
That was her work; and she had twined
His girdle's many-hues;
And he had seen his robe
Grow in Oneiza's loom.[49]
How often with a memory-mingled joy
That made her Mother live before his sight,
He watched her nimble finders thread the woof!
Or at the hand-mill[50] when she knelt and toiled,
Tost the thin cake on spreading palm,
Or fixed it on the glowing oven's side
With bare[51] wet arm, in safe dexterity.

'Tis the cool evening hour:
The Tamarind from the dew
Sheaths[52] its young fruit, yet green.
Before their Tent the mat is spread,
The old man's aweful voice
Intones[53] the holy Book.
What if beneath no lamp-illumined dome,
Its marble walls[54] bedecked with flourished truth,
Azure and gold adornment? sinks the Word
With deeper influence from the Imam's voice,
Where in the day of congregation, crowds
Perform the duty task?
Their Father is their Priest,
The Stars of Heaven their point[55] of prayer,
And the blue Firmament
The glorious Temple, where they feel
The present Deity.

Yet thro' the purple glow of eve
Shines dimly the white moon.
The slackened bow, the quiver, the long lance,
Rest on the pillar[56] of the Tent.
Knitting light palm-leaves[57] for her brother's brow
The dark-eyed damsel sits;
The Old Man tranquilly
Up his curled pipe inhales
The tranquillizing herb.
So listen they the reed[58] of Thalaba,
While his skilled fingers modulate
The low, sweet, soothing, melancholy tones,
Or if he strung the pearls[59] of Poetry
Singing with agitated face
And eloquent arms, and sobs that reach the heart,
A tale[60] of love and woe;
Then, if the brightening Moon that lit his face

In darkness favoured her's,
Oh! even with such a look, as, fables say,
The mother Ostrich[61] fixes on her egg,
Till that intense affection
Kindle its light of life,
Even in such deep and breathless tenderness
Oneiza's soul is centered on the youth,
So motionless with such an ardent gaze,
Save when from her full eyes
Quickly she wipes away the gushing tears
That dim his image there.

She called him brother: was it sister-love
That made the silver rings
Round her smooth ankles[62] and her twany arms,
Shine daily brightened? for a brother's eye
Were her long fingers[63] tinged,
As when she trimmed the lamp,
And thro' the veins and delicate skin
The light shone rosy? that the darkened lids[64]
Gave yet a softer lustre to her eye?
That with such pride she tricked
Her glossy tresses, and on holy day
Wreathed the red flower-crown[65] round their jetty waves?
How happily the years
Of Thalaba went by!

Yet was the heart of Thalaba
Impatient of repose;
Restless he pondered still
The task for him decreed,
The mighty and mysterious work announced.
Day by day with youthful ardour
He the call of Heaven awaits,
And oft in visions o'er the Murderer's head
He lifts the avenging arm,
And oft in dreams he sees
The Sword that is circled with fire.

One morn as was their wont, in sportive mood
The youth and damsel bent Hodeirah's bow,
For with no feeble hand nor erring aim
Oneiza could let loose the obedient shaft.
With head back-bending, Thalaba
Shot up the aimless arrow high in air,
Whose line in vain the aching sight pursued
Lost in the depth of heaven.
"When will the hour arrive," exclaimed the youth,
"That I shall aim these fated shafts
"To vengeance long delayed?
"Have I not strength, my father, for the deed?

"Or can the will of Providence
"Be mutable like man?
"Shall I never be called to the task?"

"Impatient boy!" quoth Moath, with a smile:
"Impatient Thalaba!" Oneiza cried,
And she too smiled, but in her smile
A mild reproachful melancholy mixed.

Then Moath pointed where a cloud
Of Locusts, from the desolated fields
Of Syria, winged their way.
"Lo! how created things
"Obey the written doom!"

Onward they came, a dark continuous cloud
Of congregated myriads numberless,
The rushing of whose wings was as the sound
Of a broad river, headlong in its course
Plunged from a mountain summit, or the roar
Of a wild ocean in the autumn storm,
Shattering its billows on a shore of rocks.
Onward they came, the winds impelled them on,
Their work was done, their path of[66] ruin past,
Their graves were ready in the wilderness.
"Behold the mighty army!" Moath cried,
"Blindly they move, impelled
"By the blind Element.
"And yonder Birds our welcome visitants,
"Lo! where they soar above the embodied host,
"Pursue their way, and hang upon their rear,
"And thin their spreading flanks,
"Rejoicing o'er their banquet! deemest thou
"The scent of water, on the Syrian mosque
"Placed with priest-mummery, and the jargon-rites
"That fool the multitude, has led them here
"From far Khorasan?[67] Allah who decreed
"Yon tribe the plague and punishment of man,
"These also hath he doomed to meet their way:
"Both passive instruments
"Of his all-acting will,
"Sole mover he, and only spring of all."

While thus he spake, Oneiza's eye looks up
Where one towards her flew,
Satiate, for so it seemed, with sport and food.
The Bird flew over her,
And as he past above,
From his relaxing grasp a Locust fell....
It fell upon the Maiden's robe,
And feebly there it stood, recovering slow.

The admiring girl surveyed
His out-spread sails of green.
His gauzy underwings,
One closely to the grass green body furled,
One ruffled in the fall, and half unclosed.
She viewed his jet-orbed eyes
His glossy gorget bright
Green-glittering in the sun;
His plumy pliant horns
That, nearer as she gazed,
Bent tremblingly before her breath.
She viewed his yellow-circled front
With lines mysterious veined;
"And knowest thou what is written here,
"My father?" said the Maid.
"Look Thalaba! perchance these lines
"Are in the letters of the Ring,
"Nature's own language written here."

The youth bent down, and suddenly
He started, and his heart
Sprung, and his cheek grew red,
For the mysterious[68] lines were legible,
WHEN THE SUN SHALL BE DARKENED AT NOON,
SON OF HODEIRAH, DEPART.
And Moath looked, and read the lines aloud;
The Locust shook his wings and fled,
And they were silent all.

Who then rejoiced but Thalaba?
Who then was troubled but the Arabian Maid?
And Moath sad of heart,
Tho' with a grief supprest, beheld the youth
Sharpen his arrows now,
And now new-plume their shafts,
Now to beguile impatient hope
Feel every sharpened point.

"Why is that anxious look," Oneiza cried,
"Still upwards cast at noon?
"Is Thalaba aweary of our tent?"
"I would be gone," the youth replied,
"That I might do my task,
"And full of glory to the tent return
"Whence I should part no more."

But on the noontide sun,
As anxious and as oft Oneiza's eye
Was upward glanced in fear.
And now as Thalaba replied, her cheek

Lost its fresh and lively hue,
For in the Sun's bright edge
She saw, or thought she saw, a little speck.
The sage Astronomer
Who with the love of science full
Trembled that day at every passing cloud,
He had not seen it, 'twas a speck so small.

Alas! Oneiza sees the spot increase!
And lo! the ready Youth
Over his shoulder the full quiver slings
And grasps the slackened bow.
It spreads, and spreads, and now
Has shaddowed half the Sun,
Whose crescent-pointed horns
Now momently decrease.

The day grows dark, the Birds retire to rest;
Forth from her shadowy haunt
Flies the large-headed[69] Screamer of the night.
Far off the affrighted African,
Deeming his God deceased,
Falls on his knees in prayer,
And trembles as he sees
The fierce Hyena's eyes
Glare in the darkness of that dreadful noon.

Then Thalaba exclaimed, "Farewell,
"My father! my Oneiza!" the Old Man
Felt his throat swell with grief.
"Where wilt thou go my Child?" he cried,
"Wilt thou not wait a sign
"To point thy destined way?"
"God will conduct me!" said the noble youth,
He said and from the Tent
In the depth of the darkness departed.
They heard his parting steps,
The quiver rattling as he past away.

THALABA THE DESTROYER

THE FOURTH BOOK

Whose is yon dawning form,
That in the darkness meets
The delegated youth?
Dim as the shadow of a fire at noon,
Or pale reflection on the evening brook

Of Glow-worm on the bank
Kindled to guide her winged paramour.

A moment, and the brightening image shaped
His Mother's form and features. "Go," she cried,
"To Babylon, and from the Angels learn
"What talisman thy task requires."
The Spirit hung towards him when she ceased,
As tho' with actual lips she would have given
A mother's kiss ... his arms outstretched,
His body bending on,
His lips unclosed and trembling into speech
He prest to meet the blessing,... but the wind
Played on his cheek: he looked, and he beheld
The darkness close. "Again! again!" he cried,
"Let me again behold thee!" from the darkness
His Mother's voice went forth;
"Thou shall behold me in the hour of death."

Day dawns, the twilight gleam dilates,
The Sun comes forth and like a God
Rides thro' rejoicing heaven.
Old Moath and his daughter from their tent
Beheld the adventurous youth,
Dark moving o'er the sands,
A lessening image, trembling thro' their tears.
Visions of high emprize
Beguiled his lonely road;
And if sometimes to Moath's tent
The involuntary mind recurred,
Fancy, impatient of all painful thoughts
Pictured the bliss should welcome his return.
In dreams like these he went,
And still of every dream
Oneiza formed a part,
And Hope and Memory made a mingled joy.

In the eve he arrived at a Well,
The Acacia bent over its side,
Under whose long light-hanging boughs
He chose his night's abode.
There, due ablutions made and prayers performed,
The youth his mantle spread,
And silently produced
His solitary meal.
The silence and the solitude recalled
Dear recollections, and with folded arms,
Thinking of other days, he sate, till thought
Had left him, and the Acacia's moving shade
Upon the sunny sand
Had caught his idle eye,

And his awakened ear
Heard the grey Lizard's chirp,
The only sound of life.

As thus in vacant quietness he sate,
A Traveller on a Camel reached the Well,
And courteous greeting gave.
The mutual salutation past,
He by the cistern too his garment spread,
And friendly converse cheered the social meal.

The Stranger was an antient man,
Yet one whose green old age
Bore the fair characters of temperate youth.
So much of manhood's strength his limbs retained,
It seemed he needed not the staff he bore.
His beard was long, and grey, and crisp;
Lively his eyes and quick,
And reaching over them
The large broad eye-brow curled....
His speech was copious, and his winning words
Enriched with knowledge, that the attentive youth
Sate listening with a thirsty joy.

So in the course of talk
The adventurer youth enquired
Whither his course was bent;
The Old Man answered, "to Bagdad I go."
At that so welcome sound a flash of joy
Kindled the eye of Thalaba;
"And I too," he replied,
"Am journeying thitherward,
"Let me become companion of thy way!"
Courteous the Old Man smiled,
And willing in assent....

OLD MAN.
Son, thou art young for travel.

THALABA.
Until now
I never past the desert boundary.

OLD MAN.
It is a noble city that we seek.
Thou wilt behold magnificent palaces,
And lofty obelisks, and high-domed Mosques,
And rich Bazars, whither from all the world
Industrious merchants meet, and market there
The World's collected wealth.

THALABA.
Stands not Bagdad
Near to the site of ancient Babylon
And Nimrod's impious temple?

OLD MAN.
From the walls
'Tis but a long day's distance.

THALABA.
And the ruins?

OLD MAN.
A mighty mass remains; enough to tell us
How great our [70]fathers were, how little we.
Men are not what they were; their crimes and follies
Have dwarfed them down from the old hero race
To such poor things as we!

THALABA.
At Babylon
I have heard the Angels expiate their guilt,
Haruth and Maruth.

OLD MAN.
'Tis a history
Handed from ages down; the nurses make it
A tale to please their children,
And as their garrulous ignorance relates
We learn it and believe ... but all things feel
The power of Time and Change! thistles and grass
Usurp the desolate palace, and the weeds
Of Falshood root in the aged pile of Truth.
How have you heard the tale?

THALABA.
Thus ... on a time
The Angels at the wickedness of man
Expressed indignant wonder: that in vain
Tokens and signs were given, and Prophets sent,...
Strange obstinacy this! a stubborness
Of sin, they said, that should for ever bar
The gates of mercy on them. Allah heard
Their unforgiving pride, and bade that two
Of these untempted Spirits should descend,
Judges on earth. Haruth and Maruth went,
The chosen Sentencers; they fairly heard
The appeals of men to their tribunal brought,
And rightfully decided. At the length
A Woman came before them ... beautiful
Zohara was, as yonder Evening star,

In the mild lustre[71] of whose lovely light
Even now her beauty shines. They gazed on her
With fleshly eyes, they tempted her to sin.
The wily woman listened, and required
A previous price, the knowledge of the name[72]
Of God. She learnt the wonder-working name
And gave it utterance, and its virtue bore her
Up to the glorious Presence, and she told
Before the aweful Judgement-Seat, her tale.

OLD MAN.
I know the rest, the accused Spirits were called:
Unable of defence, and penitent,
They owned their crime and heard the doom deserved.
Then they besought the Lord that not for ever
His wrath might be upon them; and implored
That penal ages might at length restore them
Clean from offence, since then by Babylon
In the cavern of their punishment they dwell,
Runs the conclusion so?

THALABA.
So I am taught.

OLD MAN.
The common tale! and likely thou hast heard
How that the bold and bad, with impious rites
Intrude upon their penitence, and force,
Albeit from loathing and reluctant lips,
The sorcery-secret?

THALABA.
Is it not the truth?

OLD MAN.
Son, thou hast seen the Traveller in the sands
Move in the dizzy light of the hot noon,
Huge[73] as the giant race of elder times,
And his Camel, than the monstrous Elephant,
Seem of a vaster bulk.

THALABA.
A frequent sight.

OLD MAN.
And hast thou never in the twilight, fancied
Familiar object into some strange shape
And form uncouth?

THALABA.
Aye! many a time.

OLD MAN.
Even so
Things viewed at distance thro' the mist of fear,
In their distortion terrify and shock
The abused sight.

THALABA.
But of these Angels fate
Thus in the uncreated Book is written.

OLD MAN.
Wisely from legendary fables, Heaven
Inculcates wisdom.

THALABA.
How then is the truth?
Is not the dungeon of their punishment
By ruined Babylon?

OLD MAN.
By Babylon
Haruth and Maruth may be found.

THALABA.
And there
Magician learn their impious sorcery?

OLD MAN.
Son what thou sayest is true, and it is false.
But night approaches fast; I have travelled far
And my old lids are heavy ... on our way
We shall have hours for converse, let us now
Turn to our due repose. Son, peace be with thee!

So in his loosened cloak
The Old Man wrapt[74] himself
And laid his limbs at length:
And Thalaba in silence laid him down.
Awhile he lay and watched the lovely Moon,
O'er whose broad orb the boughs
A mazy fretting framed,
Or with a pale transparent green
Lighting the restless leaves,
The thin Acacia leaves that played above.
The murmuring wind, the moving leaves
Lulled him to sleep with mingled lullabies.

Not so the dark Magician by his side,
Lobaba, who from the Domdaniel caves
Had sought the dreaded youth.

Silent he lay, and simulating sleep,
Till by the long and regular breath he knew
The youth beside him slept.
Carefully then he rose,
And bending over him, surveyed him near
And secretly he cursed
The dead Abdaldar's ring,
Armed by whose amulet
He slept from danger safe.

Wrapped in his mantle Thalaba reposed,
His loose right arm pillowing his head.
The Moon was on the Ring,
Whose crystal gem returned
A quiet, moveless light.
Vainly the Wizard vile put forth his hand
And strove to reach the gem,
Charms strong as hell could make them, made it safe.
He called his servant fiends,
He bade the Genii rob the sleeping youth.
By the virtue of the Ring,
By Mohammed's holier power,
By the holiest name of God,
Had Thalaba disarmed the evil race.

Baffled and weary, and convinced at length,
Anger, and fear, and rancour gnawing him,
The accursed Sorcerer ceased his vain attempts.
Content perforce to wait
Temptations likelier aid.
Restless he lay, and brooding many a wile,
And tortured with impatient hope,
And envying with the bitterness of hate
The innocent youth, who slept so sweetly by.

The ray of morning on his eye lids fell,
And Thalaba awoke
And folded his mantle around him,
And girded his loins for the day;
Then the due rites of holiness observed.
His comrade too arose,
And with the outward forms
Of righteousness and prayer insulted God.
They filled their water skin, they gave
The Camel his full draught.
Then on their road while yet the morn was young
And the air was fresh with dew,
Forward the travellers went,
With various talk beguiling the long way.
But soon the youth, whose busy mind
Dwelt on Lobaba's wonder-stirring words,

Renewed the unfinished converse of the night.

THALABA.
Thou saidest that it is true, and yet is false,
That men accurst, attain at Babylon
Forbidden knowledge from the Angel pair....
How mean you?

LOBABA.
All things have a double power,
Alike for good and evil, the same fire
That on the comfortable hearth at eve
Warmed the good man, flames o'er the house at night
Should we for this forego
The needful element?
Because the scorching summer Sun
Darts fever, wouldst thou quench the orb of day?
Or deemest thou that Heaven in anger formed
Iron to till the field, because when man
Had tipt his arrows for the chase, he rushed
A murderer to the war?

THALABA.
What follows hence?

LOBABA.
That nothing in itself is good or evil,
But only in its use. Think you the man
Praiseworthy who by painful study learns
The knowledge of all simples, and their power
Healing or harmful?

THALABA.
All men hold in honour
The skilful Leech. From land to land he goes
Safe in his privilege; the sword of war
Spares him, Kings welcome him with costly gifts,
And he who late had from the couch of pain
Lifted a languid look to him for aid,
Views him with brightened eyes, and blesses him
In his first thankful prayer.

LOBABA.
Yet some there are
Who to the purposes of wickedness,
Apply this knowledge, and from herbs distil
Poison to mix it in the trusted draught.

THALABA.
Allah shall cast them in the fire
Whose fuel is the cursed! there shall they

Endure the ever-burning agony
Consuming[75] still in flames, and still renewed.

LOBABA.
But is their knowledge therefore in itself
Unlawful?

THALABA.
That were foolishness to think.

LOBABA.
O what a glorious animal were Man,
Knew he but his own powers! and knowing gave them
Room for their growth and spread! the Horse obeys
His guiding will, the patient Camel bears him
Over these wastes of sand, the Pigeon wafts
His bidding thro' the sky: and with these triumphs
He rests contented! with these ministers,
When he might awe the Elements, and make
Myriads of Spirits serve him!

THALABA.
But as how!
By a league with Hell, a covenant that binds
The soul to utter death!

LOBABA.
Was Solomon
Accurst of God? yet to his talismans
Obedient, o'er his throne the birds of Heaven
Their waving wings[76] his sun-shield, fanned around him
The motionless air of noon: from place to place,
As his will reined the viewless Element
He rode the Wind: the Genii reared his temple,
And ceaselessly in fear while his dead eye
O'erlooked them, day and night pursued their toil,
So dreadful was his power.

THALABA.
But 'twas from Heaven
His wisdom came; God's special gift ... the guerdon
Of early virtue.

LOBABA.
Learn thou, O young man!
God hath appointed Wisdom the reward
Of study! 'tis a spring of living waters,
Whose inexhaustible bounties all might drink
But few dig deep enough. Son! thou art silent,...
Perhaps I say too much,... perhaps offend thee.

THALABA.

Nay, I am young, and willingly as becomes me,
Hear the wise words of age.

LOBABA.

Is it a crime
To mount the horse, because forsooth thy feet
Can serve thee for the journey? is it sin
Because the Hern soars upward in the sky
Above the arrow's flight, to train the Falcon
Whose beak shall pierce him there? the powers which All
Granted to man, were granted for his use;
All knowledge that befits not human weakness
Is placed beyond its reach.... They who repair
To Babylon, and from the Angels learn
Mysterious wisdom, sin not in the deed.

THALABA.

Know you these secrets?

LOBABA.

I? alas my Son
My age just knows enough to understand
How little all its knowledge! later years
Sacred to study, teach me to regret
Youth's unforeseeing indolence, and hours
That cannot be recalled! something I know:
The properties of herbs, and have sometimes
Brought to the afflicted comfort and relief
By the secrets of my art; under His blessing
Without whom all had failed! Also of Gems
I have some knowledge, and the characters
That tell beneath what aspect they were set.

THALABA.

Belike you can interpret then the graving
Around this Ring?

LOBABA.

My sight is feeble, Son,
And I must view it closer, let me try!

The unsuspecting Youth
Held forth his linger to draw off the spell.
Even whilst he held it forth,
There settled there a Wasp,
And just above the Gem infixed its dart.
All purple swoln the hot and painful flesh
Rose round the tightened Ring.
The baffled Sorcerer knew the hand of Heaven,
And inwardly blasphemed.

Ere long Lobaba's heart,
Fruitful in wiles, devised new stratagem.
A mist arose at noon;
Like the loose hanging skirts
Of some low cloud that, by the breeze impelled,
Sweeps o'er the mountain side.
With joy the thoughtless youth
That grateful shadowing hailed;
For grateful was the shade,
While thro' the silver-lighted haze
Guiding their way, appeared the beamless Sun.
But soon that beacon failed;
A heavier mass of cloud
Impenetrably deep,
Hung o'er the wilderness.
"Knowest thou the track?" quoth Thalaba,
"Or should we pause, and wait the wind
"To scatter this bewildering fog?"
The Sorcerer answered him
"Now let us hold right on,... for if we stray
"The Sun tomorrow will direct our course."
So saying, he towards the desert depths
Misleads the youth deceived.

Earlier the night came on,
Nor moon, nor stars, were visible in Heaven;
And when at morn the youth unclosed his eyes
He knew not where to turn his face in prayer.
"What shall we do?" Lobaba cried,
"The lights of Heaven have ceased
"To guide us on our way.
"Should we remain and wait
"More favourable skies?
"Soon would our food and water fail us here!
"And if we venture on,
"There are the dangers of the wilderness!"
"Sure it were best proceed!"
The chosen youth replies.
"So haply we may reach some tent, or grove
"Of dates, or stationed tribe.
"But idly to remain
"Were yielding effortless, and waiting death."
The wily Sorcerer willingly assents,
And farther in the sands,
Elate of heart, he leads the credulous youth.

Still o'er the wilderness
Settled the moveless mist.
The timid Antelope that heard their steps
Stood doubtful where to turn in that dim light,

The Ostrich, blindly hastening, met them full.
At night again in hope,
Young Thalaba laid down;
The morning came, and not one guiding ray
Thro' the thick mist was visible,
The same deep moveless mist that mantled all.
Oh for the Vulture's scream
That haunts for prey the abode of humankind!
Oh for the Plover's[77] pleasant cry
To tell of water near!
Oh for the Camel-driver's[78] song!
For now the water-skin grows light,
Tho' of the draught, more eagerly desired,
Imperious prudence took with sparing thirst.
Oft from the third night's broken sleep,
As in his dreams he heard
The sound of rushing winds,
Started the anxious youth, and looked abroad,
In vain! for still the deadly calm endured.
Another day past on,
The water-skin was drained,
But then one hope arrived
For there was motion in the air!
The sound of the wind arose anon
That scattered the thick mist,
And lo! at length the lovely face of Heaven!

Alas ... a wretched scene
Was opened on their view.
They looked around, no wells were near,
No tent, no human aid!
Flat on the Camel lay the water-skin,
And their dumb servant difficultly now,
Over hot sands and under the hot sun,
Dragged on with patient pain.
But oh the joy! the blessed sight!
When in the burning waste the Travellers
Saw a green meadow, fair with flowers besprent,
Azure and yellow, like the beautiful fields
Of England, when amid the growing grass
The blue-bell bends, the golden king-cup shines,
In the merry month of May!
Oh joy! the Travellers
Gaze on each other with hope-brightened eyes,
For sure thro' that green meadow flows
The living stream! and lo! their famished beast
Sees the restoring sight!
Hope gives his feeble limbs a sudden strength,
He hurries on!
The herbs so fair to eye
Were Senna, and the Gentian's blossom blue,

And kindred plants that with unwatered root
Fed in the burning sand, whose bitter leaves
Even frantic[79] Famine loathed.

In uncommunicating misery
Silent they stood. At length Lobaba cried,
"Son we must slay the Camel, or we die
"For lack of water! thy young hand is firm,
"Draw forth the knife and pierce him!"
Wretch accurst,
Who that beheld thy venerable face,
Thy features fixed with suffering, the dry lips,
The feverish eyes, could deem that all within
Was magic ease, and fearlessness secure,
And wiles of hellish import? the young man
Paused with reluctant pity: but he saw
His comrade's red and painful countenance,
And his own burning breath came short and quick,
And at his feet the gasping beast
Lies, over-worn with want.
Then from his[80] girdle Thalaba took the knife
With stern compassion, and from side to side
Across[81] the Camel's throat,
Drew deep the crooked blade.
Servant of man, that merciful deed
For ever ends thy suffering, but what doom
Waits thy deliverer! "little will thy death
"Avail us!" thought the youth,
As in the water-skin he poured
The Camel's hoarded draught:
It gave a scant supply,
The poor allowance of one prudent day.

Son of Hodeirah, tho' thy steady soul
Despaired not, firm in faith,
Yet not the less did suffering Nature feel
Her pangs and trials, long their craving thirst
Struggled with fear, by fear itself inflamed;
But drop by drop, that poor,
That last supply is drained!
Still the same burning sun! no cloud in heaven!
The hot air quivers, and the sultry mist
Floats o'er the desert, with a show
Of distant[82] waters, mocking their distress!
The youth's parched lips were black,
His tongue was[83] dry and rough,
His eye-balls red with heat.
His comrade gazed on him with looks
That seemed to speak of pity, and he said
"Let me behold thy Ring,
"It may have virtue that can save us yet!"

With that he took his hand
And viewed the writing close,
Then cried with sudden joy
"It is a stone that whoso bears
"The Genii must obey!
"Now raise thy voice, my Son,
"And bid them in his name that here is written
"Preserve us in our need."

"Nay!" answered Thalaba,
"Shall I distrust the providence of God?
"Is it not He must save?
"If Allah wills it not
"Vain were the Genii's aid."

Whilst he spake Lobaba's eye
Full on the distance fixed,
Attended not his speech.
Its fearful meaning drew
The looks of Thalaba.
Columns of sand came moving on,
Red in the burning ray
Like obelisks of fire
They rushed before the driving wind.
Vain were all thoughts of flight!
They had not hoped escape
Could they have backed the Dromedary then
Who in his rapid race
Gives to the tranquil[84] air, a drowning force.

High ... high in heaven upcurled
The dreadful[85] columns moved,
Swift, as the whirlwind that impelled their way,
They rushed towards the Travellers!
The old Magician shrieked,
And lo! the foremost bursts,
Before the whirlwind's force,
Scattering afar a burning shower of sand.
"Now by the virtue of the Ring
"Save us!" Lobaba cried.
"While yet thou hast the power
"Save us. O save us! now!"
The youth made no reply,
Gazing in aweful wonder on the scene.

"Why dost thou wait?" the Old Man exclaimed,
"If Allah and the Prophet will not save
"Call on the Powers that will!"

"Ha! do I know thee, Infidel accurst?"
Exclaimed the awakened youth.

"And thou hast led me hither, Child of Sin!
"That fear might make me sell
"My soul to endless death!"

"Fool that thou art!" Lobaba cried,
"Call upon him whose name
"Thy charmed signet bears,
"Or die the death thy foolishness deserves!"

"Servant of Hell! die thou!" quoth Thalaba.
And leaning on his bow
He fitted the loose string,
And laid the arrow in its resting-place.
"Bow of my Father, do thy duty now!"
He drew the arrow to its point,
True to his eye it fled,
And full upon the breast
It smote the wizard man.
Astonished Thalaba beheld
The blunted point recoil.

A proud and bitter smile
Wrinkled Lobaba's cheek,
"Try once again thine earthly arms!" he cried.
"Rash Boy! the Power I serve
"Abandons not his votaries.
"It is for Allah's wretched slaves, like thou,
"To serve a master, who in the hour of need
"Forsakes them to their fate!
"I leave thee!"... and he shook his staff, and called
The Chariot of his Charms.

Swift as the viewless wind,
Self-moved, the Chariot came,
The Sorcerer mounts the seat.
"Yet once more weigh thy danger!" he exclaimed,
"Ascend the car with me,
"And with the speed of thought
"We pass the desert bounds."
The indignant youth vouchsafed not to reply,
And lo! the magic car begins its course!
Hark! hark!... he screams.... Lobaba screams!
What wretch, and hast thou raised
The rushing Terrors of the Wilderness
To fall on thine own head?
Death! death! inevitable death!
Driven by the breath of God
A column of the Desert met his way.

THE FIFTH BOOK

When Thalaba from adoration rose,
The air was cool, the sky
With welcome clouds o'ercast,
That soon came down in rain.
He lifted up his fevered face to heaven,
And bared his head and stretched his hands
To that delightful shower,
And felt the coolness flow thro' every limb
Freshening his powers of life.

A loud quick panting! Thalaba looks up,
He starts, and his instinctive hand
Grasps the knife hilt: for close beside
A Tyger passes him.
An indolent and languid eye
The passing Tyger turned;
His head was hanging down,
His dry tongue lolling low,
And the short panting of his fevered breath
Came thro' his hot parched nostrils painfully.
The young Arabian knew
The purport of his hurried pace,
And following him in hope
Saw joyful from afar
The Tyger stoop and drink.

The desert Pelican had built her nest
In that deep solitude.
And now returned from distant flight
Fraught with the river stream,
Her load of water had disburthened there.
Her young in the refreshing bath
Sported all wantonness;
Dipt down their callow heads,
Filled the swoln membrane from their plumeless throat
Pendant, and bills yet soft,
And buoyant with arched breast,
Plied in unpractised stroke
The oars of their broad feet.
They, as the spotted prowler of the wild
Laps the cool wave, around their mother croud,
And nestle underneath her outspread wings.
The spotted prowler of the wild
Lapt the cool wave,[86] and satiate from the nest,
Guiltless of blood, withdrew.

The mother bird had moved not
But cowering o'er her nestlings,
Sate confident and fearless,
And watched the wonted guest.
But when the human visitant approached,
The alarmed Pelican
Retiring from that hostile shape,
Gathers her young, and menaces with wings,
And forward thrusts her threatening neck,
Its feathers ruffling in her wrath,
Bold with maternal fear.
Thalaba drank and in the water-skin
Hoarded the precious element.
Not all he took, but in the large nest left
Store that sufficed for life.
And journeying onward blest the Carrier Bird,
And blest in thankfulness,
Their common Father, provident for all.

With strength renewed and confident in faith
The son of Hodeirah proceeds;
Till after the long toil of many a day,
At length Bagdad appeared,
The City of his search.
He hastening to the gate
Roams o'er the city with insatiate eyes,
Its thousand dwellings o'er whose level roofs
Fair cupolas appeared, and high-domed mosques
And pointed minarets, and cypress groves
Every where scattered[87] in unwithering green.

Thou too art fallen, Bagdad! City of[88] Peace,
Thou too hast had thy day!
And loathsome Ignorance and brute Servitude
Pollute thy dwellings now,
Erst for the Mighty and the Wise renowned.
O yet illustrious for remembered fame,
Thy founder the [89]Victorious, and the pomp
Of Haroun, for whose name by blood defiled,
Jahia's, and the blameless Barmecides',
Genius hath wrought salvation; and the years
When Science with the good Al-Maimon dwelt;
So one day may the Crescent from thy Mosques
Be plucked by Wisdom, when the enlightened arm
Of Europe conquers to redeem the East.

Then Pomp and Pleasure dwelt within her walls
The Merchants of the East and of the West
Met in her arched[90] Bazars;
All day the active poor
Showered a cool comfort o'er her thronging streets;

Labour was busy in her looms;
Thro' all her open gates
Long troops of laden Camels lined her roads,
And Tigris on his tameless[91] current bore
Armenian harvests to her multitudes.

But not in sumptuous Caravansary
The adventurer idles there,
Nor satiates wonder with her pomp and wealth;
A long day's distance from the walls
Stands ruined Babylon!
The time of action is at hand,
The hope that for so many a year
Hath been his daily thought, his nightly dream,
Stings to more restlessness.
He loathes all lingering that delays the hour
When, full of glory, from his quest returned,
He on the pillar of the Tent beloved
Shall hang Hodeirah's sword.

The many-coloured[92] domes
Yet wore one dusky hue,
The Cranes upon the Mosque
Kept their night-clatter[93] still,
When thro' the gate the early Traveller past.
And when at evening o'er the swampy plain
The Bittern's[94] Boom came far,
Distinct in darkness seen
Above the low horizon's lingering light
Rose the near ruins of old Babylon.

Once from her lofty walls[95] the Charioteer
Looked down on swarming myriads; once she flung
Her arches o'er Euphrates conquered tide,
And thro' her brazen portals when she poured
Her armies forth, the distant nations looked
As men who watched the thunder-cloud in fear
Lest it should burst above them. She was fallen,
The Queen of Cities, Babylon was fallen!
Low lay her bulwarks; the black scorpion basked
In the palace courts, within her sanctuary
The She Wolf hid her whelps.
Is yonder huge and shapeless heap, what once
Had been the aerial[96] Gardens, height on height
Rising like Medias mountains crowned with wood,
Work of imperial dotage? where the fame
Of[97] Belus? where the Golden Image now,
Which at the sound of dulcimer and lute,
Cornet and sackbut, harp and psaltery,
The Assyrian slaves adored?
A labyrinth of ruins, Babylon

Spreads o'er the blasted plain:
The wandering Arab never sets his tent
Within her walls; the Shepherd[98] eyes afar
Her evil Towers, and devious drives his flock.
Alone unchanged, a free and bridgeless tide
Euphrates rolls along,
Eternal Nature's work.

Thro' the broken portal,
Over weedy fragments,
Thalaba went his way.
Cautious he trod, and felt
The dangerous ground before him with his bow.
The Chacal started at his steps,
The Stork, alarmed at sound of man,
From her broad nest upon the old pillar top,
Affrighted fled on flapping wings.
The Adder in her haunts disturbed
Lanced at the intruding staff her arrowy tongue.

Twilight and moonshine dimly mingling gave
An aweful light obscure,
Evening not wholly closed,
The Moon still pale and faint.
An aweful light obscure,
Broken by many a mass of blackest shade;
Long column stretching dark thro' weeds and moss,
Broad length of lofty wall
Whose windows lay in light,
And of their former shape, low-arched or square,
Rude outline on the earth
Figured, with long grass fringed.

Reclined against a column's broken shaft,
Unknowing whitherward to bend his way
He stood and gazed around.
The Ruins closed him in,
It seemed as if no foot of man
For ages had intruded there.
Soon at approaching step
Starting, he turned and saw
A warrior in the moon beam drawing near.
Forward the Stranger came
And with a curious eye
Perused the Arab youth.
"And who art thou," he cried,
"That at an hour like this
"Wanderest in Babylon?
"A way-bewildered traveller, seekest thou
"The ruinous shelter here?
"Or comest thou to hide

"The plunder of the night?
"Or hast thou spells to make
"These ruins, yawning from their rooted base
"Disclose their secret[99] wealth?"

The youth replied, "nor wandering traveller
"Nor robber of the night
"Nor skilled in spells am I.
"I seek the Angels here,
"Haruth and Maruth. Stranger in thy turn,
"Why wanderest thou in Babylon,
"And who art thou, the Questioner?"

The man was fearless, and the tempered pride
That toned the voice of Thalaba
Displeased not him, himself of haughty heart.
Heedless he answered, "knowest thou
"Their cave of punishment?"

THALABA.
Vainly I seek it.

STRANGER.
Art thou firm of foot
To tread the ways of danger?

THALABA.
Point the path!

STRANGER.
Young Arab! if thou hast a heart can beat
Evenly in danger, if thy bowels yearn not
With human fears, at scenes where undisgraced
The soldier tried in battle might look back
And tremble, follow me!... for I am bound
Into that cave of horrors. Thalaba
Gazed on his comrade, he was young, of port
Stately and strong; belike his face had pleased
A woman's eye, yet the youth read in it
Unrestrained passions, the obdurate soul
Bold in all evil daring; and it taught,
By Nature's irresistible instinct, doubt
Well timed and wary. Of himself assured,
Fearless of man, and confident in faith,
"Lead on!" cried Thalaba.
Mohareb led the way;
And thro' the ruined streets,
And thro' the farther gate
They past in silence on.

What sound is borne on the wind?

Is it the storm that shakes
The thousand oaks of the forest?
But Thalaba's long locks
Flow down his shoulders moveless, and the wind
In his loose mantle raises not one fold.
Is it the river's roar
Dashed down some rocky descent?
Along the level plain
Euphrates glides unheard.
What sound disturbs the night,
Loud as the summer forest in the storm,
As the river that roars among rocks?

And what the heavy cloud
That hangs upon the vale,
Thick as the mist o'er a well-watered plain
Settling at evening, when the cooler air
Lets its day-vapours fall;
Black as the sulphur-cloud
That thro' Vesuvius, or from Hecla's mouth
Rolls up, ascending from the infernal fires.

From Ait's bitumen[100] lake
That heavy cloud ascends;
That everlasting roar
From where its gushing springs
Boil their black billows up.
Silent the Arab youth,
Along the verge of that wide lake,
Followed Mohareb's way
Towards a ridge of rocks that banked its side.
There from a cave with torrent force,
And everlasting roar,
The black bitumen rolled.
The moonlight lay upon the rocks.
Their crags were visible,
The shade of jutting cliffs,
And where broad lichens whitened some smooth spot,
And where the ivy hung
Its flowing tresses down.
A little way within the cave
The moonlight fell, glossing the sable tide
That gushed tumultuous out.
A little way it entered, then the rock
Arching its entrance, and the winding way,
Darkened the unseen depths.
No eye of mortal man
If unenabled by enchanted spell,
Had pierced those fearful depths.
For mingling with the roar
Of the portentous torrent, oft were heard

Shrieks, and wild yells that scared
The brooding Eagle from her midnight nest.
The affrighted countrymen
Call it the Mouth of Hell;
And ever when their way leads near
They hurry with averted eyes,
And dropping their beads[101] fast
Pronounce the holy name.

There pausing at the cavern mouth
Mohareb turned to Thalaba,
"Now darest thou enter in?"
"Behold!" the youth replied,
And leading in his turn the dangerous way
Set foot within the cave.

"Stay Madman!" cried his comrade. "Wouldst thou rush
"Headlong to certain death?
"Where are thine arms to meet
"The Guardian of the Passage?" a loud shriek
That shook along the windings of the cave
Scattered the youth's reply.

Mohareb when the long reechoing ceased
Exclaimed, "Fate favoured thee,
"Young Arab! when she wrote[102] upon thy brow
"The meeting of to-night;
"Else surely had thy name
"This hour been blotted from the Book of Life!"

So saying from beneath
His cloak a bag he drew;
"Young Arab! thou art brave," he cried,
"But thus to rush on danger unprepared,
"As lions spring upon the hunter's spear,
"Is blind, brute courage. Zohak[103] keeps the cave,
"Giantly tyrant of primeval days.
"Force cannot win the passage." Thus he said
And from his wallet drew a human hand
Shrivelled, and dry, and black,
And fitting as he spake
A taper in its hold,
Pursued: "a murderer on the stake had died,
"I drove the Vulture from his limbs, and lopt
"The hand that did the murder, and drew up
"The tendon-strings to close its grasp,
"And in the sun and wind
"Parched it, nine weeks exposed.
"The Taper,... but not here the place to impart,
"Nor hast thou done the rites,
"That fit thee to partake the mystery.

"Look! it burns clear, but with the air around
"Its dead ingredients mingle deathiness.
"This when the Keeper of the Cave shall feel,
"Maugre the doom of Heaven,
"The salutary[104] spell
"Shall lull his penal agony to sleep
"And leave the passage free."

Thalaba answered not.
Nor was there time for answer now,
For lo! Mohareb leads,
And o'er the vaulted cave
Trembles the accursed taper's feeble light.
There where the narrowing chasm
Rose loftier in the hill,
Stood Zohak, wretched man, condemned to keep
His Cave of punishment.
His was the frequent scream
Which far away the prowling Chacal heard
And howled in terror back:
For from his shoulders grew
Two snakes of monster size,
That ever at his head
Aimed eager their keen teeth
To satiate raving hunger with his brain.
He in the eternal conflict oft would seize
Their swelling necks, and in his giant grasp
Bruise them, and rend their flesh with bloody nails,
And howl for agony,
Feeling the pangs he gave, for of himself
Inseparable parts, his torturers grew.

To him approaching now
Mohareb held the withered arm
The Taper of enchanted power.
The unhallowed spell in hand unholy held
Now ministered to mercy, heavily
The wretche's eyelids closed,
And welcome and unfelt
Like the release of death
A sudden sleep fell on his vital powers.

Yet tho' along the cave
Lay Zohak's giant limbs,
The twin-born serpents kept the narrow pass,
Kindled their fiery eyes,
Darted their tongues of terror, and rolled out
Their undulating length,
Like the long streamers of some gallant ship
Buoyed on the wavy air,
Still struggling to flow on and still withheld.

The scent of living flesh
Inflamed their appetite.

Prepared for all the perils of the cave
Mohareb came. He from his wallet drew
Two human heads yet warm.
O hard of heart! whom not the visible power
Of retributive Justice, and the doom
Of Zohak in his sight,
Deterred from equal crime!
Two human heads, yet warm, he laid
Before the scaly guardians of the pass.
They to their wonted banquet of old years
Turned eager, and the narrow pass was free.

And now before their path
The opening cave dilates;
They reach a spacious vault
Where the black river fountains burst their way.
Now as a whirlwind's force
Had centered on the spring,
The gushing flood rolled up;
And now the deadened roar
Echoed beneath them, as its sudden pause
Left wide a dark abyss,
Adown whose fathomless gulphs the eye was lost.
Blue flames that hovered o'er the springs
Flung thro' the Cavern their uncertain light
Now waving on the waves they lay,
And now their fiery curls
Flowed in long tresses up,
And now contracting glowed with whiter heat.
Then up they poured again
Darting pale flashes thro' the tremulous air;
The flames, the red and yellow sulphur-smoke,
And the black darkness of the vault
Commingling indivisibly.

"Here," quoth Mohareb, "do the Angels dwell,
"The Teachers of Enchantment." Thalaba
Then raised his voice and cried,
"Haruth and Maruth, hear me! not with rites
"Accursed, to disturb your penitence
"And learn forbidden lore,
"Repentant Angels, seek I your abode.
"Me Allah and the Prophet mission here,
"Their chosen servant I.
"Tell me the Talisman."...
"And dost thou think"
"Mohareb cried, as with a scornful smile
He glanced upon his comrade, "dost thou think

"To trick them of their secret? for the dupes
"Of human-kind keep this lip-righteousness!
"'Twill serve thee in the Mosque
"And in the Market-place,
"But Spirits view the heart.
"Only by strong and torturing spells enforced,
"Those stubborn Angels teach the charm
"By which we must descend."

"Descend!" said Thalaba.
But then the wrinkling smile
Forsook Mohareb's cheek,
And darker feelings settled on his brow.
"Now by my soul," quoth he, "and I believe
"Idiot! that I have led
"Some camel-kneed prayer-monger thro' the cave!
"What brings thee hither? thou shouldest have a hut
"By some Saint's[105] grave beside the public way,
"There to less-knowing fools
"Retail thy Koran[106] scraps,
"And in thy turn, die civet-like at last
"In the dung-perfume of thy sanctity!...
"Ye whom I seek! that, led by me,
"Feet uninitiate tread
"Your threshold, this atones!
"Fit sacrifice he falls!"
And forth he flashed his scymetar,
And raised the murderous blow.

Then ceased his power; his lifted arm,
Suspended by the spell,
Hung impotent to strike.
"Poor Hypocrite!" cried he,
"And this then is thy faith
"In Allah and the Prophet! they had failed
"To save thee, but for Magic's stolen aid;
"Yea, they had left thee yonder Serpent's meal,
"But that, in prudent cowardice,
"The chosen Servant of the Lord came in,
"Safe follower of my path!"

"Blasphemer! dost thou boast of guiding me?"
Kindling with pride quoth Thalaba,
"Blindly the wicked work
"The righteous will of Heaven.
"Sayest thou that diffident of God,
"In magic spell I trust?
"Liar! let witness this!"
And he drew off Abdaldar's Ring
And cast it in the gulph.
A skinny hand came up

And caught it as it fell,
And peals of devilish laughter shook the Cave.

Then joy suffused Mohareb's cheek,
And Thalaba beheld
The blue blade gleam, descending to destroy.

The undefended youth
Sprung forward, and he seized
Mohareb in his grasp,
And grappled with him breast to breast.
Sinewy and large of limb Mohareb was,
Broad-shouldered, and his joints
Knit firm, and in the strife
Of danger practised well.
Time had not thus matured young Thalaba:
But now the enthusiast mind,
The inspiration of his soul
Poured vigour like the strength
Of madness thro' his frame.
Mohareb reels before him! he right on
With knee, with breast, with arm,
Presses the staggering foe!
And now upon the brink
Of that tremendous spring,
There with fresh impulse and a rush of force
He thrust him from his hold.
The upwhirling flood received
Mohareb, then, absorbed,
Engulphed him in the abyss.

Thalaba's breath came fast,
And panting he breathed out
A broken prayer of thankfulness.
At length he spake and said,
"Haruth and Maruth! are ye here?
"Or has that evil guide misled my search?
"I, Thalaba, the Servant of the Lord,
"Invoke you. Hear me Angels! so may Heaven
"Accept and mitigate your penitence.
"I go to root from earth the Sorcerer brood,
"Tell me the needful Talisman!"

Thus as he spake, recumbent on the rock
Beyond the black abyss,
Their forms grew visible.
A settled sorrow sate upon their brows,
Sorrow alone, for trace of guilt and shame
No more remained; and gradual as by prayer
The sin was purged away,
Their robe[107] of glory, purified of stain

Resumed the lustre of its native light.

In awe the youth received the answering voice,
"Son of Hodeirah! thou hast proved it here;
"The Talisman is Faith."

THALABA THE DESTROYER

THE SIXTH BOOK

So from the inmost cavern, Thalaba
Retrod the windings of the rock.
Still on the ground the giant limbs
Of Zohak were outstretched;
The spell of sleep had ceased
And his broad eyes were glaring on the youth:
Yet raised he not his arm to bar the way,
Fearful to rouse the snakes
Now lingering o'er their meal.

Oh then, emerging from that dreadful cave,
How grateful did the gale of night
Salute his freshened sense!
How full of lightsome joy,
Thankful to Heaven, he hastens by the verge
Of that bitumen lake,
Whose black and heavy fumes,
Surge heaving after surge,
Rolled like the billowy and tumultuous sea.

The song of many a bird at morn
Aroused him from his rest.
Lo! by his side a courser stood!
More animate of eye,
Of form more faultless never had he seen,
More light of limbs and beautiful in strength,
Among the race whose blood,
Pure and unmingled, from the royal steeds
Of [108]Solomon came down.

The chosen Arab's eye
Glanced o'er his graceful shape,
His rich caparisons,
His crimson trappings gay.
But when he saw the mouth
Uncurbed, the unbridled neck,

Then flushed his cheek, and leapt his heart,
For sure he deemed that Heaven had sent
The Courser, whom no erring hand should guide.
And lo! the eager Steed
Throws his head and paws the ground,
Impatient of delay!
Then up leapt Thalaba
And away went the self-governed steed.

Far over the plain
Away went the bridleless steed;
With the dew of the morning his fetlocks were wet,
The foam frothed his limbs in the journey of noon,
Nor stayed he till over the westerly heaven
The shadows of evening had spread.
Then on a sheltered bank
The appointed Youth reposed,
And by him laid the docile courser down.
Again in the grey of the morning
Thalaba bounded up,
Over hill, over dale
Away goes the bridleless steed.
Again at eve he stops
Again the Youth descends.
His load discharged, his errand done,
Then bounded the courser away.

Heavy and dark the eve;
The Moon was hid on high,
A dim light only tinged the mist
That crost her in the path of Heaven.
All living sounds had ceased,
Only the flow of waters near was heard,
A low and lulling melody.
Fasting, yet not of want
Percipient, he on that mysterious steed
Had reached his resting place,
For expectation kept his nature up.
The flow of waters now
Awoke a feverish thirst:
Led by the sound, he moved
To seek the grateful wave.
A meteor in the hazy air
Played before his path;
Before him now it rolled
A globe of livid fire;
And now contracted to a steady light,
As when the solitary hermit prunes
His lamp's long undulating flame:
And now its wavy point
Up-blazing rose, like a young cypress-tree

Swayed by the heavy wind;
Anon to Thalaba it moved,
And wrapped him in its pale innocuous fire:
Now in the darkness drowned
Left him with eyes bedimmed,
And now emerging[109] spread the scene to sight.

Led by the sound, and meteor-flame
Advanced the Arab youth.
Now to the nearest of the many rills
He stoops; ascending steam
Timely repels his hand,
For from its source it sprung, a boiling tide.
A second course with better hap he tries,
The wave intensely cold
Tempts to a copious draught.
There was a virtue in the wave,
His limbs that stiff with toil,
Dragged heavy, from the copious draught received
Lightness and supple strength.
O'erjoyed, and deeming the benignant Power
Who sent the reinless steed,
Had blessed the healing waters to his use
He laid him down to sleep;
Lulled by the soothing and incessant sound,
The flow of many waters, blending oft
With shriller tones and deep low murmurings
That from the fountain caves
In mingled melody
Like faery music, heard at midnight, came.

The sounds that last he heard at night
Awoke his sense at morn.
A scene of wonders lay before his eyes.
In mazy windings o'er the vale
Wandered a thousand streams;
They in their endless flow[110] had channelled deep
The rocky soil o'er which they ran,
Veining its thousand islet stones,
Like clouds that freckle o'er the summer sky,
The blue etherial ocean circling each
And insulating all.
A thousand shapes they wore, those islet stones,
And Nature with her various tints
Varied anew their thousand forms:
For some were green with moss,
Some rich with yellow lichen's gold,
Or ruddier tinged, or grey, or silver-white,
Or sparkling sparry radiance to the sun.
Here gushed the fountains up,
Alternate light and blackness, like the play

Of sunbeams, on the warrior's burnished arms.
Yonder the river rolled, whose bed,
Their labyrinthine lingerings o'er
Received the confluent rills.

This was a wild and wonderous scene,
Strange and beautiful, as where
By Oton-tala, like a sea[111] of stars,
The hundred sources of Hoangho burst.
High mountains closed the vale,
Bare rocky mountains, to all living things
Inhospitable, on whose sides no herb
Rooted, no insect fed, no bird awoke
Their echoes, save the Eagle, strong of wing,
A lonely plunderer, that afar
Sought in the vales his prey.

Thither towards those mountains, Thalaba
Advanced, for well he weened that there had Fate
Destined the adventures end.
Up a wide vale winding amid their depths,
A stony vale between receding heights
Of stone, he wound his way.
A cheerless place! the solitary Bee
Whose buzzing was the only sound of life
Flew there on restless wing,
Seeking in vain one blossom, where to fix.

Still Thalaba holds on,
The winding vale now narrows on his way,
And steeper of ascent
Rightward and leftward rise the rocks,
And now they meet across the vale.
Was it the toil of human hands
That hewed a passage in the rock,
Thro' whose rude portal-way
The light of heaven was seen?
Rude and low the portal-way,
Beyond the same[112] ascending straits
Went winding up the wilds.

Still a bare, silent, solitary glen,
A fearful silence and a solitude
That made itself be felt.
And steeper now the ascent,
A rugged path, that tired
The straining muscles, toiling slowly up.
At length again a rock
Stretched o'er the narrow vale.
There also was a portal hewn,
But gates of massy iron barred the way,

Huge, solid, heavy-hinged.

There hung a horn beside the gate,
Ivory-tipt and brazen mouthed,
He took the ivory tip,
And thro' the brazen mouth he breathed;
From rock to rock rebounding rung the blast,
Like a long thunder peal!
The gates of iron, by no human arm
Unfolded, turning on their hinges slow,
Disclosed the passage of the rock.
He entered, and the iron gates
Fell to, and closed him in.
It was a narrow winding way,
Dim lamps suspended from the vault
Lent to the gloom an agitated light.
Winding it pierced the rock,
A long descending path
By gates of iron closed;
There also hung the horn beside
Of ivory tip and brazen mouth,
Again he took the ivory tip
And gave the brazen mouth his voice again.
Not now in thunder spake the horn,
But poured a sweet and thrilling melody:
The gates flew open, and a flood of light
Rushed on his dazzled eyes.

Was it to earthly Eden lost so long,
The youth had found the wonderous way?
But earthly Eden boasts
No terraced palaces,
No rich pavilions bright with woven[113] gold.
Like these that in the vale
Rise amid odorous groves.
The astonished Thalaba
Doubting as tho' an unsubstantial dream
Beguiled his passive sense,
A moment closed his eyes;
Still they were there ... the palaces and groves,
And rich pavilions glittering golden light.

And lo! a man, reverend in comely age
Advancing meets the youth.
"Favoured of Fortune," he exclaimed,
"Go taste the joys of Paradise!
"The reinless steed that ranges o'er the world
"Brings hither those alone for lofty deeds
"Marked by their horoscope; permitted here
"A foretaste of the full beatitude,
"That in heroic acts they may go on

"More ardent, eager to return and reap
"Endless enjoyment here, their destined meed.
"Favoured of Fortune thou,
"Go taste the joys of Paradise!"

This said, he turned away, and left
The Youth in wonder mute;
For Thalaba stood mute
And passively received
The mingled joy that flowed on every sense.
Where'er his eye could reach
Fair structures, rain bow-hued, arose;
And rich pavilions thro' the opening woods
Gleamed from their waving curtains sunny gold;
And winding thro' the verdant vale
Flowed streams of liquid light;
And fluted cypresses reared up
Their living obelisks;
And broad-leaved[114] Zennars in long colonades
O'er-arched delightful walks,
Where round their trunks the thousand-tendril'd vine
Wound up and hung the bows with greener wreaths,
And clusters not their own.
Wearied with endless beauty did his eyes
Return for rest? beside him teems the earth
With tulips, like the ruddy[115] evening streaked,
And here the lily hangs her head of snow,
And here amid her sable[116] cup
Shines the red eye-spot, like one brightest star
The solitary twinkler of the night,
And here the rose expands
Her paradise[117] of leaves.

Then on his ear what sounds
Of harmony arose!
Far music and the distance-mellowed song
From bowers of merriment;
The waterfall remote;
The murmuring of the leafy groves;
The single nightingale
Perched in the Rosier by, so richly toned,
That never from that most melodious bird,
Singing a love-song to his brooding mate,
Did Thracian shepherd by the grave
Of Orpheus[118] hear a sweeter song;
Tho' there the Spirit of the Sepulchre
All his own power infuse, to swell
The incense that he loves.

And oh! what odours the voluptuous vale
Scatters from jasmine bowers.

From yon rose wilderness,
From clustered henna, and from orange groves
That with such perfumes fill the breeze,
As Peris to their Sister bear,
When from the summit of some lofty tree
She hangs encaged, the captive of the Dives.
They from their pinions shake
The sweetness of celestial flowers,
And as her enemies impure
From that impervious poison far away
Fly groaning with the torment, she the while
Inhales her fragrant[119] food.
Such odours flowed upon the world
When at Mohammed's nuptials, word
Went forth in Heaven to roll
The everlasting gates of Paradise
Back on their living hinges, that its gales
Might visit all below; the general bliss
Thrilled every bosom, and the family
Of man, for once[120] partook one common joy.

Full of the joy, yet still awake
To wonder, on went Thalaba;
On every side the song of mirth,
The music of festivity,
Invite the passing youth.
Wearied at length with hunger and with heat
He enters in a banquet room,
Where round a fountain brink,
On silken[121] carpets sate the festive train.
Instant thro' all his frame
Delightful coolness spread;
The playing fount refreshed
The agitated air;
The very light came cooled thro' silvering panes
Of pearly[122] shell, like the pale moon-beam tinged;
Or where the wine-vase[123] filled the aperture,
Rosy as rising morn, or softer gleam
Of saffron, like the sunny evening mist:
Thro' every hue, and streaked by all
The flowing fountain played.
Around the water-edge
Vessels of wine, alternate placed,
Ruby and amber, tinged its little waves.
From golden goblets there[124]
The guests sate quaffing the delicious juice
Of Shiraz' golden grape.

But Thalaba took not the draught
For rightly he knew had the Prophet forbidden
That beverage the mother[125] of sins.

Nor did the urgent guests
Proffer a second time the liquid fire
For in the youth's strong eye they saw
No moveable resolve.
Yet not uncourteous, Thalaba
Drank the cool draught of innocence,
That fragrant from its dewy[126] vase
Came purer than it left its native bed.
And he partook the odorous fruits,
For all rich fruits were there.
Water-melons rough of rind,
Whose pulp the thirsty lip
Dissolved into a draught:
Pistachios from the heavy-clustered trees
Of Malavert, or Haleb's fertile soil,
And Casbin's[127] luscious grapes of amber hue,
That many a week endure
The summer sun intense,
Till by its powerful fire
All watery particles exhaled, alone
The strong essential sweetness ripens there.
Here cased in ice, the [128]apricot,
A topaz, crystal-set:
Here on a plate of snow
The sunny orange rests,
And still the aloes and the sandal-wood
From golden censers o'er the banquet room
Diffuse their dying sweets.

Anon a troop of females formed the dance
Their ancles bound with [129]bracelet-bells
That made the modulating harmony.
Transparent[130] garments to the greedy eye
Gave all their harlot limbs,
That writhed, in each immodest gesture skilled.

With earnest eyes the banqueters
Fed on the sight impure;
And Thalaba, he gazed,
But in his heart he bore a talisman
Whose blessed Alchemy
To virtuous thoughts refined
The loose suggestions of the scene impure.
Oneiza's image swam before his sight,
His own Arabian Maid.
He rose, and from the banquet room he rushed,
And tears ran down his burning cheek,
And nature for a moment woke the thought
And murmured, that from all domestic joys
Estranged, he wandered o'er the world
A lonely being, far from all he loved.

Son of Hodeirah, not among thy crimes
That murmur shall be written!

From tents of revelry,
From festal bowers, to solitude he ran,
And now he reached where all the rills
Of that well-watered garden in one tide
Rolled their collected waves.
A straight and stately bridge
Stretched its long arches o'er the ample stream.
Strong in the evening and distinct its shade
Lay on the watry mirror, and his eye
Saw it united with its parent pile
One huge fantastic fabric. Drawing near,
Loud from the chambers[131] of the bridge below,
Sounds of carousal came and song,
And unveiled women bade the advancing youth
Come merry-make with them.
Unhearing or unheeding, Thalaba
Past o'er with hurried pace,
And plunged amid the forest solitude.
Deserts of Araby!
His soul returned to you.
He cast himself upon the earth
And closed his eyes, and called
The voluntary vision up.
A cry as of distress
Aroused him; loud it came, and near!
He started up, he strung his bow,
He plucked the arrow forth.
Again a shriek ... a woman's shriek!
And lo! she rushes thro' the trees,
Her veil all rent, her garments torn!
He follows close, the ravisher....
Even on the unechoing grass
She hears his tread, so close!
"Prophet save me! save me God!
"Help! help!" she cried to Thalaba,
Thalaba drew the bow.
The unerring arrow did its work of death.
He turned him to the woman, and beheld
His own Oneiza, his Arabian Maid.

THALABA THE DESTROYER

THE SEVENTH BOOK

From fear, amazement, joy,

At length the Arabian Maid recovering speech,
Threw around Thalaba her arms and cried,
"My father! O my father!" Thalaba
In wonder lost, yet fearful to enquire,
Bent down his cheek on hers,
And their tears mingled as they fell.

ONEIZA.
At night they seized me, Thalaba! in my sleep,...
Thou wert not near,... and yet when in their grasp
I woke, my shriek of terror called on thee.
My father could not save me,... an old man!
And they were strong and many,... O my God,
The hearts they must have had to hear his prayers,
And yet to leave him childless!

THALABA.
We will seek him.
We will return to Araby.

ONEIZA.
Alas!
We should not find him, Thalaba! our tent
Is desolate, the wind hath heaped the sands
Within its door, the lizard's[132] track is left
Fresh on the untrodden dust; prowling by night
The tyger, as he passes hears no breath
Of man, and turns to search its solitude.
Alas! he strays a wretched wanderer
Seeking his child! old man, he will not rest,...
He cannot rest, his sleep is misery,
His dreams are of my wretchedness, my wrongs....
O Thalaba! this is a wicked place!
Let us be gone!

THALABA.
But how to pass again
The iron doors that opening at a breath
Gave easy entrance? armies in their strength,
Would fail to move those hinges for return!

ONEIZA.
But we can climb the mountains that shut in
This dreadful garden.

THALABA.
Are Oneiza's limbs
Equal to that long toil?

ONEIZA.
Oh I am strong

Dear Thalaba! for this ... fear gives me force,
And you are with me!
So she took his hand,
And gently drew him forward, and they went
Towards the mountain chain.
It was broad moonlight, and obscure or lost
The garden beauties lay,
But the great boundary rose, distinctly marked.
These were no little hills,
No sloping uplands lifting to the sun
Their vine-yards, with fresh verdure, and the shade
Of ancient woods, courting the loiterer
To win the easy ascent: stone mountains these
Desolate rock on rock,
The burthens of the earth,
Whose snowy summits met the morning beam
When night was in the vale, whose feet were fixed
In the world's[133] foundations. Thalaba surveyed
The heights precipitous,
Impending crags, rocks unascendible,
And summits that had tired the eagle's wing;
"There is no way!" he cried.
Paler Oneiza grew
And hung upon his arm a feebler weight.

But soon again to hope
Revives the Arabian maid,
As Thalaba imparts the sudden thought.
"I past a river," cried the youth
"A full and copious stream.
"The flowing waters cannot be restrained
"And where they find or force their way,
"There we perchance may follow, thitherward
"The current rolled along."
So saying yet again in hope
Quickening their eager steps
They turned them thitherward.

Silent and calm the river rolled along,
And at the verge arrived
Of that fair garden, o'er a rocky bed
Towards the mountain base,
Still full and silent, held its even way,
But the deep sound, the dash
Louder and louder in the distance rose,
As if it forced its stream
Struggling with crags along a narrow pass.
And lo! where raving o'er a hollow course
The ever-flowing tide
Foams in a thousand whirlpools! there adown
The perforated rock

Plunge the whole waters, so precipitous,
So fathomless a fall
That their earth-shaking roar came deadened up
Like subterranean thunders.
"Allah save us!"
Oneiza cried, "there is no path for man
"From this accursed place!"
And as she spake her joints
Were loosened, and her knees sunk under her.
"Cheer up, Oneiza!" Thalaba replied,
"Be of good heart. We cannot fly
"The dangers of the place,
"But we can conquer them!"

And the young Arab's soul
Arose within him; "what is he," he cried,
"Who has prepared this garden of delight,
"And wherefore are its snares?"

The Arabian Maid replied,
"The Women when I entered, welcomed me
"To Paradise, by Aloadin's will
"Chosen like themselves, a Houri of the Earth.
"They told me, credulous of his blasphemies,
"That Aloadin placed them to reward
"His faithful servants with the joys of Heaven.
"O Thalaba, and all are ready here
"To wreak his wicked will, and work all crimes!
"How then shall we escape?"

"Woe to him!" cried the Appointed, a stern smile
Darkening with stronger shades his countenance,
"Woe to him! he hath laid his toils
"To take the Antelope,
"The Lion is come in!"
She shook her head, "a Sorcerer he
"And guarded by so many! Thalaba,...
"And thou but one!"
He raised his hand to Heaven,
"Is there not God, Oneiza?
"I have a Talisman, that, whoso bears,
"Him, nor the Earthly, nor the Infernal Powers
"Of Evil can cast down.
"Remember Destiny
"Hath marked me from mankind!
"Now rest in faith, and I will guard thy sleep!"

So on a violet bank
The Arabian Maid lay down,
Her soft cheek pillowed upon moss and flowers.
She lay in silent prayer,

Till prayer had tranquillized her fears,
And sleep fell on her. By her side
Silent sate Thalaba,
And gazed upon the Maid,
And as he gazed, drew in
New courage and intenser faith,
And waited calmly for the eventful day.

Loud sung the Lark, the awakened Maid
Beheld him twinkling in the morning light,
And wished for wings and liberty like his.
The flush of fear inflamed her cheek,
But Thalaba was calm of soul,
Collected for the work.
He pondered in his mind
How from Lobaba's breast
His blunted arrow fell.
Aloadin too might wear
Spell perchance of equal power
To blunt the weapon's edge!
Beside the river-brink,
Rose a young poplar, whose unsteady leaves
Varying their verdure to the gale,
With silver glitter caught
His meditating eye.
Then to Oneiza turned the youth
And gave his father's bow,
And o'er her shoulders slung
The quiver arrow-stored.
"Me other weapon suits;" said he,
"Bear thou the Bow: dear Maid!
"The days return upon me, when these shafts,
"True to thy guidance, from the lofty palm
"Brought down the cluster, and thy gladdened eye
"Exulting turned to seek the voice of praise.
"Oh! yet again Oneiza, we shall share
"Our desert joys!"
So saying to the bank
He moved, and stooping low,
With double grasp, hand below hand, he clenched
And from its watry soil
Uptore the poplar trunk.
Then off he shook the clotted earth,
And broke away the head
And boughs and lesser roots,
And lifting it aloft
Wielded with able sway the massy club.
"Now for this child of Hell!" quoth Thalaba,
"Belike he shall exchange to day
"His dainty Paradise
"For other dwelling, and the fruit

"Of Zaccoum,[134] cursed tree."

With that the youth and Arab maid
Towards the garden centre past.
It chanced that Aloadin had convoked
The garden-habitants,
And with the assembled throng
Oneiza mingled, and the appointed youth.
Unmarked they mingled, or if one
With busier finger to his neighbour notes
The quivered Maid, "haply," he says,
"Some daughter of the[135] Homerites,
"Or one who yet remembers with delight
"Her native tents of Himiar!" "Nay!" rejoins
His comrade, "a love-pageant! for the man
"Mimics with that fierce eye and knotty club
"Some savage lion-tamer, she forsooth
"Must play the heroine of the years of old!"

Radiant with gems upon his throne of gold
Aloadin sate.
O'er the Sorcerer's head
Hovered a Bird, and in the fragrant air
Waved his winnowing wings,
A living canopy.
Large as the plumeless Cassowar
Was that o'ershadowing Bird;
So huge his talons, in their grasp
The Eagle would have hung a helpless prey.
His beak was iron, and his plumes
Glittered like burnished gold,
And his eyes glowed, as tho' an inward fire
Shone thro' a diamond orb.

The blinded multitude
Adored the Sorcerer,
And bent the knee before him,
And shouted out his praise,
"Mighty art thou, the Bestower of joy,
"The Lord of Paradise!"
Aloadin waved his hand,
In idolizing reverence
Moveless they stood and mute.
"Children of Earth," he cried,
"Whom I have guided here
"By easier passage than the gate of Death,
"The infidel Sultan to whose lands
"My mountains reach their roots,
"Blasphemes and threatens me.
"Strong are his armies, many are his guards,
"Yet may a dagger find him.

"Children of Earth, I tempt you not
"With the vain promise of a bliss unseen,
"With tales of a hereafter Heaven
"Whence never Traveller hath returned!
"Have ye not tasted of the cup of joy,
"That in these groves of happiness
"For ever over-mantling tempts
"The ever-thirsty lip?
"Who is there here that by a deed
"Of danger will deserve
"The eternal joys of actual Paradise?

"I!" Thalaba exclaimed,
And springing forward, on the Sorcerer's head
He dashed the knotty club.

He fell not, tho' the force
Shattered his skull; nor flowed the blood.
For by some hellish talisman
His life imprisoned still
Dwelt in the body. The astonished crowd
Stand motionless with fear, and wait
Immediate vengeance from the wrath of Heaven.
And lo! the Bird ... the monster Bird
Soars up ... then pounces down
To seize on Thalaba!
Now Oneiza, bend the bow,
Now draw the arrow home!
It fled, the arrow from Oneiza's hand,
It pierced the monster Bird,
It broke the Talisman.
Then darkness covered all,...
Earth shook, Heaven thundered, and amid the yells
Of Spirits accursed, destroyed
The Paradise[136] of Sin.

At last the earth was still;
The yelling of the Demons ceased;
Opening the wreck and ruin to their sight
The darkness rolled away. Alone in life
Amid the desolation and the dead
Stood the Destroyer and the Arabian Maid.
They looked around, the rocks were rent,
The path was open, late by magic closed.
Awe-struck and silent down the stony glen
They wound their thoughtful way.

Amid the vale below
Tents rose, and streamers played
And javelins sparkled in the sun,
And multitudes encamped

Swarmed, far as eye could follow, o'er the plain.
There in his war pavilion sate
In council with his Chiefs
The Sultan of the Land.
Before his presence there a Captain led
Oneiza and the appointed Youth.

"Obedient to our Lord's command," said he,
"We past towards the mountains, and began
"The ascending strait; when suddenly Earth shook,
"And darkness like the midnight fell around,
"And fire and thunder came from Heaven
"As tho' the Retribution day were come.
"After the terror ceased, and when with hearts
"Somewhat assured, again we ventured on,
"This youth and woman met us on the way.
"They told us that from Aloadin's haunt
"They came on whom the judgement-stroke has fallen;
"He and his sinful Paradise at once
"Destroyed by them, the agents they of Heaven.
"Therefore I brought them hither, to repeat
"The tale before thy presence; that as search
"Shall prove it false or faithful, to their merit
"Thou mayest reward them."
"Be it done to us,"
Thalaba answered, "as the truth shall prove!"

The Sultan while he spake
"Fixed on him the proud eye of sovereignty;
"If thou hast played with us,
"By Allah and by Ali, Death shall seal
"The lying lips for ever! if the thing
"Be as thou sayest it, Arab, thou shalt stand
"Next to ourself!"...
And hark! the cry
The lengthening cry, the increasing shout
Of joyful multitudes!

Breathless and panting to the tent
The bearer of good tidings comes,
"O Sultan, live for ever! be thy foes
"Like Aloadin all!
"The wrath of God hath smitten him."

Joy at the welcome tale
Shone in the Sultan's cheek
"Array the Arab in the robe
"Of honour," he exclaimed,
"And place a chain of gold around his neck,
"And bind around his brow the diadem,
"And mount him on my steed of state,

"And lead him thro' the camp,
"And let the Heralds go before and cry
"Thus shall the Sultan reward
"The man[137] who serves him well!"

Then in the purple robe
They vested Thalaba.
And hung around his neck the golden chain,
And bound his forehead with the diadem,
And on the royal steed
They led him thro' the camp,
And Heralds went before and cried
"Thus shall the Sultan reward
"The man who serves him well!"

When from the pomp of triumph
And presence of the King
Thalaba sought the tent allotted him,
Thoughtful the Arabian Maid beheld
His animated eye,
His cheek inflamed with pride.
"Oneiza!" cried the youth,
"The King hath done according to his word,
"And made me in the land
"Next to himself be named!...
"But why that serious melancholy smile?
"Oneiza when I heard the voice that gave me
"Honour, and wealth, and fame, the instant thought
"Arose to fill my joy, that thou wouldest hear
"The tidings, and be happy."

ONEIZA.
Thalaba
Thou wouldest not have me mirthful! am I not
An orphan,... among strangers?

THALABA.
But with me.

ONEIZA.
My Father,...

THALABA.
Nay be comforted! last night
To what wert thou exposed! in what a peril
The morning found us! safety, honour, wealth
These now are ours. This instant who thou wert
The Sultan asked. I told him from our childhood
We had been plighted;... was I wrong Oneiza?
And when he said with bounties he would heap
Our nuptials,... wilt thou blame me if I blest

His will, that bade me fix the marriage day!
In tears Oneiza?...

ONEIZA.
Remember Destiny
Hath marked thee from mankind!

THALABA.
Perhaps when Aloadin was destroyed
The mission ceased, else would wise Providence
With its rewards and blessings strew my path
Thus for accomplished service?

ONEIZA.
Thalaba!

THALABA.
Or if haply not, yet whither should I go?
Is it not prudent to abide in peace
Till I am summoned?

ONEIZA.
Take me to the Deserts!

THALABA.
But Moath is not there; and wouldest thou dwell
In a Stranger's tent? thy father then might seek
In long and fruitless wandering for his child.

ONEIZA.
Take me then to Mecca!
There let me dwell a servant of the Temple.
Bind thou thyself my veil,... to human eye
It never shall be lifted. There, whilst thou
Shalt go upon thine enterprize, my prayers,
Dear Thalaba! shall rise to succour thee,
And I shall live,... if not in happiness;
Surely in hope.

THALABA.
Oh think of better things!
The will of Heaven is plain: by wonderous ways
It led us here, and soon the common voice
Shall tell what we have done, and how we dwell
Under the shadow of the Sultan's wing,
So shall thy father hear the fame, and find us
What he hath wished us ever.... Still in tears!
Still that unwilling eye! nay ... nay.... Oneiza....
Has then another since I left the tent....

ONEIZA.

Thalaba! Thalaba!

With song, with music, and with dance
The bridal pomp proceeds.
Following on the veiled Bride
Fifty female slaves attend
In costly robes that gleam
With interwoven gold,
And sparkle far with gems.
An hundred slaves behind them bear
Vessels of silver and vessels of gold
And many a gorgeous garment gay
The presents that the Sultan gave.
On either hand the pages go
With torches flaring thro' the gloom,
And trump and timbrel merriment
Accompanies their way;
And multitudes with loud acclaim
Shout blessings on the Bride.
And now they reach the palace pile,
The palace home of Thalaba,
And now the marriage feast is spread
And from the finished banquet now
The wedding guests are gone.

Who comes from the bridal chamber?
It is Azrael, the Angel of Death.

WOMAN.
Go not among the Tombs, Old Man!
There is a madman there.

OLD MAN.
Will he harm me if I go?

WOMAN.
Not he, poor miserable man!
But 'tis a wretched sight to see
His utter wretchedness.
For all day long he lies on a grave,
And never is he seen to weep,
And never is he heard to groan.
Nor ever at the hour of prayer

Bends his knee, nor moves his lips.
I have taken him food for charity
And never a word he spake,
But yet so ghastly he looked
That I have awakened at night
With the dream of his ghastly eyes.
Now go not among the Tombs, Old Man!

OLD MAN.
Wherefore has the wrath of God
So sorely stricken him?

WOMAN.
He came a Stranger to the land,
And did good service to the Sultan,
And well his service was rewarded.
The Sultan named him next himself,
And gave a palace for his dwelling,
And dowered his bride with rich domains.
But on his wedding night
There came the Angel of Death.
Since that hour a man distracted
Among the sepulchres he wanders.
The Sultan when he heard the tale
Said that for some untold crime
Judgement thus had stricken him,
And asking Heaven forgiveness
That he had shewn him favour,
Abandoned him to want.

OLD MAN.
A Stranger did you say?

WOMAN.
An Arab born, like you.
But go not among the Tombs,
For the sight of his wretchedness
Might make a hard heart ache!

OLD MAN.
Nay, nay, I never yet have shunned
A countryman in distress:
And the sound of his dear native tongue
May be like the voice of a friend.

Then to the Sepulchre
The Woman pointed out,
Old Moath bent his way.
By the tomb lay Thalaba,
In the light of the setting eve.
The sun, and the wind, and the rain

Had rusted his raven locks,
His checks were fallen in,
His face bones prominent,
By the tomb he lay along
And his lean fingers played,
Unwitting, with the grass that grew beside.

The Old man knew him not,
And drawing near him cried
"Countryman, peace be with thee!"
The sound of his dear native tongue
Awakened Thalaba.
He raised his countenance
And saw the good Old Man,
And he arose, and fell upon his neck,
And groaned in bitterness.
Then Moath knew the youth,
And feared that he was childless, and he turned
His eyes, and pointed to the tomb.
"Old Man!" cried Thalaba,
"Thy search is ended there!"

The father's cheek grew white
And his lip quivered with the misery;
Howbeit, collecting with a painful voice
He answered, "God is good! his will be done!"

The woe in which he spake,
The resignation that inspired his speech,
They softened Thalaba.
"Thou hast a solace in thy grief," he cried,
"A comforter within!
"Moath! thou seest me here,
"Delivered to the Evil Powers,
"A God-abandoned wretch."

The Old Man looked at him incredulous.
"Nightly," the youth pursued,
"Thy daughter comes to drive me to despair.
"Moath thou thinkest me mad,...
"But when the Cryer[138] from the Minaret
"Proclaims the midnight hour,
"Hast thou a heart to see her?"

In the[139] Meidan now
The clang of clarions and of drums
Accompanied the Sun's descent.
"Dost thou not pray? my son!"
Said Moath, as he saw
The white flag waving on the neighbouring Mosque;
Then Thalaba's eye grew wild,

"Pray!" echoed he, "I must not pray!"
And the hollow groan he gave
Went to the Old Man's heart,
And bowing down his face to earth,
In fervent agony he called on God.

A night of darkness and of storms!
Into the Chamber[140] of the Tomb
Thalaba led the Old Man,
To roof him from the rain.
A night of storms! the wind
Swept thro' the moonless sky
And moaned among the pillared sepulchres.
And in the pauses of its sweep
They heard the heavy rain
Beat on the monument above.
In silence on Oneiza's grave
The Father and the Husband sate.

The Cryer from the Minaret
Proclaimed the midnight hour;
"Now! now!" cried Thalaba,
And o'er the chamber of the tomb
There spread a lurid gleam
Like the reflection of a sulphur fire,
And in that hideous light
Oneiza stood before them, it was She,
Her very lineaments, and such as death
Had changed them, livid cheeks, and lips of blue.
But in her eyes there dwelt
Brightness more terrible
Than all the loathsomeness of death.
"Still art thou living, wretch?"
In hollow tones she cried to Thalaba,
"And must I nightly leave my grave
"To tell thee, still in vain,
"God has abandoned thee?"

"This is not she!" the Old Man exclaimed,
"A Fiend! a manifest Fiend!"
And to the youth he held his lance,
"Strike and deliver thyself!"
"Strike HER!" cried Thalaba,
And palsied of all powers
Gazed fixedly upon the dreadful form.
"Yea! strike her!" cried a voice whose tones
Flowed with such sudden healing thro' his soul,
As when the desert shower
From death delivered him.
But unobedient to that well-known voice
His eye was seeking it,

When Moath firm of heart,
Performed the bidding; thro' the vampire[141] corpse
He thrust his lance; it fell,
And howling with the wound
Its demon tenant fled.
A sapphire light fell on them,
And garmented with glory, in their sight
Oneiza's Spirit stood.

"O Thalaba!" she cried,
"Abandon not thyself!
"Wouldst thou for ever lose me?... go, fulfill
"Thy quest, that in the Bowers of Paradise
"In vain I may not wait thee, O my Husband!"
To Moath then the Spirit
Turned the dark lustre of her Angel eyes,
"Short is thy destined path,
"O my dear father! to the abode of bliss.
"Return to Araby,
"There with the thought of death.
"Comfort thy lonely age,
"And Azrael the Deliverer, soon
"Shall visit thee in peace."

They stood with earnest eyes
And arms out-reaching, when again
The darkness closed around them.
The soul of Thalaba revived;
He from the floor the quiver took
And as he bent the bow, exclaimed,
"Was it the over-ruling Providence
"That in the hour of frenzy led my hands
"Instinctively to this?
"To-morrow, and the sun shall brace anew
"The slackened cord that now sounds loose and damp,
"To-morrow, and its livelier tone will sing
"In tort vibration to the arrow's flight.
"I ... but I also, with recovered health
"Of heart, shall do my duty.
"My Father! here I leave thee then!" he cried,
"And not to meet again
"Till at the gate of Paradise
"The eternal union of our joys commence.
"We parted last in darkness!"... and the youth
Thought with what other hopes,
But now his heart was calm,
For on his soul a heavenly hope had dawned.
The Old Man answered nothing, but he held
His garment and to the door
Of the Tomb Chamber followed him.
The rain had ceased, the sky was wild

Its black clouds broken by the storm.
And lo! it chanced that in the chasm
Of Heaven between, a star,
Leaving along its path continuous light,
Shot eastward. "See my guide!" quoth Thalaba,
And turning, he received
Old Moath's last embrace,
And his last blessing.
It was eve,
When an old Dervise, sitting in the sun
At his cell door, invited for the night
The traveller; in the sun
He spread the plain repast
Rice and fresh grapes, and at their feet there flowed
The brook of which they drank.

So as they sate at meal,
With song, with music, and with dance,
A wedding train went by;
The veiled bride, the female slaves,
The torches of festivity,
And trump and timbrel merriment
Accompanied their way.
The good old Dervise gave
A blessing as they past.
But Thalaba looked on,
And breathed a low, deep groan, and hid his face.
The Dervise had known sorrow; and he felt
Compassion; and his words
Of pity and of piety
Opened the young man's heart
And he told all his tale.

"Repine not, O my Son!" the Old Man replied,
"That Heaven has chastened thee.
"Behold this vine,[142] I found it a wild tree
"Whose wanton strength had swoln into
"Irregular twigs, and bold excrescencies,
"And spent itself in leaves and little rings,
"In the vain flourish of its outwardness
"Wasting the sap and strength
"That should have given forth fruit.
"But when I pruned the Tree,
"Then it grew temperate in its vain expence
"Of useless leaves, and knotted, as thou seest,
"Into these full, clear, clusters, to repay
"The hand whose foresight wounded it.
"Repine not, O my Son!
"In wisdom and in mercy Heaven inflicts,
"Like a wise Leech, its painful remedies."

Then pausing, "whither goest thou now?" he asked.
"I know not," answered Thalaba,
"Straight on, with Destiny my guide."
Quoth the Old Man, "I will not blame thy trust,
"And yet methinks thy feet
"Should tread with certainty.
"In Kaf the Simorg hath his dwelling place,
"The all-knowing Bird of Ages, who hath seen
"The World, with all her children, thrice destroyed.
"Long is the thither path,
"And difficult the way, of danger full;
"But his unerring voice
"Could point to certain end thy weary search."

Easy assent the youth
Gave to the words of wisdom; and behold
At dawn, the adventurer on his way to Kaf.
And he has travelled many a day
And many a river swum over,
And many a mountain ridge has crost
And many a measureless plain,
And now amid the wilds advanced,
Long is it since his eyes
Have seen the trace of man.

Cold! cold! 'tis a chilly clime
That the toil of the youth has reached,
And he is aweary now,
And faint for the lack of food.
Cold! cold! there is no Sun in heaven
But a heavy and uniform cloud
And the snows begin to fall.
Dost thou wish for thy deserts, O Son of Hodeirah?
Dost thou long for the gales of Arabia?
Cold! cold! his blood flows languid,
His hands are red, his lips are blue,
His feet are sore with the frost.
Cheer thee! cheer thee! Thalaba!
A little yet bear up!

All waste! no sign of life
But the track of the wolf and the bear!
No sound but the wild, wild wind
And the snow crunching under his feet!
Night is come; no moon, no stars,
Only the light of the snow!
But behold a fire in the cave of the hill
A heart-reviving fire;
And thither with strength renewed
Thalaba presses on.

He found a Woman in the cave,
A solitary Woman,
Who by the fire was spinning
And singing as she spun.
The pine boughs they blazed chearfully
And her face was bright with the flame.
Her face was as a Damsel's face
And yet her hair was grey.
She bade him welcome with a smile
And still continued spinning
And singing as she spun.
The thread the Woman drew
Was finer than the silkworm's,
Was finer than the gossamer.
The song she sung was low and sweet
And Thalaba knew not the words.

He laid his bow before the hearth,
For the string was frozen stiff.
He took the quiver from his neck,
For the arrow plumes were iced.
Then as the chearful fire
Revived his languid limbs,
The adventurer asked for food.
The Woman answered him,
And still her speech was song,
"The She Bear she dwells near to me,
"And she hath cubs, one, two and three.
"She hunts the deer and brings him here,
"And then with her I make good cheer,
"And she to the chase is gone
"And she will be here anon."

She ceased from her work as she spake,
And when she had answered him,
Again her fingers twirled the thread
And again the Woman began
In low, sweet, tones to sing
The unintelligible song.

The thread she spun it gleamed like gold
In the light of the odorous fire,
And yet so wonderous thin,
That save when the light shone on it
It could not be seen by the eye.
The youth sate watching it,
And she beheld his wonder.
And then again she spake to him
And still her speech was song,
"Now twine it round thy hands I say,
"Now twine it round thy hands I pray,

"My thread is small, my thread is fine,
"But he must be
"A stronger than thee,
"Who can break this thread of mine!"

And up she raised her bright blue eyes
And sweetly she smiled on him,
And he conceived no ill.
And round and round his right hand,
And round and round his left,
He wound the thread so fine.
And then again the Woman spake,
And still her speech was song,
"Now thy strength, O Stranger, strain,
"Now then break the slender chain."

Thalaba strove, but the thread
Was woven by magic hands,
And in his cheek the flush of shame
Arose, commixt with fear.
She beheld and laughed at him,
And then again she sung,
"My thread is small, my thread is fine,
"But he must be
"A stronger than thee
"Who can break this thread of mine."

And up she raised her bright blue eyes
And fiercely she smiled on him,
"I thank thee, I thank thee, Hodeirah's Son!
"I thank thee for doing what can't be undone,
"For binding thyself in the chain I have spun!"
Then from his head she wrenched
A lock of his raven hair,
And cast it in the fire
And cried aloud as it burnt,
"Sister! Sister! hear my voice!
"Sister! Sister! come and rejoice,
"The web is spun,
"The prize is won,
"The work is done,
"For I have made captive Hoderiah's Son."

Borne in her magic car
The Sister Sorceress came,
Khawla, the fiercest of the Sorcerer brood.
She gazed upon the youth,
She bade him break the slender thread,
She laughed aloud for scorn,
She clapt her hands for joy.

The She Bear from the chase came in,
She bore the prey in her bloody mouth,
She laid it at Maimuna's feet,
And she looked up with wistful eyes
As if to ask her share.
"There! there!" quoth Maimuna
And pointing to the prisoner youth
She spurned him with her foot,
And bade her make her meal.
But soon their mockery failed them
And anger and shame arose,
For the She Bear fawned on Thalaba
And quietly licked his hand.

The grey haired Sorceress stamped the ground
And called a Spirit up,
"Shall we bear the Enemy
"To the dungeon dens below?"

SPIRIT.
Woe! woe! to our Empire woe!
If ever he tread the caverns below.

MAIMUNA.
Shall we leave him fettered here
With hunger and cold to die?

SPIRIT.
Away from thy lonely dwelling fly!
Here I see a danger nigh
That he should live and thou shouldst die.

MAIMUNA.
Whither must we bear the foe?

SPIRIT.
To Mohareb's island go,
There shalt thou secure the foe,
There prevent thy future woe.

Then in the Car they threw
The fettered Thalaba,
And took their seats, and set
Their feet upon his neck,
Maimuna held the reins
And Khawla shook the scourge
And away![143] away! away!
They were no steeds of mortal race
That drew the magic car
With the swiftness of feet and of wings.
The snow-dust rises behind them,

The ice-rocks splinters fly,
And hark! in the valley below
The sound of their chariot wheels
And they are far over the mountains.
Away! away! away!
The Demons of the air
Shout their joy as the Sisters pass,
The Ghosts of the Wicked that wander by night
Flit over the magic car.
Away! away! away!
Over the hills and the plains
Over the rivers and rocks,
Over the sands of the shore;
The waves of ocean heave
Under the magic steeds,
With unwet hoofs they trample the deep
And now they reach the Island coast,
And away to the city the Monarch's abode.
Open fly the city gates,
Open fly the iron doors
The doors of the palace court.
Then stopt the charmed car.
The Monarch heard the chariot wheels
And forth he came to greet
The Mistress whom he served.
He knew the captive youth,
And Thalaba beheld
Mohareb in[144] the robes of royalty,
Whom erst his arm had thrust
Down the bitumen pit.

THALABA THE DESTROYER

THE NINTH BOOK

"Go up, my Sister Maimuna,
"Go up, and read the stars!"

Lo! on the terrace of the topmost tower
She stands; her darkening eyes,
Her fine face raised to heaven,
Her white hair flowing like the silver streams
That streak the northern night.

They hear her coming tread,
They lift their asking eyes,
Her face is serious, her unwilling lips
Slow to the tale of ill.

"What hast thou read? what hast thou read?"
Quoth Khawla in alarm.
"Danger ... death ... judgement!" Maimuna replied.

"Is that the language of the lights of Heaven?"
Exclaimed the sterner Witch.
"Creatures of Allah, they perform his will.
"And with their lying menaces would daunt
"Our credulous folly.... Maimuna,
"I never liked this uncongenial lore!
"Better befits to make the sacrifice
"Of Divination; so shall I
"Be mine own Oracle.
"Command the victims thou, O King!
"Male and female they must be,
"Thou knowest the needful rites.
"Meanwhile I purify the place."

The Sultan went; the Sorceress rose,
And North and South and East and West
She faced the points of Heaven,
And ever where she turned
She laid her hand upon the wall,
And up she looked and smote the air,
And down she stooped and smote the floor,
"To Eblis and his servants
"I consecrate the place,
"Let none intrude but they!
"Whatever hath the breath of life,
"Whatever hath the sap of life,
"Let it be blasted and die!"

Now all is prepared;
Mohareb returns,
The Circle is drawn,
The Victims have bled,
The Youth and the Maid.
She in the circle holds in either hand
Clenched by the hair, a head,
The heads of the Youth and the Maid.
"Go out ye lights!" quoth Khawla,
And in darkness began the spell.

With spreading arms she whirls around
Rapidly, rapidly
Ever around and around;
And loudly she calls the while
"Eblis! Eblis!"
Loudly, incessantly,
Still she calls "Eblis! Eblis!"
Giddily, giddily, still she whirls,

Loudly, incessantly, still she calls;
The motion is ever the same,
Ever around and around;
The calling is still the same
Still it is "Eblis! Eblis!"
And her voice is a shapeless yell,
And dizzily rolls her brain,
And now she is full of the Fiend.
She stops, she rocks, she reels!
Look! look! she appears in the darkness!
Her flamy hairs curl up
All living, like the Meteor's locks of light!
Her eyes are like the sickly Moon!

It is her lips that move,
Her tongue that shapes the sound,
But whose is the Voice that proceeds?
"Ye may hope and ye may fear,
"The danger of his stars is near.
"Sultan! if he perish, woe!
"Fate has written one death-blow
"For Mohareb and the Foe?
"Triumph! triumph! only she
"That knit his bonds can set him free."

She spake the Oracle,
And senselessly she fell.
They knelt in care beside her,
Her Sister and the King.
They sprinkled her palms with water,
They wetted her nostrils with blood.
She wakes as from a dream,
She asks the uttered Voice,
But when she heard, an anger and a grief
Darkened her wrinkling brow.
"Then let him live in long captivity!"
She answered: but Mohareb's quickened eye
Perused her sullen countenance
That lied not with the lips.
A miserable man!
What boots it, that, in central caves
The Powers of Evil at his Baptism pledged
The Sacrament of Hell?
His death secures them now.
What boots it that they gave
Abdaldar's guardian ring,
When thro' another's life
The blow may reach his own?

He sought the dungeon cell
Where Thalaba was laid.

'Twas the grey morning twilight, and the voice
Of Thalaba in prayer,
With words of hallowed import, smote
The King's alarmed sense.
The grating of the heavy hinge
Roused not the Arabian youth;
Nor lifted he his earthward face
At sound of coming feet.
Nor did Mohareb with unholy voice
Disturb the duty: silent, spirit-awed,
Envious, heart-humbled, he beheld
The dungeon-peace of piety
Till Thalaba, the perfect rite performed,
Raised his calm eye; then spake the Island-Chief.
"Arab! my guidance thro' the dangerous Cave,
"Thy service overpaid,
"An unintended friend in enmity.
"The hand that caught thy ring
"Received and bore me to the scene I sought.
"Now know me grateful. I return
"That amulet, thy only safety here."

Artful he spake, with show of gratitude
Veiling the selfish deed.
Locked in the magic chain
The powerless hand of Thalaba
Received again the Spell.
Remembering then with what an ominous faith
First he drew on the gem,
The Youth repeats his words of augury;
"In God's name and the Prophet's! be its power
"Good, let it serve the holy! if for evil
"God and my faith shall hallow it.
"Blindly the wicked work
"The righteous will of Heaven!"

So Thalaba received again
The written ring of gold.

Thoughtful awhile Mohareb stood
And eyed the captive youth.
Then, building skilfully the sophist speech,
Thus he began. "Brave art thou, Thalaba!
"And wherefore are we foes!... for I would buy
"Thy friendship at a princely price, and make thee
"To thine own welfare wise.
"Hear me! in Nature are two hostile Gods,
"Makers and Masters of existing things,
"Equal in power:... nay hear me patiently!...
"Equal ... for look around thee! the same Earth
"Bears fruit and poison; where the Camel finds

"His fragrant[145] food, the horned Viper there
"Sucks in the juice of death; the Elements
"Now serve the use of man, and now assert
"Dominion o'er his weakness; dost thou hear
"The sound of merriment and nuptial song?
"From the next house proceeds the mourner's cry
"Lamenting o'er the dead. Sayest thou that Sin
"Entered the world of Allah? that the Fiend
"Permitted for a season, prowls for prey?
"When to thy tent the venomous serpent creeps
"Dost thou not crush the reptile? even so,
"Besure, had Allah crushed his Enemy,
"But that the power was wanting. From the first,
"Eternal as themselves their warfare is,
"To the end it must endure. Evil and Good....
"What are they Thalaba but words? in the strife
"Of Angels, as of men, the weak are guilty;
"Power must decide. The Spirits of the Dead
"Quitting their mortal mansion, enter not,
"As falsely ye are preached, their final seat
"Of bliss, or bale; nor in the sepulchre
"Sleep they the long long sleep: each joins the host
"Of his great Leader, aiding in the war
"Whose fate involves his own.
"Woe to the vanquished then!
"Woe to the sons of man who followed him!
"They with their Leader, thro' eternity,
"Must howl in central fires.
"Thou Thalaba hast chosen ill thy part,
"If choice it may be called, where will was not,
"Nor searching doubt, nor judgement wise to weigh.
"Hard is the service of the Power beneath
"Whose banners thou wert born; his discipline
"Severe, yea cruel; and his wages, rich
"Only in promise; who has seen the pay?
"For us ... the pleasures of the world are ours,
"Riches and rule, the kingdoms of the Earth.
"We met in Babylon adventurers both,
"Each zealous for the hostile Power he served:
"We meet again; thou feelest what thou art,
"Thou seest what I am, the Sultan here,
"The Lord of Life and Death.
"Abandon him who has abandoned thee,
"And be as I am, great among mankind!"

The Captive did not, hasty to confute
Break of that subtle speech,
But when the expectant silence of the King
Looked for his answer, then spake Thalaba.
"And this then is thy faith! this monstrous creed!
"This lie against the Sun and Moon and Stars

"And Earth and Heaven! blind man who canst not see
"How all things work the best! who wilt not know
"That in the Manhood of the World, whate'er
"Of folly marked its Infancy, of vice
"Sullied its Youth, ripe Wisdom shall cast off,
"Stablished in good, and knowing evil safe.
"Sultan Mohareb, yes, ye have me here
"In chains; but not forsaken, tho' opprest:
"Cast down, but not destroyed. Shall danger daunt,
"Shall death dismay his soul, whose life is given
"For God and for his brethren of mankind?
"Alike rewarded, in that noble cause,
"The Conquerors and the Martyrs palm above
"Beam with one glory. Hope ye that my blood
"Can quench the dreaded flame? and know ye not
"That leagued against you are the Just and Wise,
"And all Good Actions of all ages past,
"Yea your own Crimes, and Truth, and God in Heaven!"

"Slave!" quoth Mohareb, and his lips
Quivered with eager wrath.
"I have thee! thou shalt feel my power,
"And in thy dungeon loathsomeness
"Rot piece-meal, limb from limb!"
And out the Tyrant rushes,
And all impatient of the thoughts
That cankered in his heart,
Seeks in the giddiness of boisterous sport
Short respite from the avenging power within.

What Woman is she
So wrinkled and old,
That goes to the wood?
She leans on her staff
With a tottering step,
She tells her bead-strings slow
Thro' fingers dulled by age.
The wanton boys bemock her.
The babe in arms that meets her
Turns round with quick affright
And clings to his nurse's neck.

Hark! hark! the hunter's cry
Mohareb gone to the chase!
The dogs with eager yell
Are struggling to be free;
The hawks in frequent stoop
Token their haste for flight;
And couchant on the saddle-bow,
With tranquil eyes and talons sheathed
The ounce expects his liberty.

Propt on the staff that shakes
Beneath her trembling weight,
The Old Woman sees them pass.
Halloa! halloa!
The game is up!
The dogs are loosed
The deer bounds over the plain,
The lagging dogs behind
Follow from afar!
But lo! the Falcon o'er his head.
Hovers with hostile[146] wings,
And buffets him with blinding strokes!
Dizzy with the deafening strokes
In blind and interrupted course,
Poor beast be struggles on;
And now the dogs are nigh!
How his heart pants! you see
The panting of his heart;
And tears like human tears
Roll down, along the big veins, fever-swoln;
And now the death-sweat[147] darkens his dun hide!
His fear, his groans, his agony, his death,
Are the sport and the joy and the triumph!

Halloa! another prey,
The nimble Antelope!
The Ounce[148] is freed; one spring
And his talons are sheathed in her shoulders,
And his teeth are red in her gore.
There came a sound from the wood,
Like the howl of the winter wind at night
Around a lonely dwelling,
The Ounce whose gums were warm in his prey
He hears the summoning sound.
In vain his master's voice
No longer dreaded now,
Calls and recalls with threatful tone.
Away to the forest he goes,
For that Old Woman had laid
Her shrivelled finger on her shrivelled lips,
And whistled with a long, long breath,
And that long breath was the sound
Like the howl of the winter wind at night
Around a lonely dwelling.

Mohareb knew her not,
As to the chase he went,
The glance of his proud eye
Passing in scorn o'er age and wretchedness.
She stands in the depth of the wood,

And panting to her feet
Fawning and fearful creeps the charmed ounce.
Well mayst thou fear, and vainly dost thou fawn!
Her form is changed, her visage new,
Her power, her heart the same!
It is Khawla that stands in the wood.

She knew the place where the mandrake grew,
And round the neck of the ounce,
And round the mandrake's head
She tightens the ends of her cord.
Her ears are closed with wax,
And her prest finger fastens them,
Deaf as the Adder, when with grounded head
And circled form, her avenues of sound
Barred safely, one slant eye
Watches the charmer's lips
Waste on the wind his[149] baffled witchery.
The spotted ounce so beautiful
Springs forceful from the scourge:
The dying plant all agony,
Feeling its life-strings crack,
Uttered the unimaginable groan
That none can hear and live.

Then from her victim servant Khawla loosed
The precious poison, next with naked hand
She plucked the boughs of the manchineel.
Then of the wormy wax she took,
That from the perforated[150] tree forced out,
Bewrayed its insect-parent's work within.

In a cavern of the wood she sits
And moulds the wax to human form,
And as her fingers kneaded it,
By magic accents, to the mystic shape
Imparted with the life of Thalaba,
In all its passive powers
Mysterious sympathy.
With the Mandrake and the Manchineel
She builds her pile accurst.
She lays her finger to the pile,
And blue and green, the flesh
Glows with emitted fire,
A fire[151] to kindle that strange fuel meet.
Before the fire she placed the imaged wax,
"There[152] waste away!" the Enchantress cried,
"And with thee waste Hodeirah's Son!"

Fool! fool! go thaw the everlasting ice,
Whose polar mountains bound the human reign.

Blindly the wicked work
The righteous will of Heaven!
The doomed Destroyer wears Abdaldar's ring!
Against the danger of his horoscope
Yourselves have shielded him!
And on the sympathizing wax
The unadmitted flames play powerlessly,
As the cold moon-beam on a plain of snow.

"Curse thee! curse thee!" cried the fiendly woman,
"Hast thou yet a spell of safety?"
And in the raging flames
She cast the imaged wax.
It lay amid the flames,
Like Polycarp of old,
When by the glories of the burning stake
O'er vaulted, his grey hairs
Curled, life-like, to the fire
That haloed round his saintly brow.

"Wherefore is this!" cried Khawla, and she stamped
Thrice on the cavern floor,
"Maimuna! Maimuna!"
Thrice on the floor she stamped,
Then to the rocky gateway glanced
Her eager eyes, and Maimuna was there.
"Nay Sister, nay!" quoth she, "Mohareb's life
"Is linked with Thalaba's!
"Nay Sister, nay! the plighted oath!
"The common Sacrament!"

"Idiot!" said Khawla, "one must die, or all!
"Faith kept with him were treason to the rest.
"Why lies the wax, like marble, in the fire?
"What powerful amulet
"Protects Hodeirah's son?"

Cold, marble-cold, the wax
Lay on the raging pile,
Cold in that white intensity of fire.
The Bat that with her hooked and leathery wings
Clung to the cave-roof, loosed her hold,
Death-sickening with the heat;
The Toad who to the darkest nook had crawled
Panted fast with fever pain;
The Viper from her nest came forth
Leading her quickened brood,
Who sportive with the warm delight, rolled out
Their thin curls, tender as the tendril rings,
Ere the green beauty of their brittle youth
Grows brown, and toughens in the summer sun.

Cold, marble-cold, the wax
Lay on the raging pile,
The silver quivering of the element
O'er its pale surface shedding a dim gloss.

Amid the red and fiery smoke,
Watching the strange portent,
The blue-eyed Sorceress and her Sister stood,
Seeming a ruined Angel by the side
Of Spirit born in Hell.
At length raised Maimuna her thoughtful eyes,
"Whence Sister was the wax
"The work of the worm, or the bee?
"Nay then I marvel not!
"It were as wise to bring from Ararat
"The fore-world's[153] wood to build the magic pile,
"And feed it from the balm bower, thro' whose veins
"The Martyr's blood sends such a virtue out,
"That the fond Mother from beneath its shade
"Wreathes the Cerastes[154] round her playful child.
"This the eternal, universal strife!
"There is a grave-wax,[155]... I have seen the Gouls
"Fight for the dainty at their banquetting."...

"Excellent witch!" quoth Khawla; and she went
To the cave arch of entrance, and scowled up,
Mocking the blessed Sun,
"Shine thou in Heaven, but I will shadow Earth!
"Thou wilt not shorten day,
"But I will hasten darkness!" Then the Witch
Began a magic song,
One long low tone thro' teeth half-closed,
Thro' lips slow-moving muttered slow,
One long-continued breath,
Till to her eyes a darker yellowness
Was driven, and fuller swoln the prominent veins
On her loose throat grew black.
Then looking upward thrice she breathed
Into the face of Heaven,
The baneful breath infected Heaven;
A mildewing mist it spread
Darker and darker; so the evening sun
Poured his unentering glory on the mist,
And it was night below.

"Bring now the wax," quoth Khawla, "for thou knowest
"The mine that yields it!" forth went Maimuna,
In mist and darkness went the Sorceress forth.
And she has reached the place of Tombs,
And in their sepulchres the dead
Feel[156] feet unholy trampling over them.

Thou startest Maimuna,
Because the breeze is in thy lilted locks!
Is Khawla's spell so weak?
Sudden came the breeze and strong;
The mist that in the labouring lungs was felt
So heavy late, flies now before the gale,
Thin as an Infant's breath
Seen in the sunshine of an autumn frost.
Sudden it came and soon its work was done,
And suddenly it ceased;
Cloudless and calm it left the firmament,
And beautiful in the blue sky
Arose the summer Moon.

She heard the quickened action of her blood,
She felt the fever in her cheeks.
Daunted, yet desperate, in a tomb
Entering, with impious hand she traced
Circles, and squares, and trines,
And magic characters,
Till riven by her charms the grave
Yawned and disclosed its dead,
Maimuna's eyes were opened, and she saw
The secrets of the grave.

There sate a Spirit in the vault,
In shape, in hue, in lineaments like life,
And by him couched, as if intranced,
The hundred-headed Worm that never dies.

"Nay Sorceress! not to-night!" the Spirit cried,
"The flesh in which I sinned may rest to-night
"From suffering; all things, even I to-night,
"Even the Damned repose!"

The flesh of Maimuna
Crept on her bones with terror, and her knees
Trembled with their trembling weight.
"Only this sabbath! and at dawn the Worm
"Will wake, and this poor flesh must grow to meet
"The gnawing of his hundred[157] poison-mouths!
"God! God! Is there no mercy after death?"

Soul-struck she rushed away,
She fled the place of Tombs,
She cast herself upon the earth,
All agony and tumult and despair.
And in that wild and desperate agony
Sure Maimuna had died the utter death,
If aught of evil had been possible

On this mysterious night;
For this was that most holy[158] night
When all created things know and adore
The Power that made them; insects, beasts, and birds,
The water-dwellers, herbs and trees and stones,
Yea Earth and Ocean and the infinite Heaven
With all its worlds. Man only does not know
The universal sabbath, does not join
With Nature in her homage. Yet the prayer
Flows from the righteous with intenser love,
A holier calm succeeds, and sweeter dreams
Visit the slumbers of the penitent.

Therefore on Maimuna the elements,
Shed healing; every breath she breathed was balm.
Was not a flower but sent in incense up
Its richest odours, and the song of birds
Now, like the music of the Seraphim,
Entered her soul, and now
Made silence aweful by their sudden pause.
It seemed as if the quiet moon
Poured quietness, its lovely light
Was like the smile of reconciling Heaven.

Is it the dew of night
That down her glowing cheek
Shines in the moon-beam? oh! she weeps ... she weeps
And the Good Angel that abandoned her
At her hell-baptism, by her tears drawn down
Resumes his charge, then Maimuna
Recalled to mind the double oracle;
Quick as the lightening flash
Its import glanced upon her, and the hope
Of pardon and salvation rose,
As now she understood
The lying prophecy of truth.
She pauses not, she ponders not,
The driven air before her fanned the face
Of Thalaba, and he awoke and saw
The Sorceress of the silver locks.

One more permitted spell!
She takes the magic chain.
With the wide eye of wonder, Thalaba
Watches her snowy fingers round and round
Wind the loosening chain.
Again he hears the low sweet voice,
The low sweet voice so musical,
That sure it was not strange,
If in those unintelligible tones
Was more than human potency,

That with such deep and undefined delight,
Filled the surrendered soul.
The work is done, the song is ceased;
He wakes as from a dream of Paradise
And feels his fetters gone, and with the burst
Of wondering adoration praises God.

Her charm has loosed the chain it bound,
But massy walls and iron gates
Confine Hodeirah's son.
Heard ye not, Genii of the Air, her spell,
That o'er her face there flits
The sudden flush of fear?
Again her louder lips repeat the charm,
Her eye is anxious, her cheek pale,
Her pulse plays fast and feeble.
Nay Maimuna! thy power has ceased,
And the wind scatters now
The voice that ruled it late.

"Pray for me, Thalaba," she cried,
"For death and judgement are at hand!"
All night in agony,
She feared the instant blow of Hell's revenge.
At dawn the sound of gathering multitudes
Led to the prison bars her dreading eye.
What spectacle invites
The growing multitude,
That torrent-like they roll along?
Boys and grey-headed age; the Mother comes
Leading her child, who at arm's length
Outstripping her, looks back
And bids her hasten more.

Why does the City pour her thousands forth?
What glorious pageantry
Makes her streets desolate, and silences
Her empty dwellings? comes the bridal pomp,
And have the purveyors of imperial lust
Torn from their parents arms again
The virgin beauties of the land?
Will elephants in gilded cages bear
The imprisoned victims? or may yet their eyes
With a last look of liberty, behold
Banners and guards and silk-arched palanquins.
The long procession, and the gorgeous pomp
Of their own sacrifice?
On the house tops and in the windows ranged
Face above face, they wait
The coming spectacle;
The trees are clustered, and below the dust

Thro' the thronged populace
Can find no way to rise.

He comes! the Sultan! hark the swelling horn,
The trumpet's spreading blair,
The timbrel tinkling as its silver bells
Twinkle aloft, and the shrill cymbal's sound,
Whose broad brass flashes in the morning sun
Accordant light and music! closing all
The heavy Gong is heard,
That falls like thunder on the dizzy ear.

On either hand the thick-wedged crowd
Fall from the royal path.
Recumbent in the palanquin he casts
On the wide tumult of the waving throng
A proud and idle eye.
Now in his tent alighted, he receives
Homage and worship. The slave multitude
With shouts of blasphemy adore
Him, father of his people! him their Lord!
Great King, all-wise, all-mighty, and all-good!
Whose smile was happiness, whose frown was death,
Their present Deity!

With silken cords his slaves
Wave the silk[159] fan, that waving o'er his head
Freshens the languid air.
Others the while shower o'er his robes
The rose's treasured sweets,
Rich odours burn before him, ambergrese,
Sandal and aloe wood,
And thus inhaling the voluptuous air
He sits to watch the agony,
To hear the groan of death.

At once all sounds are hushed,
All eyes take one direction, for he comes,
The object he of this day's festival,
Of all this expectation and this joy,
The Christian captive. Hark! so silently
They stand, the clanking of his chain is heard.
And he has reached the place of suffering now.
And as the death's-men round his ancles bind
The cords and to the gibbet swing him up,
The Priests begin their song, the song of praise,
The hymn of glory to their Devil-God.

Then Maimuna grew pale, as thro the bars
She saw the Martyr pendant by the feet,
His gold locks hanging downwards, and she cried,

"This is my Sister's deed!
"O Thalaba, for us,
"Not for his faith the red-haired Christian dies.
"She wants the foam[160] that in his agony,
"Last from his lips shall fall,
"The deadliest poison that the Devils know.
"Son of Hodeirah, thou and I
"Shall prove its deadly force!"

And lo! the Executioners begin
And beat his belly with alternate blows.
And these are human that look on;...
The very women that would shrink
And shudder if they saw a worm
Crushed by the careless tread,
They clap their hands for joy
And lift their children up
To see the Christian die.

Convulsing Nature with her tortures drunk
Ceases to suffer now.
His eye-lids tremble, his lips quake,
But like the quivering of a severed limb
Move no responsive pang.
Now catch the exquisite poison! for it froths
His dying lips,... and Khawla holds the bowl.

Enough the Island crimes had cried to Heaven,
The measure of their guilt was full,
The hour of wrath was come.
The poison burst the bowl,
It fell upon the earth.
The Sorceress shrieked and caught Mohareb's robe
And called the whirlwind and away!
For lo! from that accursed venom springs,
The Upas Tree of Death.

THE TENTH BOOK

Alone, beside a rivulet it stands
The Upas[161] Tree of Death.
Thro' barren banks the barren waters flow,
The fish that meets them in the unmingling sea
Floats poisoned on the waves.
Tree grows not near, nor bush, nor flower, nor herb,
The Earth has lost its parent powers of life

And the fresh dew of Heaven that there descends,
Steams in rank poison up.

Before the appointed Youth and Maimuna
Saw the first struggle of the dying throng,
Crash sunk their prison wall!
The whirlwind wrapt them round;
Borne in the Chariot of the Winds
Ere there was time to fear, their way was past,
And lo! again they stand
In the cave-dwelling of the blue-eyed Witch.

Then came the weakness of her natural age
At once on Maimuna;
The burthen of her years
Fell on her, and she knew
That her repentance in the sight of God
Had now found favour, and her hour was come.
Her death was like the righteous; "Turn my face
"To Mecca!" in her languid eyes.
The joy of certain hope
Lit a last lustre, and in death
The smile was on her cheek.

No faithful[162] crowded round her bier,
No tongue reported her good deeds,
For her no mourners wailed and wept,
No Iman o'er her perfumed corpse,
For her soul's health intoned the prayer;
No column[163] raised by the way side
Implored the passing traveller
To say a requiem for the dead.
Thalaba laid her in the snow,
And took his weapons from the hearth,
And then once more the youth began
His weary way of solitude.

The breath of the East is in his face
And it drives the sleet and the snow.
The air is keen, the wind is keen,
His limbs are aching with the cold,
His eyes are aching[164] with the snow,
His very heart is cold,
His spirit chilled within him. He looks on
If ought of life be near,
But all is sky and the white wilderness,
And here and there a solitary pine,
Its branches broken by the weight of snow.
His pains abate, his senses dull
With suffering, cease to suffer.
Languidly, languidly,

Thalaba drags along,
A heavy weight is on his lids,
His limbs move slow with heaviness,
And he full fain would sleep.
Not yet, not yet, O Thalaba!
Thy hour of rest is come;
Not yet may the Destroyer sleep
The comfortable sleep,
His journey is not over yet,
His course not yet fulfilled;...
Run thou thy race, O Thalaba!
The prize is at the goal.

It was a Cedar-tree
That woke him from the deadly drowsiness;
Its broad, round-spreading[165] branches when they felt
The snow, rose upward in a point to heaven,
And standing in their strength erect,
Defied the baffled storm.
He knew the lesson Nature gave,
And he shook off his heaviness,
And hope revived within him.

Now sunk the evening sun,
A broad, red, beamless orb,
Adown the glowing sky;
Thro' the red light the snow-flakes fell, like fire.
Louder grows the biting wind,
And it drifts the dust of the snow.
The snow is clotted in his hair,
The breath of Thalaba
Is iced upon his lips.
He looks around, the darkness,
The dizzy floating of the snow,
Close in his narrow view.

At length thro' the thick atmosphere a light
Not distant far appears.
He doubting other wiles of enmity,
With mingled joy and quicker step,
Bends his way thitherward.

It was a little, lowly dwelling place,
Amid a garden, whose delightful air
Felt mild and fragrant, as the evening wind
Passing in summer o'er the coffee-groves[166]
Of Yemen and its blessed bowers of balm.
A Fount of Fire that in the centre played,
Rolled all around its wonderous rivulets
And fed the garden with the heat of life.
Every where magic! the Arabian's heart

Yearned after human intercourse.
A light!... the door unclosed!...
All silent ... he goes in.

There lay a Damsel sleeping on a couch,
His step awoke her, and she gazed at him
With pleased and wondering look,
Fearlessly, like a yearling child
Too ignorant to fear.
With words of courtesy
The young intruder spake.
At the sound of his voice a joy
Kindled her bright black eyes;
She rose and took his hand,
But at the touch the smile forsook her cheek,
"Oh! it is cold!" she cried,
"I thought I should have felt it warm like mine,
"But thou art like the rest!"

Thalaba stood mute awhile
And wondering at her words:
"Cold? Lady!" then he said; "I have travelled long
"In this cold wilderness,
"Till life is almost spent!"

LAILA.
Art thou a Man then?

THALABA.
I did not think
Sorrow and toil could so have altered me,
That I seem otherwise.

LAILA.
And thou canst be warm
Sometimes? life-warm as I am?

THALABA.
Surely Lady
As others are, I am, to heat and cold
Subject like all, you see a Traveller,
Bound upon hard adventure, who requests
Only to rest him here to-night, to-morrow
He will pursue his way.

LAILA.
Oh ... not to-morrow!
Not like a dream of joy, depart so soon!
And whither wouldst thou go? for all around
Is everlasting winter, ice and snow,
Deserts unpassable of endless frost.

THALABA.
He who has led me here will still sustain me
Thro' cold and hunger.

"Hunger?" Laila cried;
She clapt her lilly hands,
And whether from above or from below
It came, sight could not see,
So suddenly the floor was spread with food.

LAILA.
Why dost thou watch with hesitating eyes
The banquet? 'tis for thee! I bade it come.

THALABA.
Whence came it?

LAILA.
Matters it from whence it came
My father sent it: when I call, he hears.
Nay ... thou hast fabled with me! and art like
The forms that wait upon my solitude,
Human to eye alone;... thy hunger would not
Question so idly else.

THALABA.
I will not eat!
It came by magic! fool to think that aught
But fraud and danger could await me here!
Let loose my cloak!...

LAILA.
Begone then, insolent!
Why dost thou stand and gaze upon my face?
Aye! watch the features well that threaten thee
With fraud and danger! in the wilderness
They shall avenge me,... in the hour of want
Rise on thy view, and make thee feel
How innocent I am:
And this remembered cowardice and insult
With a more painful shame will burn thy cheek
Than now beats mine in anger!

THALABA.
Mark me Lady!
Many and restless are my enemies;
My daily paths have been beset with snares
Till I have learnt suspicion, bitter sufferings
Teaching the needful vice, if I have wronged you,
And yours should be the face of innocence,

I pray you pardon me! in the name of God,
And of his Prophet, I partake your food.

LAILA.
Lo now! thou wert afraid of sorcery,
And yet hast said a charm!

THALABA.
A charm?

LAILA.
And wherefore?
Is it not not delicate food? what mean thy words?
I have heard many spells and many names
That rule the Genii and the Elements,
But never these.

THALABA.
How! never heard the names
Of God and of the Prophet?

LAILA.
Never ... nay now
Again that troubled eye? thou art a strange man
And wonderous fearful ... but I must not twice
Be charged with fraud! if thou suspectest still,
Depart and leave me!

THALABA.
And you do not know
The God that made you?

LAILA.
Made me, man! my Father
Made me. He made this dwelling, and the grove,
And yonder fountain-fire, and every morn
He visits me, and takes the snow, and moulds
Women and men, like thee; and breathes into them
Motion, and life, and sense,... but to the touch
They are chilling cold, and ever when night closes
They melt away again, and leave me here
Alone and sad. Oh then how I rejoice
When it is day and my dear Father comes,
And chears me with kind words and kinder looks!
My dear, dear, Father! were it not for him,
I am so weary of this loneliness,
That I should wish I also were of snow
That I might melt away, and cease to be.

THALABA.
And have you always had your dwelling here

Amid this solitude of snow?

LAILA.
I think so.
I can remember with unsteady feet
Tottering from room to room, and finding pleasure
In flowers and toys and sweetmeats, things that long
Have lost their power to please; that when I see them
Raise only now a melancholy wish
I were the little trifler once again
That could be pleased so lightly!

THALABA.
Then you know not
Your Father's art?

LAILA.
No. I besought him once
To give me power like his, that where he went
I might go with him: but he shook his head,
And said it was a power too dearly bought,
And kist me with the tenderness of tears.

THALABA.
And wherefore has he hidden you thus far
From all the ways of humankind?

LAILA.
'Twas fear,
Fatherly fear and love. He read[167] the stars
And saw a danger in my destiny,
And therefore placed me here amid the snows,
And laid a spell that never human eye,
If foot of man by chance should reach the depth
Of this wide waste, shall see one trace of grove,
Garden, or dwelling-place, or yonder fire,
That thaws and mitigates the frozen sky.
And more than this, even if the enemy
Should come, I have a guardian here.

THALABA.
A guardian?

LAILA.
'Twas well that when my sight unclosed upon thee
There was no dark suspicion in thy face.
Else I had called his succour! wilt thou see him?
But if a Woman can have terrified thee,
How wilt thou bare his unrelaxing brow
And lifted lightnings?

THALABA.
Lead me to him, Lady!

She took him by the hand
And thro' the porch they past.
Over the garden and the grove
The fountain streams of fire
Poured a broad light like noon.
A broad unnatural light
That made the Rose's blush of beauty pale,
And dimmed the rich Geranium's scarlet blaze.
The various verdure of the grove
Now wore one undistinguishable grey,
Checqured with blacker shade.
Suddenly Laila stopt,
"I do not think thou art the enemy,"
She said, "but He will know!
"If thou hast meditated wrong
"Stranger, depart in time....
"I would not lead thee to thy death!"

The glance of Laila's eye
Turned anxiously toward the Arabian youth.
"So let him pierce my heart," cried Thalaba,
"If it hide thought to harm you!"

LAILA.
'Tis a figure,
Almost I fear to look at!... yet come on.
'Twill ease me of a heaviness that seems
To sink my heart; and thou mayest dwell here then.
In safety;... for thou shalt not go to-morrow,
Nor on the after, nor the after day,
Nor ever! it was only solitude
That made my misery here,...
And now that I can see a human face,
And hear a human voice....
Oh no! thou wilt not leave me!

THALABA.
Alas I must not rest!
The star that ruled at my nativity
Shone with a strange and blasting influence.
O gentle Lady! I should draw upon you
A killing curse.

LAILA.
But I will ask my Father
To save you from all danger, and you know not
The wonders he can work, and when I ask
It is not in his power to say me nay.

Perhaps thou knowest the happiness it is
To have a tender father?

THALABA.
He was one
Whom like a loathsome leper I have tainted
With my contagious destiny. At evening
He kist me as he wont, and laid his hands
Upon my head, and blest me ere I slept.
His dying groan awoke me, for the Murderer
Had stolen upon our sleep! for me was meant
The midnight blow of death; my father died,
The brother play-mates of my infancy,
The baby at the breast, they perished all,
All in that dreadful hour: but I was saved
To remember and revenge.

She answered not, for now
Emerging from the o'er-arched avenue
The finger of her upraised hand
Marked where the Guardian of the garden stood.
It was a brazen[168] Image, every limb
And swelling vein and muscle, true to life:
The left knee bending on,
The other straight, firm planted, and his hand
Lifted on high to hurl
The Lightning that it grasped.

When Thalaba approached,
The charmed Image knew Hodeirah's son,
And hurled the lightning at the dreaded foe.
The Ring! the saviour Ring!
Full in his face the lightning-bolt was driven,
The scattered fire recoiled.
Like the flowing of a summer gale he felt
Its ineffectual force,
His countenance was not changed,
Nor a hair of his head was singed.

He started and his glance
Turned angrily upon the Maid,
The sight disarmed suspicion ... breathless, pale,
Against a tree she stood.
Her wan lips quivering, and her eye
Upraised, in silent supplicating fear.

She started with a scream of joy
Seeing her Father there,
And ran and threw her arms around his neck,
"Save me!" she cried, "the Enemy is come!
"Save me! save me! Okba!"

"Okba!" repeats the youth,
For never since that hour
When in the Tent the Spirit told his name,
Had Thalaba let slip
The memory of his Father's murderer;
"Okba!"... and in his hand
He graspt an arrow-shaft.
And he rushed on to strike him.

"Son of Hodeirah!" the Old Man replied,
"My hour is not yet come."
And putting forth his hand
Gently he repelled the Youth.
"My hour is not yet come!
"But thou mayest shed this innocent Maiden's blood,
"That vengeance God allows thee."

Around her Father's neck
Still Laila's hands were clasped.
Her face was turned to Thalaba,
A broad light floated o'er its marble paleness,
As the wind waved the fountain fire.
Her large, dilated eye in horror raised
Watched his every movement.
"Not upon her," said he,
"Not upon her Hodeirah's blood cries out
"For vengeance!" and again his lifted arm
Threatened the Sorcerer,
Again withheld it felt
The barrier that no human strength could burst.

"Thou dost not aim the blow more eagerly,"
Okba replied, "than I would rush to meet it!
"But that were poor revenge.
"O Thalaba, thy God
"Wreaks on the innocent head
"His vengeance;... I must suffer in my child!
"Why dost thou pause to strike thy victim? Allah
"Permits, commands the deed."

"Liar!" quoth Thalaba.
And Laila's wondering eye
Looked up, all anguish to her Father's face,
"By Allah and the Prophet," he replied,
"I speak the words of truth.
"Misery, misery,
"That I must beg mine enemy to speed
"The inevitable vengeance now so near!
"I read it in her horoscope,
"Her birth-star warned me of Hodeirah's race.

"I laid a spell, and called a Spirit up.
"He answered one must die
"Laila or Thalaba....
"Accursed Spirit! even in truth
"Giving a lying hope!
"Last, I ascended the seventh Heaven
"And on the everlasting[169] Table there
"In characters of light,
"I read her written doom.
"The years that it has gnawn me! and the load
"Of sin that it has laid upon my soul!
"Curse on this hand that in the only hour
"The favouring stars allowed
"Reeked with other blood than thine.
"Still dost thou stand and gaze incredulous?
"Young man, be merciful, and keep her not
"Longer in agony!"

Thalaba's unbelieving frown
Scowled on the Sorcerer,
When in the air the rush of wings was heard
And Azrael stood among them.
In equal terror at the sight
The Enchanter, the Destroyer stood,
And Laila, the victim maid.

"Son of Hodeirah!" said the Angel of Death,
"The accursed fables not.
"When from the Eternal Hand I took
"The yearly[170] scroll of fate,
"Her name was written there.
"This is the hour, and from thy hands
"Commissioned to receive the Maid I come."

"Hear me O Angel!" Thalaba replied,
"To avenge my Father's death,
"To work the will of Heaven,
"To root from earth the accursed sorcerer race,
"I have dared danger undismayed,
"I have lost all my soul held dear,
"I am cut off from all the ties of life,
"Unmurmuring; for whate'er awaits me still,
"Pursuing to the end the enterprize,
"Peril or pain, I bear a ready heart.
"But strike this Maid! this innocent!
"Angel, I dare not do it."

"Remember," answered Azrael, "all thou sayest
"Is written down for judgement! every word
"In the balance of[171] thy trial must be weighed!"

"So be it!" said the Youth.
"He who can read the secrets of the heart
"Will judge with righteousness!
"This is no doubtful path,
"The voice of God within me cannot lie....
"I will not harm the innocent."

He said, and from above,
As tho' it were the Voice of Night,
The startling answer came.
"Son of Hodeirah, think again!
"One must depart from hence,
"Laila, or Thalaba;
"She dies for thee, or thou for her,
"It must be life for life!
"Son of Hodeirah, weigh it well,
"While yet the choice is thine!"

He hesitated not,
But looking upward spread his hands to Heaven,
"Oneiza, in thy bower of Paradise
"Receive me, still unstained!"

"What!" exclaimed Okba, "darest thou disobey,
"Abandoning all claim
"To Allah's longer aid?"

The eager exultation of his speech
Earthward recalled the thoughts of Thalaba.
"And dost thou triumph, Murderer? dost thou deem
"Because I perish, that the unsleeping lids
"Of Justice shall be closed upon thy crime?
"Poor, miserable man! that thou canst live
"With such beast-blindness in the present joy
"When o'er thy head the sword of God
"Hangs for the certain stroke!"

"Servant of Allah, thou hast disobeyed,
"God hath abandoned thee,
"This hour is mine!" cried Okba,
And shook his Daughter off,
And drew the dagger from his vest.
And aimed the deadly blow.

All was accomplished. Laila rushed between
To save the saviour Youth.
She met the blow and sunk into his arms,
And Azrael from the hands[172] of Thalaba
Received her parting soul.

THE ELEVENTH BOOK

O fool to think thy human hand
Could check the chariot-wheels of Destiny
To dream of weakness in the all-knowing Mind
That his decrees should change!
To hope that the united Powers
Of Earth, and Air, and Hell,
Might blot one letter from the Book of Fate,
Might break one link of the eternal chain!
Thou miserable, wicked, poor old man,
Fall now upon the body of thy child,
Beat now thy breast, and pluck the bleeding hairs
From thy grey beard, and lay
Thine ineffectual hand to close her wound.
And call on Hell to aid,
And call on Heaven to send
Its merciful thunderbolt!

The young Arabian silently
Beheld his frantic grief.
The presence of the hated youth
To raging anguish stung
The wretched Sorcerer.
"Aye! look and triumph!" he exclaimed,
"This is the justice of thy God!
"A righteous God is he, to let
"His vengeance fall upon the innocent head!
"Curse thee, curse thee, Thalaba!"

All feelings of revenge
Had left Hodeirah's son.
Pitying and silently he heard
The victim of his own iniquities,
Not with the busy hand
Of Consolation, fretting the sore wound
He could not hope to heal.

So as the Servant of the Prophet stood,
With sudden motion the night air
Gently fanned his cheek.
'Twas a Green Bird whose wings
Had waved the quiet air.
On the hand of Thalaba
The Green Bird perched, and turned
A mild eye up, as if to win
The Adventurer's confidence.

Then springing on flew forward,
And now again returns
To court him to the way;
And now his hand perceives
Her rosy feet press firmer, as she leaps
Upon the wing again.

Obedient to the call,
By the pale moonlight Thalaba pursued
O'er trackless snows his way;
Unknowing he what blessed messenger
Had come to guide his steps,
That Laila's Spirit went before his path.
Brought up in darkness and the child of sin,
Yet as the meed of spotless innocence,
Just Heaven permitted her by one good deed
To work her own redemption, after death;
So till the judgement day
She might abide in bliss,
Green[173] warbler of the Bowers of Paradise.

The morning sun came forth,
Wakening no eye to life
In this wide solitude;
His radiance with a saffron hue, like heat,
Suffused the desert snow.
The Green Bird guided Thalaba,
Now oaring with slow wing her upward way,
Descending now in slant descent
On out-spread pinions motionless,
Floating now with rise and fall alternate,
As if the billows of the air
Heaved her with their sink and swell.

And when, beneath the noon,
The icey glitter of the snow
Dazzled his aching sight,
Then on his arm alighted the Green Bird
And spread before his eyes
Her plumage of refreshing hue.
Evening came on; the glowing clouds
Tinged with a purple ray the mountain ridge
That lay before the Traveller.
Ah! whither art thou gone,
Guide and companion of the youth, whose eye
Has lost thee in the depth of Heaven?
Why hast thou left alone
The weary wanderer in the wilderness?
And now the western clouds grow pale
And Night descends upon his solitude.

The Arabian youth knelt down,
And bowed his forehead to the ground
And made his evening prayer.
When he arose the stars were bright in heaven,
The sky was blue, and the cold Moon
Shone over the cold snow.
A speck in the air!
Is it his guide that approaches?
For it moves with the motion of life!
Lo! she returns and scatters from her pinions
Odours diviner than the gales of morning
Waft from Sabea.

Hovering before the youth she hung,
Till from her rosy feet that at his touch
Uncurled their grasp, he took
The fruitful bough they bore.
He took and tasted, a new life
Flowed thro' his renovated frame;
His limbs that late were sore and stiff
Felt all the freshness of repose,
His dizzy brain was calmed.
The heavy aching of his lids
At once was taken off,
For Laila from the Bowers of Paradise
Had borne the healing[174] fruit.

So up the mountain steep
With untired foot he past,
The Green Bird guiding him
Mid crags, and ice, and rocks,
A difficult way, winding the long ascent.
How then the heart of Thalaba rejoiced
When bosomed in the mountain depths,
A sheltered Valley opened on his view!
It was the Simorg's vale,
The dwelling of the ancient Bird.

On a green and mossy bank.
Beside a rivulet
The Bird of Ages stood.
No sound intruded on his solitude,
Only the rivulet was heard
Whose everlasting flow
From the birth-day of the world had made
The same unvaried murmuring.
Here dwelt the all-knowing Bird
In deep tranquillity,
His eyelids ever closed
In full enjoyment of profound repose.

Reverently the youth approached
That old and only[175] Bird,
And crossed his arms upon his breast,
And bowed his head and spake.
"Earliest of existing things,
"Earliest thou, and wisest thou,
"Guide me, guide me, on my way!
"I am bound to seek the caverns
"Underneath the roots of Ocean
"Where the Sorcerer brood are nurst.
"Thou the eldest, thou the wisest,
"Guide me, guide me, on my way!"

The ancient Simorg on the youth
Unclosed his thoughtful eyes,
And answered to his prayer.
"Northward by the stream proceed,
"In the fountain of the rock
"Wash away thy worldly stains,
"Kneel thou there, and seek the Lord
"And fortify thy soul with prayer.
"Thus prepared ascend the Sledge,
"Be bold, be wary, seek and find!
"God hath appointed all."
The ancient Simorg then let fall his lids
Returning to repose.

Northward along the rivulet
The adventurer went his way,
Tracing its waters upward to their source.
Green Bird of Paradise
Thou hast not left the youth;...
With slow associate flight
She companies his way,
And now they reach the fountain of the rock.

There in the cold clear well
Thalaba washed away his earthly stains,
And bowed his face before the Lord,
And fortified his soul with prayer.
The while upon the rock
Stood the celestial Bird,
And pondering all the perils he must pass,
With a mild melancholy eye
Beheld the youth beloved.

And lo! beneath yon lonely pine, the sledge....
And there they stand the harnessed Dogs,
Their wide eyes watching for the youth,
Their ears erected turned towards his way.
They were lean as lean might be,

Their furrowed ribs rose prominent,
And they were black from head to foot,
Save a white line on every breast
Curved like the crescent moon.
And he is seated in the sledge,
His arms are folded on his breast,
The bird is on his knees;
There is fear in the eyes of the Dogs,
There is fear in their pitiful moan,
And now they turn their heads,
And seeing him there, Away!

The Youth with the start of their speed
Falls back to the bar of the sledge,
His hair floats straight in the stream of the wind
Like the weeds in the running brook.
They wind with speed the upward way,
An icey path thro' rocks of ice,
His eye is at the summit now,
And thus far all is dangerless,
And now upon the height
The black Dogs pause and pant,
They turn their eyes to Thalaba
As if to plead for pity,
They moan and moan with fear.

Once more away! and now
The long descent is seen,
A long, long, narrow path.
Ice-rocks aright and hills of snow,
Aleft the giddy precipice.
Be firm, be firm, O Thalaba!
One motion now, one bend,
And on the crags below
Thy shattered flesh will harden in the frost.
Why howl the Dogs so mournfully?
And wherefore does the blood flow fast
All purple o'er their sable hair?
His arms are folded on his breast,
Nor scourge nor goad has he,
No hand appears to strike,
No sounding lash is heard:
But piteously they moan and moan
And track their way with blood.

And lo! on yonder height
A giant Fiend aloft
Waits to thrust down the tottering Avalanche!
If Thalaba looks back he dies,
The motion of fear is death.
On ... on ... with swift and steady pace

Adown that dreadful way!
The youth is firm, the Dogs are fleet,
The Sledge goes rapidly,
The thunder of the avalanche
Re-echoes far behind.
On ... on ... with swift and steady pace
Adown that dreadful way!
The Dogs are fleet, the way is steep
The Sledge goes rapidly,
They reach the plain below.

A wide, wide plain, all desolate,
Nor tree, nor bush, nor herb!
On go the Dogs with rapid step,
The Sledge slides after rapidly,
And now the Sun went down.
They stopt and looked at Thalaba,
The Youth performed his prayer;
They knelt beside him as he prayed
They turned their heads to Mecca
And tears ran down their cheeks.
Then down they laid them in the snow
As close as they could lie,
They laid them down and slept.
And backward in the sledge
The Adventurer laid him down,
There peacefully slept Thalaba,
And the Green Bird of Paradise
Lay in his bosom warm.

The Dogs awoke him at the dawn,
They knelt and wept again;
Then rapidly they journeyed on,
And still the plain was desolate,
Nor tree, nor bush, nor herb!
And ever at the hour of prayer
They stopt, and knelt, and wept;
And still that green and graceful Bird
Was as a friend to him by day,
And ever when at night he slept
Lay in his bosom warm.
In that most utter solitude
It cheered his heart to hear
Her soft and soothing voice;
Her voice was soft and sweet,
It swelled not with the blackbird's thrill,
Nor warbled rich like the dear bird, that holds
The solitary man
A loiterer in his thoughtful walk at eve;
But if no overflowing joy
Spake in its tones of tenderness

They soothed the softened soul.
Her bill was not the beak of blood;
There was a human meaning in her eye,
Its mild affection fixed on Thalaba
Woke wonder while he gazed
And made her dearer for the mystery.

Oh joy! the signs of life appear,
The first and single Fir
That on the limits of the living world
Strikes in the ice its roots.
Another, and another now;
And now the Larch that flings its arms
Down arching like the falling wave;
And now the Aspin's scattered leaves
Grey glitter on the moveless twig;
The Poplar's varying verdure now,
And now the Birch so beautiful,
Light as a Lady's plumes.
Oh joy! the signs of life! the Deer
Hath left his slot beside the way;
The little Ermine now is seen
White wanderer of the snow;
And now from yonder pines they hear
The clatter of the Grouse's wings:
And now the snowy Owl pursues
The Traveller's sledge in hope of food;
And hark! the rosy-breasted bird
The Throstle of sweet song!
Joy! joy! the winter-wilds are left!
Green bushes now and greener grass,
Red thickets here all berry-bright,
And here the lovely flowers!

When the last morning of their way arrived,
After the early prayer,
The Green Bird fixed on Thalaba
A sad and supplicating eye,
And with a human voice she spake,
"Servant of God, I leave thee now.
"If rightly I have guided thee,
"Give me the boon I beg!"

"O gentle Bird," quoth Thalaba,
"Guide and companion of my dangerous way,
"Friend and sole solace of my solitude,
"How can I pay thee benefits like these!
"Ask what thou wilt that I can give,
"O gentle Bird, the poor return
"Will leave me debtor still!"

"Son of Hodeirah!" she replied,
"When thou shalt see an Old Man crushed beneath
"The burthen of his earthly punishment,
"Forgive him, Thalaba!
"Yea, send a prayer to God on his behalf!"

A flush o'erspread the young Destroyer's cheek,
He turned his eye towards the Bird
As if in half repentance; for he thought
Of Okba; and his Father's dying groan
Came on his memory. The celestial Bird
Saw and renewed her speech.
"O Thalaba, if she who in thine arms
"Received the dagger-blow and died for thee,
"Deserve one kind remembrance ... save, O save
"The Father that she loved from endless death!"

"Laila! and is it thou?" the youth replied:
"What is there that I durst refuse to thee?
"This is no time to harbour in my heart
"One evil thought ... here I put off revenge,
"The last rebellious feeling ... be it so!
"God grant to me the pardon that I need
"As I do pardon him!
"But who am I that I should save
"The sinful soul alive?"

"Enough!" said Laila. "When the hour shall come
"Remember me! my task is done.
"We meet again in Paradise!"
She said and shook her wings, and up she soared
With arrow-swiftness thro' the heights of Heaven.

His aching eye pursued her path,
When starting onward went the Dogs,
More rapidly they hurried on
In hope of near repose.
It was the early morning yet
When by the well-head of a brook
They stopt, their journey done.
The spring was clear, the water deep,
A venturous man were he and rash
That should have probed its depths,
For all its loosened bed below
Heaved strangely up and down,
And to and fro, from side to side
It heaved, and waved, and tossed,
And yet the depths were clear,
And yet no ripple wrinkled o'er
The face of that fair Well.

And on that Well so strange and fair
A little boat there lay,
Without on oar, without a sail,
One only seat it had, one seat
As if for only Thalaba.
And at the helm a Damsel stood
A Damsel bright and bold of eye,
Yet did a maiden modesty
Adorn her fearless brow.
She seemed sorrowful, but sure
More beautiful for sorrow.
To her the Dogs looked wistful up,
And then their tongues were loosed,
"Have we done well, O Mistress dear!
"And shall our sufferings end?"

The gentle Damsel made reply,
"Poor Servants of the God I serve,
"When all this witchery is destroyed
"Your woes will end with mine.
"A hope, alas! how long unknown!
"This new adventurer gives:
"Now God forbid that he, like you,
"Should perish for his fears!
"Poor Servants of the God I serve
"Wait ye the event in peace."
A deep and total slumber as she spake
Seized them. Sleep on, poor sufferers! be at rest!
Ye wake no more to anguish. Ye have borne
The Chosen, the Destroyer! soon his hand
Shall strike the efficient blow,
Soon shaking off your penal forms shall ye
With songs of joy amid the Eden groves
Hymn the Deliverer's praise!

Then did the Damsel say to Thalaba,
"The morn is young, the Sun is fair
"And pleasantly thro' pleasant banks
"The quiet brook flows on....
"Wilt thou embark with me?
"Thou knowest not the water's way,
"Think Stranger well! and night must come,...
"Wilt thou embark with me?
"Thro' fearful perils thou must pass,...
"Stranger, the oppressed ask thine aid!
"Thou wilt embark with me!"

She smiled in tears upon the youth,...
What heart were his who could gainsay
That melancholy smile?
"Sail on, sail on," quoth Thalaba,

"Sail on, in Allah's name!"

He sate him on the single seat,
The little boat moved on.
Thro' pleasant banks the quiet brook
Went winding pleasantly;
By fragrant fir groves now it past,
And now thro' alder-shores,
Thro' green and fertile meadows now
It silently ran by.
The flag-flower blossomed on its side,
The willow tresses waved,
The flowing current furrowed round
The water-lilly's floating leaf,
The fly of green and gauzy wing
Fell sporting down its course.
And grateful to the voyager
The freshness of the running stream,
The murmur round the prow.
The little boat falls rapidly
Adown the rapid brook.

But many a silent spring meantime,
And many a rivulet
Had swoln the growing brook,
And when the southern Sun began
To wind the downward way of heaven,
It ran a river deep and wide
Thro' banks that widened still.
Then once again the Damsel spake,
"The stream is strong, the river broad,
"Wilt thou go on with me?
"The day is fair but night must come....
"Wilt thou go on with me?
"Far far away the mourner's eye
"Is watching; for our little boat....
"Thou wilt go on with me!"
"Sail on, sail on," quoth Thalaba,
"Sail on, in Allah's name!"
The little boat falls rapidly
Adown the river-stream.

A broader and a broader stream.
That rocked the little boat!
The Cormorant stands upon its shoals,
His black and dripping wings
Half opened to the wind.
The Sun goes down, the crescent Moon
Is brightening in the firmament;
And what is yonder roar
That sinking now and swelling now,

But roaring, roaring still,
Still louder, louder, grows?
The little boat falls rapidly
Adown the rapid tide,
The Moon is bright above,
And the wide Ocean opens on their way!

Then did the Damsel speak again
"Wilt thou go on with me?
"The Moon is bright, the sea is calm
"And I know well the ocean-paths;...
"Wilt thou go on with me?
"Deliverer! yes! thou dost not fear!
"Thou wilt go on with me!"
"Sail on, sail on!" quoth Thalaba
"Sail on, in Allah's name!"

The Moon is bright, the sea is calm,
The little boat rides rapidly
Across the ocean waves;
The line of moonlight on the deep
Still follows as they voyage on;
The winds are motionless;
The gentle waters gently part
In murmurs round the prow.
He looks above, he looks around,
The boundless heaven, the boundless sea,
The crescent moon, the little boat,
Nought else above, below.

The Moon is sunk, a dusky grey
Spreads o'er the Eastern sky,
The Stars grow pale and paler;
Oh beautiful! the godlike Sun
Is rising o'er the sea!
Without an oar, without a sail
The little boat rides rapidly;...
Is that a cloud that skirts the sea?
There is no cloud in heaven!
And nearer now, and darker now....
It is ... it is ... the Land!
For yonder are the rocks that rise
Dark in the reddening morn,
For loud around their hollow base
The surges rage and roar.

The little boat rides rapidly,
And now with shorter toss it heaves
Upon the heavier swell;
And now so near they see
The shelves and shadows of the cliff,

And the low-lurking rocks
O'er whose black summits hidden-half
The shivering billows burst.
And nearer now they feel the breaker's spray.
Then spake the Damsel, "yonder is our path
"Beneath the cavern arch.
"Now is the ebb, and till the ocean-flow
"We cannot over-ride the rocks.
"Go thou and on the shore
"Perform thy last ablutions, and with prayer
"Strengthen thy heart.... I too have need to pray."

She held the helm with steady hand
Amid the stronger waves,
Thro' surge and surf she drove,
The adventurer leapt to land.

THE TWELFTH BOOK

Then Thalaba drew off Abdaldar's ring,
And cast it in the sea, and cried aloud,
"Thou art my shield, my trust, my hope, O God!
"Behold and guard me now,
"Thou who alone canst save.
"If from my childhood up, I have looked on
"With exultation to my destiny,
"If, in the hour of anguish, I have felt
"The justice of the hand that chastened me,
"If, of all selfish passions purified,
"I go to work thy will, and from the world
"Root up the ill-doing race,
"Lord! let not thou the weakness of my arm
"Make vain the enterprize!"

The Sun was rising all magnificent,
Ocean and Heaven rejoicing in his beams.
And now had Thalaba
Performed his last ablutions, and he stood
And gazed upon the little boat
Riding the billows near,
Where, like a sea-bird breasting the broad waves,
It rose and fell upon the surge;
Till from the glitterance of the sunny main
He turned his aching eyes,
And then upon the beach he laid him down
And watched the rising tide.

He did not pray, he was not calm for prayer;
His spirit troubled with tumultuous hope
Toiled with futurity.
His brain, with busier workings, felt
The roar and raving of the restless sea,
The boundless waves that rose and rolled and rocked;
The everlasting sound
Opprest him, and the heaving infinite,
He closed his lids for rest.

Meantime with fuller reach and stronger swell
Wave after wave advanced;
Each following billow lifted the last foam
That trembled on the sand with rainbow hues;
The living flower, that, rooted to the rock,
Late from the thinner element
Shrunk down within its purple stem to sleep,
Now feels the water, and again
Awakening blossoms out
All its green anther-necks.

Was there a Spirit in the gale
That fluttered o'er his cheek?
For it came on him like the gentle sun
That plays and dallies o'er the night-closed flower,
And woos it to unfold anew to joy;
For it came on him as the dews of eve
Descend with healing and with life
Upon the summer mead;
Or liker the first sound of seraph song
And Angel hail, to him
Whose latest sense had shuddered at the groan
Of anguish, kneeling by his death bed-side.

He starts and gazes round to seek
The certain presence. "Thalaba!" exclaimed
The Voice of the Unseen;...
"Father of my Oneiza!" he replied,
"And have thy years been numbered? art thou too
"Among the Angels?" "Thalaba!"
A second and a dearer voice repeats,
"Go in the favour of the Lord
"My Thalaba go on!
"My husband. I have drest our bower of bliss.
"Go and perform the work,
"Let me not longer suffer hope in heaven!"

He turned an eager glance towards the sea,
"Come!" quoth the Damsel, and she drove
Her little boat to land.
Impatient thro' the rising wave

He rushed to meet its way,
His eye was bright, his cheek was flushed with joy.
"Hast thou had comfort in thy prayers?" she cried,
"Yea," answered Thalaba,
"A heavenly visitation." "God be praised!"
She uttered, "then I do not hope in vain!"
And her voice trembled, and her lips
Quivered, and tears ran down.
"Stranger," quoth she, "in years long past
"Was one who vowed himself
"The Champion of the Lord like thee
"Against the race of Hell.
"Young was he, as thyself,
"Gentle, and yet so brave!
"A lion-hearted man.
"Shame on me, Stranger! in the arms of love
"I held him from his calling, till the hour
"Was past, and then the Angel who should else
"Have crowned him with his glory-wreath,
"Smote him in anger ... years and years are gone....
"And in his place of penance he awaits
"Thee the Deliverer, surely thou art he!
"It was my righteous punishment
"In the same youth unchanged and changeless love,
"And fresh affliction and keen penitence
"To abide the written hour when I should waft
"The doomed Destroyer and Deliverer here.
"Remember thou that thy success involves
"No single fate, no common misery."

As thus she spake, the entrance of the cave
Darkened the boat below.
Around them from their nests,
The screaming sea-birds fled.
Wondering at that strange shape
Yet unalarmed at sight of living man,
Unknowing of his sway and power misused;
The clamours of their young
Echoed in shriller yells
That rung in wild discordance round the rock.
And farther as they now advanced
The dim reflection of the darkened day
Grew fainter, and the dash
Of the out-breakers deadened; farther yet
And yet more faint the gleam,
And there the waters at their utmost bound
Silently rippled on the rising rock.
They landed and advanced, and deeper in
Two adamantine doors
Closed up the cavern pass.

Reclining on the rock beside
Sate a grey-headed man
Watching an hour-glass by.
To him the Damsel spake,
"Is it the hour appointed?" the old man
Nor answered her awhile,
Nor lifted he his downward eye,
For now the glass ran low,
And like the days of age
With speed perceivable,
The latter sands descend:
And now the last are gone.
Then he looked up, and raised his arm, and smote
The adamantine gates.

The gates of adamant
Unfolding at the stroke
Opened and gave the entrance. Then She turned
To Thalaba and said
"Go in the name of God!
"I cannot enter,... I must wait the end
"In hope and agony.
"God and Mohammed prosper thee,
"For thy sake and for ours!"

He tarried not,... he past
The threshold, over which was no return.
All earthly thoughts, all human hopes
And passions now put off,
He cast no backward glance
Towards the gleam of day.
There was a light within,
A yellow light, as when the autumnal Sun
Through travelling rain and mist
Shines on the evening hills.
Whether from central fires effused,
Or if the sunbeams day by day,
From earliest generations, there absorbed,
Were gathering for the wrath-flame. Shade was
In those portentous vaults;
Crag overhanging, nor the column-rock
Cast its dark outline there.
For with the hot and heavy atmosphere
The light incorporate, permeating all,
Spread over all its equal yellowness.
There was no motion in the lifeless air,
He felt no stirring as he past
Adown the long descent,
He heard not his own footsteps on the rock
That thro' the thick stagnation sent no sound.
How sweet it were, he thought,

To feel the flowing wind!
With what a thirst of joy
He should breathe in the open gales of heaven!

Downward and downward still, and still the way,
The long, long, way is safe.
Is there no secret wile
No lurking enemy?
His watchful eye is on the wall of rock,...
And warily he marks the roof
And warily surveyed
The path that lay before.
Downward and downward still, and still the way,
The long, long, way is safe;
Rock only, the same light,
The same dead atmosphere,
And solitude, and silence like the grave.

At length the long descent
Ends on a precipice;
No feeble ray entered its dreadful gulphs,
For in the pit profound
Black Darkness, utter Night,
Repelled the hostile gleam,
And o'er the surface the light atmosphere
Floated and mingled not.
Above the depth four overawning wings,
Unplumed and huge and strong,
Bore up a little car;
Four living pinions, headless, bodyless,
Sprung from one stem that branched below
In four down-arching limbs,
And clenched the car-rings endlong and aside
With claws of griffin grasp.

But not on these, the depths so terrible,
The wonderous wings, fixed Thalaba his eye,
For there upon the brink,
With fiery fetters fastened to the rock,
A man, a living man, tormented lay,
The young Othatha; in the arms of love,
He who had lingered out the auspicious hour
Forgetful of his call.
In shuddering pity Thalaba exclaimed
"Servant of God, can I not succour thee?"
He groaned and answered, "Son of Man,
"I sinned and am tormented; I endure
"In patience and in hope.
"The hour that shall destroy the Race of Hell,
"That hour shall set me free."

"Is it not come?" quoth Thalaba,
"Yea! by this omen." And with fearless hand
He grasped the burning fetters, "in the name
"Of God!" and from the rock
Rooted the rivets, and adown the gulph
Hurled them. The rush of flames roared up,
For they had kindled in their fall
The deadly vapours of the pit profound,
And Thalaba bent on and looked below.
But vainly he explored
The deep abyss of flame
That sunk beyond the plunge of mortal eye,
Now all ablaze as if infernal fires
Illumed the world beneath.
Soon was the poison-fuel spent,
The flame grew pale and dim,
And dimmer now it fades and now is quenched,
And all again is dark,
Save where the yellow air
Enters a little in and mingles slow.

Meantime the freed Othatha clasped his knees
And cried, "Deliverer!" struggling then
With joyful hope, "and where is she," he cried,
"Whose promised coming for so many a year...."
"Go!" answered Thalaba,
"She waits thee at the gates."
"And in thy triumph," he replied,
"There thou wilt join us?" the Deliverer's eye
Glanced on the abyss, way else was none....
The depth was unascendable.
"Await not me," he cried,
"My path hath been appointed, go ... embark!
"Return to life,... live happy!"

OTHATHA.
But thy name,...
That thro' the nations we may blazon it,
That we may bless thee.

THALABA.
Bless the Merciful!

Then Thalaba pronounced the name of God
And leapt into the car.
Down, down, it sunk,... down down....
He neither breathes nor sees;
His eyes are closed for giddiness
His breath is sinking with the fall.
The air that yields beneath the car
Inflates the wings above.

Down ... down ... a mighty depth!...
And was the Simorgh with the Powers of ill
Associate to destroy?
And was that lovely mariner
A fiend as false as fair?
For still he sinks down ... down....
But ever the uprushing wind
Inflates the wings above,
And still the struggling wings
Repel the rushing wind.
Down ... down ... and now it strikes.

He stands and totters giddily,
All objects round, awhile,
Float dizzy on his sight.
Collected soon he gazes for the way.
There was a distant light that led his search;
The torch a broader blaze,
The unpruned taper flames a longer flame,
But this was fierce as is the noon-tide sun,
So in the glory of its rays intense
It quivered with green glow.
Beyond was all unseen,
No eye could penetrate
That unendurable excess of light.
It veiled no friendly form, thought Thalaba,
And wisely did he deem,
For at the threshold of the rocky door,
Hugest and fiercest of his kind accurst,
Fit warden of the sorcery gate
A rebel Afreet lay.
He scented the approach of human food
And hungry hope kindled his eye of flame.
Raising his hand to save the dazzled sense
Onward held Thalaba,
And lifted still at times a rapid glance.
Till, the due distance gained,
With head abased, he laid
The arrow in its rest.
With steady effort and knit forehead then,
Full on the painful light
He fixed his aching eye, and loosed the bow.

An anguish yell ensued,
And sure no human voice had scope or power
For that prodigious shriek
Whose pealing echoes thundered up the rock.
Dim grew the dying light,
But Thalaba leapt onward to the doors
Now visible beyond,
And while the Afreet warden of the way

Was writhing with his death-pangs, over him
Sprung and smote the stony doors,
And bade them in the name of God give way.

The dying Fiend beneath him at that name
Tossed in worse agony,
And the rocks shuddered, and the rocky doors
Rent at the voice asunder. Lo ... within....
The Teraph and the fire,
And Khawla, and in mail complete
Mohareb for the strife.
But Thalaba with numbing force
Smites his raised arm, and rushes by,
For now he sees the fire amid whose flames
On the white ashes of Hodeirah lies
Hodeirah's holy Sword.

He rushes to the fire,
Then Khawla met the youth
And leapt upon him, and with clinging arms
Clasps him, and calls Mohareb now to aim
The effectual vengeance. O fool! fool! he sees
His Father's Sword, and who shall bar his way?
Who stand against the fury of that arm
That spurns her to the earth?
She rises half, she twists around his knees,
A moment ... and he vainly strives
To shake her from her hold,
Impatient then into her cursed breast
He stamps his crushing heel,
And from her body, heaving now in death
Springs forward to the Sword.

The co-existent flame
Knew the Destroyer; it encircled him,
Rolled up his robe and gathered round his head,
Condensing to intenser splendour there,
His crown of glory and his light of life
Hovered the irradiate wreath.
The moment Thalaba had laid his hand
Upon his Father's Sword,
The Living Image in the inner cave
Smote the Round Altar. The Domdaniel rocked
Thro' all its thundering vaults;
Over the surface of the reeling Earth
The alarum shock was felt:
The Sorcerer brood, all, all, where'er dispersed,
Perforce obeyed the summons; all, they came
Compelled by Hell and Heaven,
By Hell compelled to keep
Their baptism-covenant,

And with the union of their strength
Oppose the common danger; forced by Heaven
To share the common doom.

Vain are all spells! the Destroyer
Treads the Domdaniel floor.
They crowd with human arms and human force
To crush the single foe;
Vain is all human force!
He wields his Father's Sword,
The vengeance of awakened Deity!
But chief on Thalaba Mohareb prest,
The language of the inspired Witch
Announced one fatal blow for both,
And desperate of self-safety, yet he hoped
To serve the cause of Eblis, and uphold
His empire true in death.

Who shall withstand his way?
Scattered before the sword of Thalaba
The sorcerer throng recede
And leave him space for combat. Wretched man
What shall the helmet or the shield avail
Against Almighty anger! wretched man,
Too late Mohareb finds that he has chosen
The evil part! he rears his shield
To meet the Arabian's sword,...
Under the edge of that fire-hardened steel
The shield falls severed; his cold arm
Rings with the jarring blow,...
He lifts his scymetar,
A second stroke, and lo! the broken hilt
Hangs from his palsied hand!
And now he bleeds! and now he flies!
And fain would hide himself amid the throng,
But they feel the sword of Hodeirah,
But they also fly from the ruin!
And hasten to the inner cave,
And fall all fearfully
Around the Giant Idol's feet,
Seeking salvation from the Power they served.

It was a Living Image, by the art
Of magic hands of flesh and bones composed,
And human blood thro' veins and arteries
That flowed with vital action. In the shape
Of Eblis it was made,
Its stature such and such its strength
As when among the Sons of God
Pre-eminent, he raised his radiant head,
Prince of the Morning. On his brow

A coronet of meteor flames,
Flowing in points of light.
Self-poised in air before him,
Hung the Round Altar, rolling like the World
On its diurnal axis, like the World
Checquered with sea and shore,
The work of Demon art.
For where the sceptre in the Idol's hand
Touched the Round Altar, in its answering realm
Earth felt the stroke, and Ocean rose in storms,
And ruining Cities shaken from their seat
Crushed all their habitants.
His other arm was raised, and its spread palm
Up-bore the ocean-weight
Whose naked waters arched the sanctuary,
Sole prop and pillar he.

Fallen on the ground around his feet
The Sorcerers lay. Mohareb's quivering arms
Clung to the Idol's knees;
The Idol's face was pale
And calm in terror he beheld
The approach of the Destroyer.

Sure of his stroke, and therefore in pursuit
Following, nor blind, nor hasty on his foe,
Moved the Destroyer. Okba met his way,
Of all that brotherhood
He only fearless, miserable man,
The one that had no hope.
"On me, on me," the childless Sorcerer cried,
"Let fall the weapon! I am he who stole
"Upon the midnight of thy Father's tent,
"This is the hand that pierced Hodeirah's heart,
"That felt thy brethren's and thy sister's blood
"Gush round the dagger-hilt. Let fall on me
"The fated sword! the vengeance hour is come!
"Destroyer, do thy work!"

Nor wile, nor weapon, had the desperate wretch,
He spread his bosom to the stroke.
"Old man, I strike thee not!" said Thalaba,
"The evil thou hast done to me and mine
"Brought its own bitter punishment.
"For thy dear Daughter's sake I pardon thee,
"As I do hope Heaven's pardon. For her sake
"Repent while time is yet! thou hast my prayers
"To aid thee; thou poor sinner, cast thyself
"Upon the goodness of offended God!
"I speak in Laila's name, and what if now
"Thou canst not think to join in Paradise

"Her spotless Spirit,... hath not Allah made
"Al-Araf[176] in his wisdom? where the sight
"Of Heaven shall kindle in the penitent
"The strong and purifying fire of hope,
"Till at the day of judgement he shall see
"The Mercy-Gates unfold."

The astonished man stood gazing as he spake,
At length his heart was softened, and the tears
Gushed, and he sobbed aloud.
Then suddenly was heard
The all-beholding Prophet's aweful voice,
"Thou hast done well, my Servant!
"Ask and receive thy reward!"

A deep and aweful joy
Seemed to distend the heart of Thalaba;
With arms in reverence crost upon his breast,
Upseeking eyes suffused with transport-tears
He answered to the Voice, "Prophet of God,
"Holy, and good, and bountiful!
"One only earthly wish have I, to work
"Thy will, and thy protection grants me that.
"Look on this Sorcerer! heavy are his crimes,
"But infinite is mercy! if thy servant
"Have now found favour in the sight of God,
"Let him be touched with penitence, and save
"His soul from utter death."

"The groans of penitence," replied the Voice
"Never arise unheard!
"But for thyself prefer the prayer,
"The Treasure-house of Heaven
"Is open to thy will."

"Prophet of God!" then answered Thalaba,
"I am alone on earth.
"Thou knowest the secret wishes of my heart!
"Do with me as thou wilt! thy will is best."

There issued forth no Voice to answer him,
But lo! Hodeirah's Spirit comes to see
His vengeance, and beside him, a pure form
Of roseate light, the Angel mother hangs.
"My Child, my dear, my glorious, blessed Child,
"My promise is performed ... fufil thy work!"

Thalaba knew that his death-hour was come,
And on he leapt, and springing up,
Into the Idol's heart
Hilt-deep he drove the Sword.

The Ocean-Vault fell in, and all were crushed.
In the same moment at the gate
Of Paradise, Oneiza's Houri-form
Welcomed her Husband to eternal bliss.

END.

[1] The Lord gave, and the Lord taketh away; blessed be the name of the Lord.— Job. i. 21.

I have placed a scripture phrase in the mouth of a Mohammedan; but it is a saying of Job, and there can be no impropriety in making a modern Arab speak like an ancient one. Resignation is particularly inculcated by Mohammed, and of all his precepts it is that which his followers have best observed: it is even the vice of the East. It had been easy to have made Zeinab speak from the Koran, if the tame language of the Koran could be remembered by the few who have toiled through its dull tautology. I thought it better to express a feeling of religion in that language with which our religious ideas are connected.

[2] La mer n'est plus qu'un cercle aux yeux des Matelots,
Ou le Ciel forme un dôme appuyé sur les flots.
Le Nouveau Monde. par M. Le Suire.

[3] The magnificent Mosque Tauris is faced with varnished bricks of various colours, like most fine buildings in Persia, says Tavernier. One of its domes is covered with white flower work upon a green ground, the other has a black ground, spotted with white stars. Gilding is also common upon Oriental buildings. At Boghar in Bactria our old traveller Jenkinson[a] saw "many houses, temples, and monuments of stone sumptuously builded and gilt."

[a] Hakluyt.

In Pegu "they consume about their Varely or idol houses great store of leafe-gold, for that they overlay all the tops of the houses with gold, and some of them are covered with gold from the top to the foote; in covering whereof there is great store of gold spent, for that every ten years they new overlay them with gold, from the top to the foote, so that with this vanetie they spend great aboundance of golde. For every ten years the rain doeth consume the gold from these houses."

Cæsar Frederick,
in Hakluyt.

A waste of ornament and labour characterises all the works of the Orientalists. I have seen illuminated Persian manuscripts that must each have been the toil of many years, every page painted, not with representations of life and manners, but usually like the curves and lines of a Turkey carpet, conveying no idea whatever, as absurd to the eye as nonsense-verses to the ear. The little of their literature that has reached us is equally worthless. Our barbarian scholars have called Ferdusi the Oriental Homer. We have a specimen of his poem; the translation is said to be bad, and certainly must be unfaithful, for it is in rhyme; but the vilest copy of a picture at least represents the subject and the composition. To make this Iliad of the East, as they have sacrilegiously stiled it, a good poem, would be realizing the dreams of Alchemy, and transmuting lead into gold.

The Arabian Tales certainly abound with genius; they have lost their metaphorical rubbish in passing through the filter of a French translation.

[4] The Arabians call this palace one of the wonders of the world. It was built for Nôman-al-Aôuar, one of those Arabian Kings who reigned at Hirah. A single stone fastened the whole structure; the colour of the walls varied frequently in a day. Nôman richly rewarded the architect Sennamar; but recollecting afterwards that he might build palaces equal, or superior in beauty for his rival kings, ordered that he should be thrown from the highest tower of the edifice.

D'Herbelot.

[5] The tribe of Ad were descended from Ad, the son of Aus or Uz, the son of Irem, the son of Shem, the son of Noah, who after the confusion of tongues, settled in Al Ahkâf, or the winding sands, in the province of Hadramaut, where his posterity greatly multiplied. Their first King was Shedad, the son of Ad, of whom the eastern writers deliver many fabulous things, particularly that he finished the magnificent city his father had begun, wherein he built a fine palace, adorned with delicious gardens, to embellish which he spared neither cost nor labour, proposing thereby to create in his subjects a superstitious veneration of himself as a God. This garden or paradise was called the garden of Irem, and is mentioned in the Koran, and often alluded to by the Oriental writers. The city they tell us, is still standing in the desarts of Aden, being preserved by providence as a monument of divine justice, though it be invisible, unless very rarely, when God permits it to be seen: a favour one Colabah pretended to have received in the reign of the Khalif Moâwiyah, who sending for him to know the truth of the matter, Colabah related his whole adventure; that is he was seeking a Camel he had lost, he found himself on a sudden at the gates of this city, and entering it, saw not one inhabitant, at which being terrified, he stayed no longer than to take with him some fine stones which he shewed the Khalif.

Sale.

The descendants of Ad in process of time falling from the worship of the true God into idolatry, God sent the prophet Houd (who is generally agreed to be Heber) to preach the unity of his essence and reclaim them. Houd preached for many years to this people without effect, till God at last was weary of waiting for their repentance. The first punishment which he inflicted was a famine of three years continuance, during all which time the heavens were closed upon them. This, with the evils which it caused, destroyed a great part of this people, who were then the richest and most powerful of all in Arabia.

The Adites seeing themselves reduced to this extremity, and receiving no succour from their false Gods, resolved to make a pilgrimage to a place in the province of Hegiaz, where at present Mecca is situated. There was then a hillock of red sand there, around which a great concourse of different people might always be seen; and all these nations, the faithful as well as the unfaithful, believed that by visiting this spot with devotion, they should obtain from God whatever they petitioned for, respecting the wants and necessities of life.

The Adites having then resolved to undertake this religious journey, chose seventy men, at whose head they appointed Mortadh and Kail, the two most considerable personages of the country, to perform this duty in the name of the whole nation, and by this means procure rain from Heaven, without which their country must be ruined. The deputees departed, and were hospitably received by Moâwiyah, who at that time reigned in the province of Hegiaz. They explained to him the occasion of their journey, and demanded leave to proceed and perform their devotions at the Red Hillock, that they might procure rain.

Mortadh, who was the wisest of this company, and who had been converted by the Prophet Houd, often remonstrated with his associates that it was useless to take this journey for the purpose of praying at this chosen spot, unless they had previously adopted the truths which the Prophet preached, and seriously repented of their unbelief. For how, said he, can you hope that God will shed upon us the abundant showers of his mercy, if we refuse to hear the voice of him whom he hath sent to instruct us?

Kail who was one of the most obstinate in error, and consequently of the Prophets worst enemies, hearing the discourses of his colleague, requested King Moâwiyah to detain Mortadh prisoner, whilst he and the remainder of his companions proceeded to make their prayers upon the Hillock. Moâwiyah consented, and detaining Mortadh captive, permitted the others to pursue their journey and accomplish their vow.

Kail, now the sole chief of the deputation, having arrived at the place, prayed thus, Lord give to the people of Ad such rains as it shall please thee. And he had scarcely finished when there appeared three clouds in the sky, one white, one red, the third black. At the same time these words were heard to proceed from Heaven, chuse which of the three thou wilt. Kail chose the black, which he imagined the fullest, and most abundant in water, of which they were in extreme want. After having chosen, he immediately quitted the place and took the road to his own country, congratulating himself on the happy success of his pilgrimage.

As soon as Kail arrived in the valley of Magaith, a part of the territory of the Adites, he informed his countrymen of the favourable answer he had received, and of the cloud which was soon to water all their lands. The senseless people all came out of their houses to receive it, but this cloud, which was big with the divine vengeance produced only a wind, most cold and most violent, which the Arabs call Sarsar; it continued to blow for seven days and seven nights, and exterminated all the unbelievers of the country, leaving only the Prophet Houd alive, and those who had heard him and turned to the faith.

D'Herbelot

[6] Al-Ahkaf signifies the Winding Sands.

[7] I have heard from a certain Cyprian botanist, that the Ebony does not produce either leaves or fruit, and that it is never seen exposed to the sun: that its roots are indeed under the earth, which the Æthiopians dig out, and that there are men among them skilled in finding the place of its concealment.

Pausanias, translated by Taylor.

[8] The Adites worshipped four Idols, Sakiah the dispenser of rain, Hafedah the protector of travellers, Razecah the giver of food, and Salemah the preserver in sickness.

D'Herbelot. Sale.

[9] Mecca was thus called. Mohammed destroyed the other superstitions of the Arabs, but he was obliged to adopt their old and rooted veneration for the Well and the Black Stone, and transfer to Mecca the respect and reverence which he had designed for Jerusalem.

[10] Some of the Pagan Arabs when they died, had their Camel tied by their sepulchre, and so left without meat or drink to perish, and accompany them to the other world, lest they should be obliged at the Resurrection to go on foot, which was accounted very scandalous.

Ali affirmed that the pious when they come forth from their sepulchres shall find ready prepared for them white-winged Camels with saddles of gold. Here are some footsteps of the doctrine of the ancient Arabians.

Sale.

[11] "She stared me in the face."

This line is in one of the most beautiful passages of our old Ballads, so full of beauty. I have never seen the Ballad in print, and with some trouble, have procured only an imperfect copy from memory. It is necessary to insert some of the preceding stanzas. The title is

Old Poulter's mare.

At length old age came on her
And she grew faint and poor,
Her master he fell out with her
And turned her out of door,
Saying, if thou wilt not labour,
I prithee go thy way,—
And never let me see thy face
Until thy dying day.

These words she took unkind
And on her way she went,
For to fulfill her master's will
Always was her intent,
The hills were very high
The vallies very bare,
The summer it was hot and dry,—
It starved Old Poulter's Mare.

Old Poulter he grew sorrowful
And said to his kinsman Will,
I'd have thee go and seek the Mare
O'er valley and o'er hill,
Go, go, go, go, says Poulter,
And make haste back again,
For until thou hast found the Mare
In grief I shall remain.

Away went Will so willingly,
And all day long he sought:

Till when it grew towards the night,
He in his mind bethought,
He would go home and rest him
And come again to-morrow,
For if he could not find the Mare
His heart would break with sorrow.

He went a little farther
And turned his head aside,
And just by goodman Whitfield's gate
Oh there the Mare he spied.
He asked her how she did,
She stared him in the face,
Then down she laid her head again,—
She was in wretched case.

[12] Concerning the Pyramids, "I shall put down, says Greaves, that which is confessed by the Arabian writers to be the most probable relation, as is reported by Ibn Abd Alhokm, whose words out of the Arabick are these. "The greatest part of chronologers agree, that he which built the Pyramids, was, Saurid Ibn Salhouk, King of Egypt, who lived three hundred years before the flood. The occasion of this was, because he saw in his sleep, that the whole earth was turned over with the inhabitants of it, the men lying upon their faces, and the stars falling down and striking one another, with a terrible noise; and being troubled, he concealed it. After this he saw the fixed stars falling to the earth, in the similitude of white fowl, and they snatched up men, carrying them between two great mountains; and these mountains closed upon them, and the shining stars were made dark. Awaking with great fear, he assembles the chief priests of all the provinces of Egypt, an hundred and thirty priests, the chief of them was called Aclimum. Relating the whole matter to them, they took the altitude of the stars, and making their prognostication, foretold of a deluge. The King said, will it come to our country? they answered, yea, and will destroy it. And there remained a certain number of years for to come, and he commanded in the mean space to build the Pyramids, and a vault to be made, into which the river Nilus entering should run into the countries of the west, and into the land Al-Said. And he filled them with telesmes,[b] and with strange things, and with riches and treasures and the like. He engraved in them all things that were told him by wise men, as also all profound sciences, the names of alakakirs,[c] the uses and hurts of them; the science of astrology and of arithmetick, and of geometry, and of physick. All this may be interpreted by him that knows their characters and language. After he had given order for this building, they cut out vast columns and wonderful stones. They fetch massy stones from the Æthiopians, and made with these the foundation of the three Pyramids, fastening them together with lead and iron. They built the gates of them forty cubits under ground, and they made the height of the Pyramids one hundred royal cubits, which are fifty of ours in these times; he also made each side of them an hundred royal cubits. The beginning of this building was in a fortunate horoscope. After that he had finished it, he covered it with coloured satten from the top to the bottom; and he appointed a solemn festival, at which were present all the inhabitants of his kingdom. Then he built in the western Pyramid thirty treasures, filled with store of riches, and utensils, and with signatures made of precious stones, and with instruments of iron, and vessels of earth, and with arms that rust not, and with glass which might be bended and yet not broken, and with several kind of alakakirs, single and double, and with deadly poisons, and with other things besides. He made also in the east Pyramid divers celestial spheres and stars, and what they severally operate in their aspects, and the perfumes which are to be used to them, and the books which treat of these matters. He also put in the coloured Pyramid the commentaries of the Priests, in chests of black marble, and with every Priest a book, in which

were the wonders of his profession, and of his actions, and of his nature, and what was done in his time, and what is, and what shall be, from the beginning of time to the end of it. He placed in every Pyramid a treasurer. The treasurer of the westerly Pyramid was a statue of marble stone, standing upright with a lance, and upon his head a serpent wreathed. He that came near it, and stood still, the serpent bit him of one side, and wreathing round about his throat and killing him, returned to his place. He made the treasurer of the east Pyramid, an idol of black agate, his eyes open and shining, sitting upon a throne with a lance; when any looked upon him, he heard of one side of him a voice, which took away his sense, so that he fell prostrate upon his face, and ceased not till he died. He made the treasurer of the coloured Pyramid a statue of stone, called Albut, sitting: he which looked towards it was drawn by the statue, till he stuck to it, and could not be separated from it, till such time as he died. The Coptites write in their books, that there is an inscription engraven upon them, the exposition of which in Arabick is this, I KING SAURID built the Pyramids in such and such a time, and finished them in six years: he that comes after me, and says that he is equal to me, let him destroy them in six hundred years; and yet it is known, that it is easier to pluck down, than to build up: I also covered them, when I had finished them, with satten; and let him cover them with mats. After that ALMAMON the Calif entered Ægypt, and saw the Pyramids. He desired to know what was within, and therefore would have them opened. They told him it could not possibly be done. He replied I will have it certainly done. And that hole was opened for him, which stands open to this day, with fire and vinegar. Two smiths prepared and sharpened the iron and engines, which they forced in, and there was a great expence in the opening of it. The thickness of the wall was found to be twenty cubits; and when they came to the end of the wall, behind the place they had digged, there was an ewer of green emerald; in it were a thousand dinars very weighty, every dinar was an ounce of our ounces: they wondered at it, but knew not the meaning of it. Then ALMAMON said, cast up the account, how much hath been spent in making the entrance; they cast it up, and lo it was the same sum which they found, it neither exceeded nor was defective. Within they found a square well, in the square of it there were doors, every door opened into a house (or vault) in which there were dead bodies wrapped up in linen. They found towards the top of the Pyramid, a chamber, in which there was an hollow stone: in it was a statue of stone like a man, and within it a man, upon whom was a breast-plate of gold set with jewels; upon his breast was a sword of invaluable price, and at his head a carbuncle of the bigness of an egg, shining like the light of the day; and upon him were characters written with a pen, no man knows what they signify. After ALMAMON had opened it, men entered into it for many years, and descended by the slippery passage which is in it; and some of them came out safe, and others died."

Greaves's Pyramidographia.

[b] That which the Arabians commonly mean by telesmes, are certain sigilla or amuleta, made under such and such an aspect, or configuration of the stars and planets, with several characters accordingly inscribed.

[c] Alakakir, amongst other significations, is the name of a precious stone; and therefore in Abulfeda it is joined with yacut, a ruby. I imagine it here to signify some magical spell, which it may be was engraven on this stone.

[13] The Carbuncle is to be found in most of the subterranean palaces of Romance. I have no where seen so circumstantial an account of its wonderful properties as in a passage of Thuanus, quoted by Setphanius in his notes to Saxo Grammaticus.

"Whilst the King was at Bologna a stone wonderful in its species and nature was brought to him from the East Indies, by a man unknown, who appeared by his manners to be a Barbarian. It sparkled as tho' all burning with an incredible splendour, flashing radiance, and shooting on every side its beams, it filled the surrounding air to a great distance with a light scarcely by any eyes endurable. In this also it was wonderful, that being most impatient of the earth, if it was confined, it would force its way and immediately fly aloft; neither could it be contained by any art of man in a narrow place, but appeared only to love those of ample extent. It was of the utmost purity stained by no soil nor spot. Certain shape it had none, for its figure was inconstant and momentarily changing, and tho' at a distance it was beautiful to the eye, it would not suffer itself to be handled with impunity, but hurt those who obstinately struggled with it, as many persons before many spectators experienced. If by chance any part of it was broken off, for it was not very hard, it become nothing less.

Thuanus. Lib. 8.

In the Mirror of Stones, Carbuncles are said to be male and female. The females throw out their brightness: the stars appear burning within the males.

Like many other jewels the Carbuncle was supposed to be an animal substance, formed in the serpent. The serpent's ingenious method of preserving it from the song of the charmer is related in an after note. Book 9.

[14] Adam, says a Moorish Author, after having eaten the forbidden fruit, sought to hide himself under the shade of the trees that form the bowers of Paradise: the Gold and Silver trees refused their shade to the father of the human race. God asked them why they did so: because, replied the trees, Adam has transgressed against your commandment. Ye have done well, answered the Creator; and that your fidelity may be rewarded, 'tis my decree that men shall hereafter become your slaves, and that in search of you they shall dig into the very bowels of the earth.

Chenier.

[15] A great number of stringy fibres seem to stretch out from the boughs of the Palm, on each side, which cross one another in such a manner, that they take out from between the boughs, a sort of bark like close net-work, and this they spin out with the hand, and with it make cords of all sizes, which are mostly used in Egypt. They also make of it a sort of brush for cloaths.

Pococke.

[16] Shedad was the first King of the Adites. I have ornamented his palace less profusely than the oriental writers who describe it. In the notes to the Bahar-Danush is the following account of its magnificence from the Tofet al Mujalis.

A pleasant and elevated spot being fixed upon, Shuddaud dispatched an hundred chiefs to collect skilful artists and workmen from all countries. He also commanded the monarchs of Syria and Ormus to send him all their jewels and precious stones. Forty camel loads of gold, silver, and jewels, were daily used in the building, which contained a thousand spacious quadrangles of many thousand rooms. In the areas were artificial trees of gold and silver, whose leaves were emeralds, and fruit clusters of pearls and jewels. The ground was strewed with ambergris, musk, and saffron. Between every two of the artificial trees was planted one of delicious fruit. This romantic abode took up five hundred years in the completion. When finished, Shuddaud marched to view it; and, when arrived near, divided two hundred thousand youthful slaves, whom he had brought with him from Damascus, into four detachments, which were stationed in cantonments prepared for their reception on each side of the garden, towards which he proceeded with his favourite courtiers. Suddenly was heard in the air a voice like thunder, and Shuddaud looking up, beheld a personage of majestic figure and stern aspect, who said, "I am the Angel of Death, commissioned to seize thy impure soul."

Shuddaud exclaimed, "give me leisure to enter the garden," and was descending from his horse, when the seizer of life snatched away his impure spirit, and he fell dead upon the ground. At the same time lightnings flashed and destroyed the whole army of the infidel; and the rose garden of Irim became concealed from the sight of man.

[17] Lamai relates that a great Monarch, whom he does not name, having erected a superb Palace, wished to show it to every man of talents and taste in the city; he therefore invited them to a banquet, and after the repast was finished asked them if they knew any building more magnificent and more perfect, in the architecture, in the ornaments and in the furniture. All the guests contented themselves with expressing their admiration, and lavishing praise, except one, who led a retired and austere life, and was one of those persons whom the Arabians call Zahed.

This man spoke very freely to the Prince and said to him, I find a great defect in this building, it is, that the foundation is not good, nor the walls sufficiently strong, so that Azrael can enter on every side, and the Sarsar can easily pass thro'. And when they showed him the walls of the Palace ornamented with azure and gold, of which the marvellous workmanship surpassed in costliness the richness of the materials, he replied, there is still a great inconvenience here! it is that we can never estimate these works well, till we are laid backwards. Signifying by these words that we never understand these things rightly, till we are upon our death-bed, when we discover their vanity.

D'Herbelot.

[18] Las horrendas palabras parecian
salir por una trompa resontane,
y que los yertos labios no movian.
Lupercio Leonardo.

[19] Death is come up into our windows, and entered into our palaces, to cut off the children from without, and the young men from the streets.

Jeremiah IX. 21.

The Trees shall give fruit and who shall gather them? The Grapes shall ripen and who shall tread them? for all places shall be desolate of men.

2. Esdras. XVI. 25.

For strong is his right hand that bendeth the Bow, his arrows that he shooteth are sharp, and shall not miss when they begin to be shot into the ends of the world.

2. Esdras. XVI. 13.

[20] There are several trees or shrubs of the genus Mimosa. One of these trees drops its branches whenever any person approaches it, seeming as if it saluted those who retire under its shade, this mute hospitality has so endeared this tree to the Arabians that the injuring or cutting of it down is strictly prohibited.

Niebuhr.

[21] The Angel of Death, say the Rabbis, holdeth his sword in his hand at the bed's head, having on the end thereof three drops of gall, the sick man spying this deadly Angel, openeth his mouth with fear and then those drops fall in, of which one killeth him, the second maketh him pale, the third rotteth and putrifieth.

Purchas.

Possibly the expression to taste the bitterness of death, may refer to this.

[22] The manner how the Teraphim were made is fondly conceited thus among the Rabbies. They killed a man that was a first born son, and wrung off his head, and seasoned it with salt and spices, and wrote upon a plate of gold the name of an uncleane spirit, and put it under the head upon a wall, and lighted candles before it and worshipped it.

Godwyn's Moses and Aaron.

In Rabbi Eleazar it is said to be the head of a child.

[23] The Devil, whom Mohammed names Eblis, from his dispair, was once one of those Angels who are nearest to God's presence, called Azazil; and fell (according to the doctrine of the Koran) for refusing to pay homage to Adam at the command of God.

Koran. Chap. 2. 7. 15.

God created the body of Adam of Salsal, that is of dry but unbaked clay; and left it forty nights, or according to others, forty years, lying without a soul; and the Devil came to it, and kicked it, and it sounded. And God breathed into it a soul with his breath, sending it in at his eyes, and he himself saw his nose still dead clay, and the soul running thro him, till it reached his feet, when he stood upright.

Maracci.

In the Nuremberg Chronicle is a print of the creation of Adam, the body is half made, growing out of a heap of clay under the Creator's hands. A still more absurd print represents Eve half way out of his side.

[24] These lines contain the various opinions of the Mohammedans respecting the intermediate state of the Blessed, till the Day of Judgment.

[25] Excepting in this line I have avoided all resemblances to the powerful poetry of Lucan.

Aspicit astantem projecti corporis umbram,
Exanimes artus, invisaque claustra timentem
Carceris antiqui, pavet ire in pectus apertum,
Visceraque, et ruptas letali vulnere fibras.
Ah miser, extremum cui mortis munus iniquæ
Eripitur, non posse mori! miratur Erichtho
Has fatis licuisse moras, irataque morti
Verberat immotum vivo serpente cadaver.

Protinus astrictus caluit cruor, atraque fovit
Vulnera, et in venas extremaque membra cucurrit.
Percussæ gelido trepidant sub pectore fibræ;
Et nova desuetis subrepens vita medullis,
Miscetur morti, tunc omnis palpitat artus;
Tenduntur nervi; nec se tellure cadaver
Paulatim per membra levat, terraque repulsum est,
Erectumque simul. Distento lumina rictu
Nudantur. Nondum facies viventis in illo,
Jam morientis erat; remanet pallorque rigorque,
Et stupet illatus mundo.
Lucan.

A curious instance of French taste occurs in this part of Brebeuf's translation. The re-animated corpse is made the corpse of Burrhus, of whose wife Octavia Sextus is enamoured. Octavia hears that her husband has fallen in battle, she seeks his body, but in vain. A light at length leads her to the scene of Erichtho's incantations, and she beholds Burrhus, to all appearance living. The witch humanely allows them time for a long conversation, which is very complimentary on the part of the husband.

Brebeuf was a man of genius. The Pharsalia is as well told in his version as it can be in the detestable French heroic couplet, which epigrammatizes every thing. He had courage enough, tho' a Frenchman, to admire Lucan, and yet could not translate him without introducing a love-story.

[26] This was one of the superstitions of the Pagan Arabs forbidden by Mohammed.

[27] Some imagine that the crystal is snow turned to ice which has been hardening thirty years, and is turned to a rock by age.

Mirror of Stones, by Camillus Leonardus
Physician of Pisaro, dedicated to Cæsar Borgia.

"In the cabinet of the Prince of Monaco among other rarities are two pieces of crystal each larger than both hands clenched together. In the middle of one is about a glass full of water, and in the other is some moss, naturally enclosed there when the crystals congealed. These pieces are very curious.

Tavernier.

Crystal, precious stones, every stone that has a regular figure, and even flints in small masses and consisting of concentric coats, whether found in the perpendicular fissures of rocks, or elsewhere, are only exudations, or the concreting juices of flint in large masses; they are, therefore, new and spurious productions, the genuine stalactites of flint or of granite.

Buffen.

[28] With the Arabs either a round skin is laid on the ground for a small company, or large course woollen cloths for a great number spread all over the room, and about ten dishes repeated six or

seven times over, laid round at a great feast, and whole sheep and lambs boild and roasted in the middle. When one company has done, another sits round, even to the meanest, till all is consumed. And an Arab Prince will often dine in the street before his door and call to all that pass even beggars, in the usual expression, Bisimillah, that is, in the name of God; who come and sit down and when they have done, give their Hamdellilah, that is, God be praised, for the Arabs who are great levellers, put every body on a footing with them, and it is by such generosity and hospitality that they maintain their interest.

Pococke.

[29] 'Tis the custom of Persia to begin their feasts with fruits and preserves. We spent two hours in eating only those and drinking beer, hydromel and aquavitæ. Then was brought up the meat in great silver dishes, they were full of rice of divers colours, and upon that, several sorts of meat boild and roasted, as beef, mutton, tame fowl, wild ducks, fish and other things, all very well ordered and very delicate.

The Persians use no knives at table, but the Cooks send up the meat ready cut up into little bits, so that it was no trouble to us to accustome ourselves to their manner of eating. Rice serves them instead of bread. They take a mouthful of it, with the two fore-fingers and the thumb, and so put it into their mouths. Every table had a carver, whom they call Suffret-zi, who takes the meat brought up in the great dishes, to put it into lesser ones, which he fills with 3 or 4 sorts of meat, so as that every dish may serve 2 or at most 3 persons. There was but little drunk till towards the end of the repast, and then the cups went about roundly, and the dinner was concluded with a vessel of porcelane, full of a hot blackish kind of drink, which they call Kahawa.

Ambassadors Travels.

They laid upon the floor of the Ambassadors room a fine silk cloth, on which there set one and 30 dishes of silver, filled with several sorts of conserves, dry and liquid, and raw fruits, as Melons, Citrons, Quinces, Pears, and some others not known in Europe. Some time after that cloth was taken away that another might be laid in the room of it, and upon this was set rice of all sorts of colours and all sorts of meat boyld and roasted in above fifty dishes of the same metal.

Amb. Tra.

There is not any thing more ordinary in Persia than rice soaked in water, they call it Plau and eat of it at all their meals, and serve it up in all their dishes. They sometimes put thereto a little of the juice of pomegranates or cherries and saffron, insomuch that commonly you have rice of several colours in the same dish.

Amb. Tra.

[30] The Tamarind is equally useful and agreable, it has a pulp of a vineous taste, of which a wholesome refreshing liquor is prepared, its shade shelters houses from the torrid heat of the sun, and its fine figure greatly adorns the scenery of the country.

Niebuhr.

[31] Of pumpkins and melons several sorts grow naturally in the woods, and serve for feeding Camels. But the proper melons are planted in the fields, where a great variety of them is to be found, and in such abundance, that the Arabians of all ranks use them, for some part of the year, as

their principal article of food. They afford a very agreeable liquor. When its fruit is nearly ripe, a hole is pierced into the pulp, this hole is then stopped with wax, and the melon left upon the stalk. Within a few days the pulp is in consequence of this process, converted into a delicious liquor.

Niebuhr.

[32] l'aspect imprévu de tant de Castillans, D'étonnement, d'effroi, peint ses regards brillans; Ses mains du choix des fruits se formant une etude, Demeurent un moment dans la même attitude.

Madame Boccage. La Colombiade.

[33] The Arabians divide their day into twenty four hours, and reckon them from one setting sun to another. As very few among them know what a watch is, and as they conceive, but imperfectly the duration of an hour, they usually determine time almost as when we say, it happened about noon, about evening, &c. The moment when the Sun disappears is called Maggrib, about two hours afterwards they call it El ascha; two hours later, El märfa; midnight Nus el lejl: the dawn of morning El fadsjer: sun rise Es subhh. They eat about nine in the morning, and that meal is called El ghadda; noon El duhhr; three hours after noon El asr. Of all these divisions of time only noon and midnight are well ascertained; they both fall upon the twelfth hour. The others are earlier or later as the days are short or long. The five hours appointed for prayer are Maggrib, Nus el lejl, El fedsjer, Duhhr, and El asr.

Niebuhr. Desc. del Arabie.

[34] The use of the bath was forbidden the Moriscoes in Spain, as being an anti-christian custom! I recollect no superstition but the Catholic in which nastiness is accounted a virtue; as if, says Jortin, piety and filth were synonimous, and religion like the itch, could he caught by wearing foul cloaths.

[35] The effects of the Simoom are instant suffocation to every living creature that happens to be within the sphere of its activity, and immediate putrefaction of the carcases of the dead. The Arabians discern its approach by an unusual redness in the air, and they say that they feel a smell of sulphur as it passes. The only means by which any person can preserve himself from suffering by these noxious blasts, is by throwing himself down with his face upon the earth, till this whirlwind of poisonous exhalations has blown over, which always moves at a certain height in the atmosphere. Instinct even teaches the brutes to incline their heads to the ground on these occasions.

Niebuhr.

The Arabs of the desert call these winds Semoum or poison, and the Turks Shamyela, or wind of Syria, from which is formed the Samiel.

Their heat is sometimes so excessive that it is difficult to form any idea of its violence without having experienced it; but it may be compared to the heat of a large oven at the moment of drawing out the bread. When these winds begin to blow, the atmosphere assumes an alarming aspect. The sky at other times so clear, in this climate, becomes dark and heavy; the sun loses his splendour and appears of a violet colour. The air is not cloudy, but grey and thick, and is in fact filled with an extremely subtile dust, which penetrates every where. This wind, always light and rapid, is not at first remarkably hot, but it increases in heat in proportion as it continues. All animated bodies soon discover it, by the change it produces in them. The lungs which a too rarefied air no longer expands, are contracted and become painful. Respiration is short and difficult, the skin parched and dry, and the body consumed by an internal heat. In vain is recourse had to large draughts of water; nothing can restore perspiration. In vain is coolness sought for; all bodies in which it is usual to find it, deceives the hand that touches them. Marble, iron, water, notwithstanding the sun no longer appears, are hot. The streets are deserted, and the dead silence of night reigns every where. The inhabitants of houses and villages shut themselves up in their houses, and those of the desert in their tents, or in pits they dig in the earth, where they wait the termination of this destructive heat. It usually lasts three days, but if it exceeds that time it becomes insupportable. Woe to the traveller whom this wind surprizes remote from shelter! he must suffer all its dreadful consequences which sometimes are mortal. The danger is most imminent when it blows in squalls, for then the rapidity of the wind increases the heat to such degree as to cause sudden death. This death is a real suffocation; the lungs being empty, are convulsed, the circulation disordered, and the whole mass of blood driven by the heart towards the head and breast; whence that hæmorrhage at the nose and mouth which happens after death. This wind is especially fatal to persons of a plethoric habit, and those in whom fatigue has destroyed the tone of the muscles and the vessels. The corpse remains a long time warm, swells, turns blue and is easily separated; all which are signs of that putrid fermentation which takes place in animal bodies when the humours become stagnant. These accidents are to be avoided by stopping the nose and mouth with handkerchiefs; an efficacious method likewise is that practised by the camels, who bury their noses in the sand and keep them there till the squall is over.

Another quality of this wind is its extreme aridity; which is such, that water sprinkled on the floor evaporates in a few minutes. By this extreme dryness it withers and strips all the plants, and by exhaling too suddenly the emanations from animal bodies, crisps the skin, closes the pores, and causes that feverish heat which is the invariable effect of suppressed perspiration.

Volney.

[36] From the Mirror of Stones I extract a few specimens of the absurd ideas once prevalent respecting precious stones.

The Amethyst drives away drunkenness; for being bound on the navel, it restrains the vapour of the wine, and so disolves the ebriety.

Alectoria is a stone of a christalline colour, a little darkish, somewhat resembling limpid water; and sometimes it has veins of the colour of flesh. Some call it Gallinaceus, from the place of its generation, the intestines of capons, which were castrated at three years old, and had lived seven, before which time the stone ought not to be taken out, for the older it is, so much the better. When the stone is become perfect in the Capon, he do'nt drink. However tis never found bigger than a large bean. The virtue of this stone is to render him who carries it invisible, being held in the mouth it allays thirst, and therefore is proper for wrestlers; makes a woman agreable to her husband; bestows honors and preserves those already acquired; it frees such as are bewitched; it renders a man eloquent, constant, agreable and amiable; it helps to regain a lost Kingdom, and acquire a foreign one.

Borax, Nosa, Crapondinus, are names of the same stone, which is extracted from a toad. There are two species; that which is the best is rarely found; the other is black or dun with a cerluean glow, having in the middle the similitude of an eye, and must be taken out while the dead toad is yet panting, and these are better than those which are extracted from it after a long continuance in the ground. They have a wonderful efficacy in poisons. For whoever has taken poison, let him swallow this; which being down, rolls about the bowels, and drives out every poisonous quality that is lodged in the intestines, and then passes thro' the fundament, and is preserved.

Corvia or Corvina, is a Stone of a reddish colour, and accounted artificial. On the calends of April boil the eggs taken out of a Crow's nest till they are hard: and being cold let them be placed in the nest as they were before. When the crow knows this, she flies a long way to find the stone, and having found it returns to the nest, and the eggs being touched with it, they become fresh and prolific, the Stone must immediately be snatched out of the nest, its virtue is to increase riches, to bestow honors, and to foretell many future events.

Kinocetus is a stone not wholly useless—since it will cast out Devils.

[37] Giafar, the founder of the Barmecides, being obliged to fly from Persia his native country, took refuge at Damascus, and implored the protection of the Caliph Soliman. When he was presented to that Prince, the Caliph suddenly changed colour and commanded him to retire, suspecting that he had poison about him. Soliman had discovered it by means of ten stones which he wore upon his arm. They were fastened there like a bracelet, and never failed to strike one against the other and make a slight noise when any poison was near. Upon enquiry it was found that Giafar carried poison in his ring, for the purpose of self-destruction in case he had been taken by his enemies.

Marigny.

These foolish old superstitions have died away, and gems are now neither pounded as poison nor worn as antidotes. But the old absurdities respecting poisons have been renewed in our days, by Authors who have revived the calumnies alledged against the Knights-Templar, with the hope of exciting a more extensive persecution.

[38] In the country called Panten or Tathalamasin, "there be canes called Cassan, which overspread the earth like glasse, and out of every knot of them spring foorth certaine branches, which are continued upon the ground almost for the space of a mile. In the sayd canes there are found certaine stones, one of which stones whosoever carryeth about with him, cannot be wounded with any yron: and therefore the men of that country for the most part carry such stones with them, withersoever they goe. Many also cause one of the armes of their children, while they are young, to be launced, putting one of the said stones into the wound, healing also, and closing up the said wound with the powder of a certain fish (the name whereof I do not know) which powder doth immediately consolidate and cure the said wound. And by the vertue of these stones, the people aforesaid doe for the most part triumph both on sea and land. Howbeit there is one kind of stratageme which the enemies of this nation, knowing the vertue of the sayd stones, doe practise against them: namely, they provide themselves armour of yron or steele against their arrowes, and weapons also poisoned with the poyson of trees, and they carry in their hands wooden stakes most sharp and hard-pointed, as if they were yron: likewise they shoot arrowes without yron heades, and so they confound and slay some of their unarmed foes trusting too securely unto the vertue of their stones.

Odoricus in Hakluyt.

We are obliged to Jewellers for our best accounts of the East. In Tavernier there is a passage curiously characteristic of his profession. A European at Delhi complained to him that he had polished and set a large diamond for Aureng-zebe, who had never paid him for his work. But he did not understand his trade, says Tavernier, for if he had been a skilful Jeweller he would have known how to take two or three pieces out of the stone, and pay himself better than the Mogul would have done.

[39] And Elisha died, and they buried him. And the bands of the Moabites invaded the land at the coming in of the year.

And it came to pass as they were burying a man, that behold they spied a band of men; and they cast the man into the sepulchre of Elisha: and when the man was let down, and touched the bones of Elisha, he revived and stood up on his feet.

II. Kings. XIII. 20. 21.

I must remind my readers that an allusion to the Old Testament is no ways improper in a Mohammedan.

It happened the dead corps of a man was cast ashore at Chatham, and being taken up was buried decently in the Church yard; now there was an image or rood in the Church called our Lady of Chatham, this Lady, say the Monks, went the next night and roused up the Clerk, telling him that a sinful person was buried near the place where she was worshipped, who offended her eyes with his ghastly grinning, and unless he were removed, to the great grief of good people she must remove from thence and could work no more miracles. Therefore she desired him to go with her to take him up, and throw him into the river again: which being done, soon after the body floated again, and was taken up and buried in the Church yard; but from that time all miracles ceased, and the place where he was buried did continually sink downwards. This tale is still remembered by some aged people, receiving it by tradition from the popish times of darkness and idolatry.

Admirable Curiosities, Rarites and Wonders in England.

[40] Matthew of Westminister says the history of the Old Woman of Berkeley, will not appear incredible, if we read the dialogue of St. Gregory in which he relates how the body of a man buried in the church was thrown out by the Devils: Charles Martel also because he had appropriated great part of the tythes to pay his soldiers, was most miserably by the wicked Spirits taken bodily out of his grave. The Turks report, as a certain truth, that the corps of Heyradin Barbarossa was found, four or five times, out of the ground, lying by his sepulchre, after he had been there inhumed: nor could they possibly make him lie quiet in his grave, till a Greek wizzard counselled them to bury a black dog together with the body; which done, he lay still, and gave them no farther trouble.

Morgan's History of Algiers.

In supernatural affairs dogs seem to possess a sedative virtue. When peace was made, about the year 1170, between the Earls of Holland, and Flanders, "it was concluded that Count Floris should send unto Count Philip, a thousand men, expert in making of ditches, to stop the hole which had beene made neere unto Dam, or the Sluce, whereby the countrey was drowned round about at everie high sea; the which the Flemings could by no meanes fil up, neither with wood, nor any other matter, for that all sunke as in a gulfe without any bottome; whereby, in succession of time, Bruges and all that jurisdiction, had been in danger to have bin lost by inundation, and to become all sea, if it were not speedily repaired. Count Floris having taken possession of the isle of Walchran, returned into Holland, from whence hee sent the best workmen he could find in all his countries, into Flanders, to make dikes and causeies, and to stop the hole neere unto this Dam, or Sluce, and to recover the drowned land. These diggers being come to the place, they found at the entrie of this bottomlesse hole a Sea-dog, the which for six dayes together, did nothing but crie out and howle very fearefully. They, not knowing what it might signifie, having consulted of this accident, they resolved to cast this dogge into the hole. There was a mad-headed Hollander among the rest, who going into the bottome of the dike, tooke the dogge by the taile, and cast him into the middest of the gulfe; then speedily they cast earth and torfe into it, so as they found a bottome, and by little and little filled it up. And for that many workemen came to the repairing of this dike, who for that they would not be far from their worke, coucht in Cabines, which seemed to be a pretie towne. Count Philip gave unto all these Hollanders, Zeelanders and others, that would inhabit there, as much land as they could recover from Dam to Ardenbourg, for them and their successors, for ever, with many other immunities and freedoms. By reason whereof many planted themselves there, and in succession of time, made a good towne there, the which by reason of this dog, which they cast into the hole, they named Hondtsdam, that is to say, a dog's sluce; Dam in Flemish signifying a sluce, and Hondt a dog: and therefore at this day, the said towne (which is simply called Dam) carrieth a dog in their armes and blason.

Grimestone's Historie of the Netherlands, 1608.

[41] The Vulture is very serviceable in Arabia, clearing the earth of all carcases, which corrupt very rapidly in hot countries. He also destroys the field mice which multiply so prodigiously in some provinces, that were it not for this assistance, the peasant might cease from the culture of the fields as absolutely vain. Their performance of these important services induced the antient Egyptians to pay those birds divine honours, and even at present it is held unlawful to kill them in all the countries which they frequent.

Niebuhr.

[42] The Bedouins, who, at all points, are less superstitious than the Turks, have a breed of very tall greyhounds, which likewise mount guard around their tents; but they take great care of these useful servants, and have such an affection for them, that to kill the dog of a Bedouin would be to endanger your own life.

Sonnini.

[43] The Arabs call the West and South West winds which prevail from November to February, the fathers of the rains.

Volney.

[44] See Note 15. Book I.

Of the Palm leaves they make mattresses, baskets and brooms; and of the branches, all sorts of cage work, square baskets for packing that serve for many uses instead of boxes; and the ends of the boughs that grow next to the trunk being beaten like flax, the fibres separate, and being tied together at the narrow end, they serve for brooms.

Pococke.

[45] The Doum, or wild palm tree, grows in abundance, from which these people when necessity renders them industrious, find great advantage. The shepherds, mule drivers, camel drivers, and travellers, gather the leaves, of which they make mats, fringes, baskets, hats, shooaris or large wallets to carry corn, twine, ropes, girths and covers for their pack saddles. This plant, with which also they heat their ovens, produces a mild and resinous fruit, that ripens in Sept. and Oct. It is in form like the raisin, contains a kernel and is astringent, and very proper to temper and counteract the effects of the watery and laxative fruits, of which these people in summer make an immoderate

use. That Power which is ever provident to all, has spread this wild plant over their deserts to supply an infinity of wants that would otherwise heavily burthen a people so poor.

Chenier.

[46] "We passed two of those vallies so common in Arabia, which when heavy rains fall, are filled with water, and are then called wadi or rivers, altho' perfectly dry at other times of the year.—We now drew nearer to the river of which a branch was dry, and having its channel filled with reeds growing to the height of 20 feet, served as a line of road which was agreably shaded by the reeds.

Niebuhr.

My brethren have dealt deceitfully as a brook, and as the stream of brooks they pass away.

Which are blackish by reason of the ice, and wherein the snow is hid:

What time they wax warm they vanish; when it is hot they are consumed out of their place.

The paths of their way are turned aside; they go to nothing and perish.

Job. VI. 15.

[47] The simplicity, or, perhaps, more properly, the poverty, of the lower class of the Bedouins, is proportionate to that of their chiefs. All the wealth of a family consists of moveables, of which the following is a pretty exact inventory. A few male and female camels, some goats and poultry, a mare and her bridle and saddle, a tent, a lance sixteen feet long, a crooked sabre, a rusty musket, with a flint or matchlock; a pipe, a portable mill, a pot for cooking, a leathern bucket, a small coffee roaster, a mat, some clothes, a mantle of black woollen, and a few glass or silver rings, which the women wear upon their legs and arms; if none of these are wanting, their furniture is complete. But what the poor man stands most in need of, and what he takes most pleasure in, is his mare; for this animal is his principal support. With his mare the Bedouin makes his excursions against hostile tribes, or seeks plunder in the country, and on the highways. The mare is preferred to the horse, because she does not neigh, is more docile, and yields milk, which on occasion, satisfies the thirst and even the hunger of her master.

Volney.

The Shaik, says Volney, with whom I resided in the country of Gaza, about the end of 1784, passed for one of the most powerful of those districts; yet it did not appear to me that his expenditure was greater than that of an opulent farmer. His personal effects, consisting in a few pelisses, carpets, arms, horses, and camels, could not be estimated at more than fifty thousand livres (a little above two thousand pounds); and it must be observed that in this calculation four mares of the breed of racers are valued at six thousand livres, (two hundred and fifty pounds), and each camel at ten pounds sterling. We must not therefore, when we speak of the Bedouins, affix to the words Prince and Lord, the ideas they usually convey; we should come nearer the truth by comparing them to substantial farmers, in mountainous countries, whose simplicity they resemble in their dress as well as in their domestic life and manners. A Shaik, who has the command of five hundred horse, does not disdain to saddle and bridle his own, nor to give him his barley and chopped straw. In his tent, his wife makes the coffee, kneeds the dough, and superintends the dressing of the victuals. His daughters and kinswomen wash the linen, and go with pitchers on their heads, and veils over their faces, to draw water from the fountain. These manners agree precisely with the descriptions in

Homer, and the history of Abraham, in Genesis. But it must be owned that it is difficult to form a just idea of them without having ourselves been eye witnesses.

Volney.

[48] Thus confined to the most absolute necessaries of life, the Arabs have as little industry as their wants are few; all their arts consist in weaving their clumsy tents, and in making mats and butter. Their whole commerce only extends to the exchanging camels, kids, stallions and milk; for arms, clothing, a little rice or corn, and money, which they bury.

Volney.

[49] The chief manufacture among the Arabs is the making of Hykes as they call woollen blankets, and webs of goat's hair for their Tents. The Women alone are employed in this work, as Andromache and Penelope were of old; who make no use of a shuttle, but conduct every thread of the woof with their fingers.

Shaw.

[50] If mine heart have been deceived by a woman, or if I have laid wait at my neighbour's door. Then let my wife grind unto another.

Job. XXXI. 9. 10.

[51] I was much amused by observing the dexterity of the Arab women in baking their bread. They have a small place built with clay, between two and three feet high, having a hole at the bottom, for the convenience of drawing out the ashes, something similar to that of a lime kiln. The oven (which I think is the most proper name for this place) is usually about fifteen inches wide at the top, and gradually grows wider to the bottom. It is heated with wood, and when sufficiently hot, and perfectly clear from smoke, having nothing but clear embers at bottom (which continue to reflect great heat), they prepare the dough in a large bowl, and mould the cakes to the desired size on a board or stone placed near the oven. After they have kneaded the cake to a proper consistence, they pat it a little, then toss it about with great dexterity in one hand, till it is as thin as they choose to make it. They then wet one side of it with water, at the same time wetting the hand and arm, with which they put it into the oven. The wet side of the cake adheres fast to the side of the oven till it is sufficiently baked when if not paid sufficient attention to, it would fall down among the embers. If they were not exceedingly quick at this work, the heat of the oven would burn the skin from off their hands and arms; but with such amazing dexterity do they perform it, that one woman will continue keeping three or four cakes at a time in the oven till she has done baking. This mode, let me add, does not require half the fuel that is made use of in Europe.

Jackson.

[52] Tamarinds grow on great trees, full of branches whereof the leaves are not bigger than, nor unlike to the leaves of pimpernel, only something longer. The flower at first is like the peaches, but at last turns white, and puts forth its fruit at the end of certain strings: as soon as the sun is set, the leaves close up the fruit, to preserve it from the dew, and open as soon as that luminary appears again. The fruit at first is green, but ripening it becomes of a dark grey, drawing towards a red, inclosed in husks, brown or twany, of taste a little bitter, like our prunelloes. The tree is as big as a walnut-tree, full of leaves, bearing its fruit at the branches, like the sheath of a knife, but not so straight, rather bent like a bow.

Mandelslo.

[53] I have often, says Niebuhr, heard the Sheiks sing passages from the Koran, they never strain the voice by attempting to raise it too high, and this natural music pleased me very much.

The airs of the Orientals are all grave and simple. They chuse their singers to sing so distinctly that every word may be comprehended. When several instruments are played at once and accompanied by the voice, you hear them all render the same melody, unless some one mingles a running base, either singing or playing, always in the same key. If this music is not greatly to our taste, ours is as little to the taste of the Orientals.

Niebuhr. Description.

[54] The Mosques, which they pronounce Mesg jid, are built exactly in the fashion of our Churches, where instead of such Seats and Benches as we make use of, they only strew the Floor with Mats, upon which they perform the several sittings and prostrations that are enjoyned in their religion. Near the middle, particularly of the principal Mosque of each city, there is a large pulpit erected, which is ballustraded round, with about half a dozen steps leading up to it. Upon these (for I am told none are permitted to enter the pulpit) the Mufty or one of the Im-ams placeth himself every Friday, the day of the congregation, as they call it, and from thence either explaineth some part or other of the Coran, or else exhorteth the people to piety and good works. That end of these Mosques, which regards Mecca, whither they direct themselves throughout the whole course of their devotions, is called the Kiblah, in which there is commonly a nich, representing as a judicious writer conjectures, the presence, and at the same time the invisibility of the Deity. There is usually a square tower erected at the other end, with a flag-staff upon the top of it. Hither the cryer ascends at the appointed times, and displaying a small flag, advertised the people with a loud voice, from each side of the battlements, of the hour of prayer. These places of the Mahometan worship, together with the Mufty, Im-ams and other persons belonging to them, are maintained out of certain revenues arising from the rents of lands and houses, either left by will or set apart by the public for that use.

Shaw.

All the Mosques are built nearly in the same style. They are of an oblong square form, and covered in the middle with a large dome, on the top of which is fixed a gilt crescent. In front there is a handsome portico covered with several small cupolas, and raised one step above the pavement of the court. The Turks sometimes in the hot season, perform their devotions there; and between the columns, upon cross iron bars, are suspended a number of lamps, for illuminations on the Thursday nights and on all festivals. The entrance into the Mosque is by one large door. All these edifices are solidly built of freestone, and in several the domes are covered with lead. The minarets stand on one side adjoining to the body of the Mosque. They are sometimes square, but more commonly round and taper, the gallery for the maazeen, or cryers, projecting a little from the column near the top, has some resemblance to a rude capital; and from this the spire tapering more in proportion than before, soon terminates in a point crowned with a crescent.

Russel's Aleppo.

[55] The Keabé is the point of direction and the centre of union for the prayers of the whole human race, as the Beïth-mâmour[d] is for those of all the celestial beings; the Kursy[e] for those of the four Arch angels, and the Arsch[f] for those of the cherubims and seraphims who guard the throne of the Almighty. The inhabitants of Mecca, who enjoy the happiness of contemplating the Keabé, are

obliged when they pray to fix their eyes upon the sanctuary; but they who are at a distance from this valuable privilege are required only during prayer to direct their attention towards that hallowed edifice. The believer who is ignorant of the position of the Keabé must use every endeavour to gain a knowledge of it; and after he has shown great solicitude, whatever be his success, his prayer is valid.

D'Ohsson.

[d] Beïth mâmour, which means the house of prosperity and felicity, is the ancient Keabé of Mecca, which according to tradition, was taken up into heaven by the Angels at the deluge, where it was placed perpendicularly over the present sanctuary.

[e] Kursy, which signifies a seat, is the 8th firmament.

[f] Arsch is the throne of the Almighty, which is thought to be placed on the ninth, which is the higher of the firmaments.

[56] The Bedoweens live in tents, called Hhymas, from the shade they afford the inhabitants, and Beet el Shar, Houses of hair, from the matter they are made of. They are the same with what the Antients called Mapalia, which being then, as they are to this day, secured from the heat and inclemency of the weather, by a covering only of such hair cloth, as our coal sacks are made of, might very justly be described by Virgil to have thin roofs. When we find any number of them together (and I have seen from 3 to 300) then they are usually placed in a circle, and constitute a Dou-war. The fashion of each tent is the same, being of an oblong figure, not unlike the bottom of a ship turned upside down, as Satlust hath long ago described them. However they differ in bigness, according to the number of people who live in them: and are accordingly supported, some with one pillar, others with two or three: whilst a curtain or carpet placed, upon occasion, at each of these divisions, separateth the whole into so many apartments. The pillar which I have mentioned, is a straight pole, 8 or 10 feet high and 3 or 4 inches in thickness, serving, not only to support the tent, but being full of hooks fixd there for the purpose, the Arabs hang upon it their cloaths, baskets, saddles, and accoutrements of war. Holofernes, as we read in Judith, 13. 16. made the like use of the pillar of his tent, by hanging his fauchin upon it, it is there called the pillar of the bed, from the custom perhaps, that hath always prevailed, of having the upper end of the carpet, matrass, or whatever else they lie upon, turned from the skirts of the tent that way. But the [Greek: Kônôpeion], Canopy as we render it (ver. 9) should I presume, be rather called the gnat or muskeeta net, which is a close curtain of gauze or fine linnen, used all over the Levant, by people of better fashion, to keep out the flies. The Arabs have nothing of this kind; who in taking their rest, lie horizontally upon the ground, without bed, matrass or pillow, wrapping themselves up only in their Hykes, and lying, as they find room upon a mat or carpet, in the middle or corner of the tent. Those who are married, have each of them a corner of the tent, cantoned off with a curtain.

Shaw.

The tents of the Moors are somewhat of a conic form, are seldom more than 8 or 10 feet high in the centre, and from 20 to 25 in length. Like those of the remotest antiquity, their figure is that of a ship overset, the keel of which is only seen. These tents are made of twine, composed of goat's hair, camel's wool, and the leaves of the wild palm, so that they keep out water; but, being black, they produce a disagreable effect at a distant view.

Chenier.

[57] In the kingdom of Imam the men of all ranks shave their heads. In some other countries of Yemen all the Arabs, even the Sheiks themselves, let their hair grow and wear neither bonnet nor Sasch, but a handkerchief instead, in which they tie the hair behind. Some let it fall upon their shoulders and bind a small cord round their heads instead of a turban. The Bedouins upon the frontiers of Hedsjas and of Yemen wear a bonnet of palm leaves, neatly platted.

Niebuhr.

[58] The music of the Bedoweens rarely consists of more than one strain, suitable to their homely instruments, and to their simple invention. The Arabebbah as they call the bladder and string, is in the highest vogue, and doubtless of great antiquity, as is also the Gaspah, which is only a common reed, open at each end, having the side of it bored, with three or more holes, according to the ability of the Person who is to touch it: tho' the compass of their tunes rarely or ever exceeds an octave. Yet sometimes, even in this simplicity of harmony, they observe something of method and ceremony, for in their historical Cantatas especially, they have their preludes and symphonies; each stanza being introduced with a flourish from the Arabebbah, while the narration itself is accompanied with the softest touches they are able to make, upon the Gaspah. The Tarr, another of their instruments, is made like a Sive, consisting (as Isidore describeth the Tympanum) of a thin rim or hoop of wood, with a skin of parchment stretched over the top of it. This serves for the Bass in all their Concerts, which they accordingly touch very artfully with their fingers, and the knuckles or palms of their hands, as the time and measure require, or as force and softness are to be communicated to the several parts of the performance. The Tarr is undoubtedly the Tympanum of the Antients, which appears as well from the general use of it all over Barbary, Egypt and the Levant, as from the method of playing upon it, and the figure of the instrument itself, being exactly of the same fashion, with what we find in the hands of Cybele and the Bacchanals among the Basso Relievos and Statues of the Antiets.

Shaw.

The Arabs have the Cussuba, or cane, which is only a piece of large cane, or reed, with stops, or holes, like a flute, and somewhat longer, which they adorn with tossels of black silk and play upon like the German flute.

Morgan's Hist. of Algiers.

The young fellows, in several towns, play prettily enough on pipes made, and sounding very much like our flagelet, of the thigh bones of cranes, storks, or such large fowl.

Morgan's Hist. of Algiers.

How great soever may have been the reputation the Libyans once had, of being famous musicians, and of having invented the pipe or flute, called by Greek author Hippophorbos, I fancy few of them would be now much liked at our Opera. As for this tibicen, flute or pipe, it is certainly lost, except it be the gayta, somewhat like the hautbois, called zurna, in Turkish, a martial instrument. Julius Pollux, in a chapter entitled de tibiarum specie, says, Hippophorbos quam quidem Libyes Scenetes invenerunt, and again, shewing the use and quality thereof, hæc verò apud equorum pascua utuntur, ejusque materia decorticata laurus est, cor enim ligni extractum acutissimam dat sonum. The sound of the gayta agrees well with this description, tho' not the make. Several Poets mention the tibicen Libycus and Arabicus: and Alhenæus quotes Duris, and says, Libycas tibia Poetæ appellant, ut inquit Duris, libro secundo de rebus gestis Agathoclis, quod Scirites, primus, ut credunt, tibicinum artis inventor, è gente Nomadum Libycorum fuerit, primusque tibiä Cerealium hymnorum cantor.

Morgan's Hist. of Algiers.

[59] Persæ "pulcherrimâ usi translatione, pro versús facere dicunt margaritas nectere; quemadmodum in illo Ferdusii versiculo "Siquidem calami acumine adamantine margaritas nexi; in scientiæ mare penitus me immersi."

Poeseos Asiaticæ Commentarii.

This is a favourite Oriental figure. "After a little time lifting his head from the collar of reflection, he removed the talisman of silence from the treasure of speech, and scattered skirts-full of brilliant gems and princely pearls before the company in his mirth-exciting deliveries."

Bahar Danush.

Again in the same work—"he began to weigh his stored pearls in the scales of delivery."

Abu Temam, who was an excellent poet himself, used to say, that, "fine sentiments delivered in prose were like gems scattered at random; but that when they were confined in a poetical measure, they resembled bracelets and strings of pearls."

Sir W. Jones. Essay on the Poetry of the Eastern nations.

In Mr. Carlyle's translations from the Arabic, a Poet says of his friends and himself

They are a row of Pearls, and I
The silken thread on which they lie.

I quote from memory, and recollect not the Author's name. It is somewhat remarkable that the same metaphor is among the quaintnesses of Fuller. "Benevolence is the silken thread, that should run thro' the pearl chain of our virtues."

Holy State.

It seems the Arabs are still great rhymers, and their verses are sometimes rewarded, but I should not venture to say that there are great Poets among them. Yet I was assured in Yemen that it is not uncommon to find them among the wandering Arabs in the country of Dsjâf. It is some few years since a Sheik of these Arabs was in prison at Sana: seeing by chance a bird upon a roof opposite to him, he recollected that the devout Mohammedans believe they perform an action agreable to God in giving liberty to a bird encaged. He thought therefore he had as much right to liberty as a bird, and made a poem upon the subject, which was first learnt by his guards, and then became so popular that at last it reached the Imam. He was so pleased with it that he liberated the Sheik, whom he had arrested for his robberies.

Niebuhr. Desc. de L'Arabie.

[60] They are fond of singing with a forced voice in the high tones, and one must have lungs like theirs to support the effort for a quarter of an hour. Their airs, in point of character and execution, resemble nothing we have heard in Europe, except the Seguidillas of the Spaniards. They have

divisions more laboured even than those of the Italians, and cadences and inflections of tone impossible to be imitated by European throats. Their performance is accompanied with sighs and gestures, which paint the passions in a more lively manner than we should venture to allow. They may be said to excel most in the melancholy strain. To behold an Arab with his head inclined, his hand applied to his ear, his eye brows knit, his eyes languishing; to hear his plaintive tones, his lengthened notes, his sighs and sobs, it is almost impossible to refrain from tears, which as their expression is, are far from bitter: and indeed they must certainly find a pleasure in shedding them, since among all their songs, they constantly prefer that which excites them most, as among all accomplishments singing is that they most admire.

Volney.

All their literature consists in reciting tales and histories, in the manner of the Arabian Nights Entertainments. They have a peculiar passion for such stories: and employ in them almost all their leisure, of which they have a great deal. In the evening they seat themselves on the ground at the door of their tents, or under cover if it be cold, and there, ranged in a circle, round a little fire of dung, their pipes in their mouths, and their legs crossed, they sit awhile in silent meditation, till, on a sudden, one of them breaks forth with, Once upon a time,—and continues to recite the adventures of some young Shaik and female Bedouin: he relates in what manner the youth first got a secret glimpse of his mistress, and how he became desperately enamoured of her: he minutely describes the lovely fair, extols her black eyes, as large and soft as those of the gazelle; her languid and empassioned looks; her arched eye brows, resembling two bows of ebony; her waist, straight and supple as a lance; he forgets not her steps, light as those of the young filley, nor her eye-lashes blackened with kohl, nor her lips painted blue, nor her nails, tinged with the golden coloured henna, nor her breasts, resembling two pomegranates, nor her words, sweet as honey. He recounts the sufferings of the young lover, so wasted with desire and passion, that his body no longer yields any shadow. At length, after detailing his various attempts to see his mistress, the obstacles on the part of the parents, the invasions of the enemy, the captivity of the two lovers, &c. he terminates, to the satisfaction of the audience, by restoring them, united and happy, to the paternal tent, and by receiving the tribute paid to his eloquence, in the ma sha allah[g] he has merited. The Bedouins have likewise their love songs, which have more sentiment and nature in them than those of the Turks, and inhabitants of the towns; doubtless because the former, whose manners are chaste, know what love is; while the latter, abandoned to debauchery, are acquainted only with enjoyment.

Volney.

[g] An exclamation of praise, equivalent to admirably well!

[61] We read in an old Arabian Manuscript, that when the Ostrich would hatch her eggs, she does not cover them as other fowls do, but both the male and female contribute to hatch them by the efficacy of their looks only; and therefore when one has occasion to go to look for food, it advertises its companion by its cry, and the other never stirs during its absence, but remains with its eyes fixed upon the eggs, till the return of its mate, and then goes in its turn to look for food, and this care of theirs is so necessary that it cannot be suspended for a moment, for if it should their eggs would immediately become addle.

Vanslebe. Harris's Collection.

This is said to emblem the perpetual attention of the Creator to the Universe.

[62] "She had laid aside the rings which used to grace her ankles, lest the sound of them should expose her to calamity."

Asiatic Researches.

Most of the Indian women have on each arm, and also above the ankle, ten or twelve rings of gold, silver, ivory, or coral. They spring on the leg, and when they walk make a noise with which they are much pleased. Their hands and toes are generally adorned with large rings.

Sonnerat.

"In that day the Lord will take away the bravery of their tinkling ornaments about their feet, and their cauls, and their round tires like the moon."

"The chains, and the bracelets and the mufflers, The bonnets, and the ornaments of the legs, &c."

Isaiah. III. 18.

[63] His fingers, in beauty and slenderness appearing as the Yed Bieza,[h] or the rays of the sun, being tinged with Hinna, seemed branches of transparent red coral.

Bahar Danush.

[h] The miraculously shining hand of Moses.

She dispenses gifts with small delicate fingers, sweetly glowing at their tips, like the white and crimson worm of Dabia, or dentifrices made of Esel wood.

Moallakat. Poem of Amriolkais.

The Hinna, says the translator of the Bahar-Danush, is esteemed not merely ornamental, but medicinal: and I have myself often experienced in India a most refreshing coolness thro' the whole habit, from an embrocation, or rather plaster of Hinna, applied to the soles of my feet, by prescription of a native physician. The effect lasted for some days.

This unnatural fashion is extended to animals.

Departing from the town of Anna we met about five hundred paces from the gate a young man of good family followed by two servants, and mounted in the fashion of the country, upon an Ass, whose rump was painted red.

Tavernier.

In Persia, "they dye the tails of those horses which are of a light colour with red or orange."

Hanway.

Ali the Moor, to whose capricious cruelty Mungo Park was so long exposed, "always rode upon a milk white horse, with its tail dyed red."

Alfenado, a word derived from alfena the Portugueze or Moorish name of this plant, is still used in Portugal as a phrase of contempt for a fop.

[64] The blackened eye-lids and the reddened fingers were Eastern customs, in use among the Greeks. They are still among the tricks of the Grecian toilette, the females of the rest of Europe have never added them to their list of ornaments.

[65] The Mimosa Selam produces splendid flowers of a beautiful red colour with which the Arabians crown their heads on their days of festival.

Niebuhr.

[66] The large locusts, which are near three inches long, are not the most destructive; as they fly, they yield to the current of the wind which hurries them into the sea, or into sandy deserts where they perish with hunger or fatigue. The young locusts, that cannot fly, are the most ruinous; they are about fifteen lines in length; and the thickness of a goose quill. They creep over the country in such multitudes that they leave not a blade of grass behind; and the noise of their feeding announces their approach at some distance. The devastations of locusts increase the price of provisions, and often occasion famines; but the Moors find a kind of compensation in making food of these insects; prodigious quantities are brought to market salted and dried like red herrings. They have an oily and rancid taste, which habit only can render agreeable; they are eat here, however, with pleasure.

Chenier.

In 1778 the empire of Morocco was ravaged by these insects. In the summer of that year, such clouds of locusts came from the south that they darkened the air, and devoured a part of the harvest. Their offspring, which they left on the ground, committed still much greater mischief. Locusts appeared and bred anew in the following year, so that in the spring the country was wholly covered, and they crawled one over the other in search of their subsistence.

It has been remarked, in speaking of the climate of Morocco, that the young locusts are those which are the most mischievous; and that it seems almost impossible to rid the land of these insects and their ravages, when the country once becomes thus afflicted. In order to preserve the houses and gardens in the neighbourhood of cities, they dig a ditch two feet in depth and as much in width. This they pallisade with reeds close to each other, and inclined inward toward the ditch; so that the insects unable to climb up the slippery reed, fall back into the ditch, where they devour one another.

This was the means by which the gardens and vineyards of Rabat, and the city itself were delivered from this scourge, in 1779. The intrenchment, which was, at least, a league in extent, formed a semicircle from the sea to river, which separates Rabat from Sallee. The quantity of young locusts here assembled was so prodigious that, on the third day, the ditch could not be approached because of the stench. The whole country was eaten up, the very bark of the fig, pomegranate, and orange tree, bitter, hard, and corrosive as it was could not escape the voracity of these insects.

The lands, ravaged throughout all the western provinces, produced no harvest, and the Moors being obliged to live on their stores, which the exportation of corn (permitted till 1774) had drained, began to feel a dearth. Their cattle, for which they make no provision, and which in these climates, have no other subsistance than that of daily grazing, died with hunger; nor could any be preserved but those which were in the neighbourhood of mountains, or in marshy grounds, where the regrowth of pasturage is more rapid.

In 1780, the distress was still farther increased. The dry winter had checked the products of the earth, and given birth to a new generation of locusts, who devoured whatever had escaped from the inclemency of the season. The husbandman did not reap even what he had sowed, and found himself destitute of food, cattle, or seed corn. In this time of extreme wretchedness the poor felt all the horrors of famine. They were seen wandering over the country to devour roots, and, perhaps, abridged their days by digging into the entrails of the earth in search of the crude means by which they might be preserved.

Vast numbers perished of indigestible food and want. I have beheld country people in the roads, and in the streets, who had died of hunger, and who were thrown across asses to be taken and buried. Fathers sold their children. The husband, with the consent of his wife, would take her into another province, there to bestow her in marriage as if she were his sister, and afterwards come and reclaim her when his wants were no longer so great. I have seen women and children run after camels, and rake in their dung to seek for some indigested grain of barley, which, if they found, they devoured with avidity.

Chenier.

[67] The Abmelec or eater of Locusts, or grasshoppers, is a bird which better deserves to be described, perhaps, than most others of which travellers have given us an account, because the facts relating to it are not only strange, in themselves, but so well and distinctly attested, that however surprising they may seem, we cannot but afford them our belief. The food of this creature is the locust, or the grasshopper: it is of the size of an ordinary hen, its feathers black, its wings large, and its flesh of a greyish colour; they fly generally in great flocks, as the starlings are wont to do with us: but the thing which renders these birds wonderful is, that they are so fond of the water of a certain fountain in Corasson, or Bactria, that where-ever that water is carried, they follow; on which account it is carefully preserved; for where ever the locusts fall, the Armenian priests, who are provided with this water, bring a quanity of it, and place in jars, or pour it into little channels in the fields, the next day whole troops of these birds arrive and quickly deliver the people from the locusts.

Universal History.

Sir John Chardin has given us, the following passage from an antient traveller, in relation to this bird. In Cyprus about the time that the corn was ripe for the sickle, the earth produced such a quantity of cavalettes, or locusts, that they obscured sometimes the splendour of the sun. Wherever these came, they burnt and eat up all; for this there was no remedy, since, as fast as they were destroyed, the earth produced more: God, however, raised them up a means for their deliverance, which happened thus. In Persia, near the city of Cuerch there is a fountain of water, which has a wonderful property of destroying these insects; for a pitcher full of this being carried in the open air, without passing through house or vault, and being set on an high place, certain birds which follow it, and fly and cry after the men who carry it from the fountain, come to the place where it is fixed. These birds are red and black, and fly in great flocks together, like starlings; the Turks and Persians call them Musulmans. These birds no sooner came to Cyprus, but they destroyed the locusts with which the Island was infested; but if the water be spilt or lost these creatures immediately disappear; which accident fell out when the Turks took this Island; for one of them going up into the steeple of Famagusta, and finding there a pitcher of this water, he, fancying that it contained gold or silver, or some precious thing, broke it, and spilt what was therein; since which the Cypriots have been as much tormented as ever by the locusts.

On the confines of the Medes and of Armenia, at certain times a great quantity of Birds are seen who resemble our blackbirds, and they have a property sufficiently curious to make me mention it.

When the corn in these parts begins to grow, it is astonishing to see the number of Locusts with which all the fields are covered. The Armenians have no other method of delivering themselves from these insects, than by going in procession round the fields and sprinkling them with a particular water which they take care to preserve in their houses. For this water comes from a great distance, they fetch it from a Well belonging to one of their Convents near the frontiers, and they say that the bodies of many Christian martyrs were formerly thrown into this well. These processions and the sprinkling continue three or four days, after which the Birds that I have mentioned come in great flights, and whether it be that they eat the locusts, or drive them away, in two or three days the country is cleared of them.

Tavernier.

At Mosul and at Haleb, says Niebuhr, I heard much of the Locust Bird, without seeing it. They there call it Samarmar, or as others pronounce it, Samarmog. It is said to be black, larger than a sparrow, and no ways pleasant to the palate. I am assured that it every day destroys an incredible number of Locusts; they pretend nevertheless that the Locusts sometimes defend themselves, and devour the Bird with its feathers, when they have overpowered it by numbers. When the children in the frontier towns of Arabia catch a live Locust, they place it before them and cry Samarmog! And because it stoops down terrified at the noise, or at the motion of the child, or clings more closely to its place, the children believe that it fears the name of its enemy, that it hides itself, and attempts to throw stones. The Samarmog is not a native of Mosul or Haleb, but they go to seek it in Khorasan with much ceremony. When the Locusts multiply very greatly, the government sends persons worthy of trust to a spring near the village of Samarûn, situated in a plain between four mountains, by Mesched, or Musa er ridda, in that province of Persia. The deputies with the ceremonies prescribed fill a chest with this water, and pitch the chest so that the water may neither evaporate nor be spilt before their return. From the spring to the Town whence they were sent, the chest must always be between heaven and earth: they must neither place it on the ground, nor under any roof, lest it should lose all its virtue. Mosul being surrounded with a wall, the water must not pass under the gate way, but it is received over the wall, and the chest placed upon the Mosque Nebbi Gurgis, a building which was formerly a church, and which in preference to all the other buildings has had from time immemorial the honour to possess this chest upon its roof. When this precious water has been brought from Khorasan with the requisite precautions, the common Mohammedans, Christians and Jews of Mosul believe that the Samarmog follows the water, and remains in the country as long as there is a single drop left in the chest of Nebbi-Gurgis. Seeing one day a large stork's nest upon this vessel, I told a Christian of some eminence in the town, how much I admired the quick smell of the Samarmog, who perceived the smell of the water thro' such a quantity of ordure, he did not answer me, but was very much scandalized that the government should have permitted the stork to make her nest upon so rare a treasure, and still more angry, that for more than nine years, the government had not sent to procure fresh water.

Niebuhr. Desc. de l'Arabie.

Dr. Russell describes this bird as about the size of a starling, the body of a flesh colour, the rest of its plumage black, the bill and legs black also.

[68] The Locusts are remarkable for the hieroglyphic that they bear upon the forehead, their colour is green throughout the whole body, excepting a little yellow rim that surrounds their head, which is lost at their eyes. This insect has two upper wings pretty solid: they are green like the rest of the body, except that there is in each a little white spot. The Locust keeps them extended like great sails of a ship going before the wind, it has besides two other wings underneath the former, and which resemble a light transparent stuff pretty much like a cobweb, and which it makes use of in the

manner of smack sails that are along a vessel; but when the Locust reposes herself she does like a vessel that lies at anchor, for she keeps the second sails furled under the first.

Norden.

The Mohammedans believe some mysterious meaning is contained in the lines upon the Locust's forehead.

I compared the description in the Poem with a Locust, which was caught in Leicestershire. It is remarkable that a single insect should have found his way so far inland.

[69] An Arabian expression from the Moallakat. "She turns her right side, as if she were in fear of some large-headed Screamer of the night."

Poem of Antara.

[70] The Mussulmans are immutably prepossessed, that as the Earth approaches its dissolution, its sons and daughters gradually decrease in their dimensions. As for Dagjial, they say, he will find the race of mankind dwindled into such diminutive pigmies, that their habitations in cities, and all the best towns, will be of no other fabrick than the shoes and slippers made in these present ages, placed in rank and file, in seemly and regular order; allowing one pair for two round families.

Morgan's Hist. of Algiers.

[71] The story of Haruth and Maruth as in the Poem, may be found in D'Herbelot, and in Sale's notes to the Koran. Of the differing accounts I have preferred that which makes Zohara originally a woman, and metamorphoses her into the planet Venus to that which says the planet Venus descended as Zohara to tempt the Angels.

The Arabians have so childish a love of rhyme, that when two names are usually coupled they make them jingle, as in the case of Haruth and Maruth. Thus they call Cain and Abel, Abel and Kabel. I am informed that the Koran is crowded with rhymes, more particularly at the conclusion of the chapters.

[72] The Ism-Ablah—The Science of the Name of God. They pretend that God is the lock of this science, and Mohammed the key, that consequently none but Mohammedans can attain it; that it discovers what passes in distant countries, that it familiarizes the possessors with the Genii, who are at the command of the initiated and who instruct them; that it places the winds and the seasons at their disposal, that it heals the bile of serpents, the lame, the maimed, and the blind. They say that some of their greatest Saints, such as Abdulkadir Cheilani of Bagdat, and Ibn Alwan who resided in the south of Yemen, were so far advanced in this science by their devotion, that they said their prayers every noon in the Kaba of Mecca, and were not absent from their own houses any other part of the day. A merchant of Mecca, who had learnt it in all its forms from Mohammed el Dsjanâdsjeni (at present so famous in that city) pretended that he himself being in danger of perishing at sea, had fastened a billet to the mast with the usual ceremonies, and that immediately the tempest ceased. He showed me at Bombay, but at a distance, a book which contained all sorts of figures and mathematical tables, with instructions how to arrange the billets and the appropriate prayers for every circumstance. But he would neither suffer me to touch the Book, nor copy the title.

There are some Mohammedans who shut themselves up in a dark place without eating and drinking for a long time, and there with a loud voice repeat certain short prayers till they faint. When they recover they pretend to have seen not only a crowd of Spirits, but God himself, and even the Devil. But the true initiated in the Ism-Allah do not seek these visions. The secret of discovering hidden treasures, belong also, if I mistake not, to the Ism Allah.

Niebuhr.

[73] One of the Arabs whom we saw from afar, and who was mounted upon a Camel, seemed higher than a tower and to be moving in the air, at first this was to me a strange appearance, however it was only the effect of refraction. The Camel which the Arab was upon touched the ground like all others. There was nothing then extraordinary in this phenomenon, and I afterwards saw many appearances exactly similar in the dry Countries.

Niebuhr.

"They surprized you, not indeed by a sudden assault; but they advanced, and the sultry vapour of noon thro' which you saw them, increased their magnitude."

Moallakat. Poem of Hareth.

[74] One of these Hykes is usually six yards long and 5 or 6 foot broad, serving the Arab for a compleat dress in the day, and for his bed and covering in the night. It is a loose but troublesome kind of garment, being frequently disconcerted and falling upon the ground, so that the person who wears it, is every moment obliged to tuck it up, and fold it anew about his body. This shews the great use there is for a girdle in attending any active employment, and in consequence thereof, the force of the scripture injunction alluding thereunto, of having our loyns girded. The method of wearing these garments, with the use they are at other times put to, in serving for coverlets to their beds, should induce us to take the finer sort of them at least, such as are wore by the Ladies and persons of distinction, to be the peplus of the antients. It is very probable likewise, that the loose folding garment, (the Toga I take it to be) of the Romans, was of this kind: for if the drapery of their statues is to instruct us, this is actually no other than what the Arabs appear in, when they are folded up in their Hykes. Instead of the fibula, they join together, with thread or a wooden bodkin, the two upper corners of this garment, which being first placed over one of their shoulders, they fold the rest of it afterwards round their bodies.

Shaw.

The employment of the women is to prepare their wool, spin, and weave in looms hung lengthways in their tents. These looms are formed by a list of an ell and a half long, to which the threads of the warp are fixed at one end, and at the other on a roller of equal length; the weight of which, being suspended, keeps them stretched. The threads of the warp are so hung as to be readily intersected. Instead of shuttles, the women pass the thread of the woof thro' the warp with their fingers, and with an iron comb, having a handle, press the woof to give a body to their cloth. Each piece of about 5 ells long, and an ell and a half wide, is called a haick; it receives neither dressing, milling nor dying, but is immediately fit for use: it is the constant dress of the Moors of the country, is without seam, and incapable of varying according to the caprices of fashion. When dirty it is washed: the Moor is wrapped up in it day and night, and this haick is the living model of the drapery of the ancients.

Chenier.

If thou at all take thy neighbour's raiment to pledge, thou shalt deliver it unto him by that the Sun goeth down.

For that is his covering only, it is his raiment for his skin: wherein shall he sleep?

Exodus. XXII. 26. 27.

[75] Fear the fire whose fuel is men, and stones prepared for the unbelievers.

Koran. Chap. 2.

Verily those who disbelieve our signs, we will surely cast to be broiled in hell fire; so often as their skins shall be well burned, we will give them other skins in exchange, that they may take the sharper torment.

Koran. Chap. 4.

[76] The Arabians attribute to Solomon a perpetual enmity and warfare against wicked Genii and Giants; on the subject of his wonder-working Ring their tales are innumerable. They have even invented a whole race of Pre-Adamite Solomons, who according to them governed the world successively to the number of 40, or as others affirm, as many as 72. All these made the evil Genii their unwilling Drudges.

D'Herbelot.

Anchieta was going in a canoe to the mouth of the river Aldea, a delightful spot, surrounded with mango trees, and usually abounding with birds called goarazes, that breed there. These birds are about the size of a hen, their colour a rich purple, inclining to red. They are white when hatched, and soon become black, but as they grow larger lose that colour and take this rich and beautiful purple. Our navigators had reached the place, but when they should have enjoyed the fine prospect which delights all who pass it, the sun was excessively hot, and this eye-pleasure was purchased dearly when the whole body was in a profuse perspiration, and the rowers were in a fever. Their distress called upon Joseph, and the remedy was no new one to him. He saw three or four of these birds perched upon a mango, and calling to them in the Brazilian language which the rowers understood, said, go you, call your companions, and come to shade these hot servants of the Lord. The birds stretched out their necks as if in obedience, and away they went to seek for others, and in a short time they came flying in the shape of an elegant cloud, and they shadowed the canoe a good league out to sea till the fresh sea breeze sprung up. Then they told them they might go about their business, and they separated with a clamor of rude but joyful sounds, which were only understood by the Author of Nature who created them. This was a greater miracle than that of the cloud with which God defended his chosen people in the wilderness from the heat of the sun, inasmuch as it was a more elegant and fanciful parasol. Acho que foy maior portento este que o da nuvem, com que deos defendes no deserto a seu Povo minoso do calor do sol, tanto quanto mais tem de gracioso & aprasivel este chapeo de sol, que aquelle.

This was a common miracle of Anchietus. Jacob Biderman has an epigram upon the subject, quoted in the Jesuit's life.

Hesperii peterent cum barbara littora mystæ,
Et sociis æger pluribus unus erat,
Ille suum extincto, Phoebi quia lampadis æstu
Occultoque uri, questus ab igne caput
Quæsiit in prora, si quam daiet angulus umbram,

Nulla sed in proræ partibus umbra fuit.
Quæsiit in puppi, nihil umbræ puppis habebat,
Summa sed urebant solis, & ima faces.
His cupiens Anchieta malis succurrere, solam
Aera per medium tendere vidit avem.
Vidit, ei socias, ait, i, quære cohortes
Aliger atque redux cum legione veni.
Dicta probavit avis, celerique citatior Euro,
Cognatum properat, quærere jussa gregem.
Milleque mox sociis comitata revertitur alis,
Mille sequi visæ, mille præire ducem.
Mille supra, & totidem, juxtaque, infraque volabant,
Omnis ad Anchietæ turba vocata preces.
Et simul expansis facta testudine pennis,
Desuper in tostas incubuere rates.
Et procul inde diem, & lucem pepulere diei,
Debile dum molis conderet umbra caput.
Scilicet hæc fierent, ut canopea repente
Anchieta artifices, esse coegit aves.

Vida do Veneravel Padre Joseph de Anchieta, da companhia de Jesu, Taumaturgo do Novo Mundo,
na Provincia do Brasil. composta pello P. Simam de Vasconcellos, da mesma companhia.

Lisboa. 1672.

Father Simam de Vasconcellos probably stole this miracle from the Arabian story of Solomon, not
that he is deficient in invention, but a Jesuit cannot be suspected of ignorance. In a very old book,
the Margarita Philosophica, is an account of a parasol more convenient, tho' not in so elegant a taste
as that of the wonder worker Anchieta. There is said to be a nation of one legged men, and one of
these unipods is represented in a print lying on his back, under the shade of his own great foot. It is
probably a classical lie.

The most quaint account of Solomon's wisdom is in Du Bartas.

Hee knowes—
Whether the Heavens sweet-sweating kisse appear
To be Pearls parent, and the Oysters pheer,
And whether, dusk, it makes them dim withall,
Cleer breeds the cleer, and stormy brings the pale:
Whether from sea the amber-greece be sent,
Or be some fishes pleasant excrement.
He knowes why the Earth's immoveable and round,
The lees of Nature, center of the mound;
Hee knows her mesure: and hee knows beside
How Coloquintida (duely apply'd)
Within the darknesse of the Conduit-pipes,
Amid the winding of our inward tripes,
Can so discreetly the white humour take.
Sylvester's Du Bartas.

[77] In places where there was water we found a beautiful variety of the plover.

Niebuhr.

[78] The Camels of the hot countries are not fastened one to the tail of the other as in cold climates, but suffered to go at their will like herds of cows. The Camel driver follows singing, and from time to time giving a sudden whistle. The louder he sings and whistles, the faster the Camels go, and they stop as soon as he ceases to sing. The Camel-drivers to relieve each other sing alternately, and when they wish their beasts to brouze for half an hour on what they can find, they amuse themselves by smoking a pipe, after which beginning again to sing, the Camels immediately proceed.

Tavernier.

[79] At four in the afternoon we had an unexpected entertainment, which filled our hearts with a very short-lived joy. The whole plain before us seemed thick covered with green grass and yellow daisies. We advanced to the place with as much speed as our lame condition would suffer us, but how terrible was our disapointment, when we found the whole of that verdure to consist in senna and coloquintida, the most nauseous of plants, and the most incapable of being substituted as food for man or beast.

Bruce.

[80] The girdles of these people are usually of worsted, very artfully woven into a variety of figures, and made to wrap several times about their bodies, one end of them, by being doubled and sown along the edges, serves them for a purse, agreeable to the acceptation of the word [Greek: Zônê] in the Holy Scriptures, the Turks and Arabs make a further use of their girdles by fixing their knives and poiniards in them; whilst the Hojias, i. e. the writers and secretaries, are distinguished by having an inkhorn, the badge of their office, suspended in the like situation.

Shaw.

[81] On the road we passed the skeleton of a camel, which now and then happens in the desert. These are poor creatures that have perished with fatigue: for those which are killed for the sustenance of the Arabs, are carried away bones and all together. Of the hides are made the soles of the slippers which are worn in Egypt, without any dressing, but what the sun can give them. The circumstances of this animal's death, when his strength fails him on the road, have something in them affecting to humanity. Such are his patience and perseverance, that he pursues his journey without flagging, as long as he has power to support its weight; and such are his fortitude and spirit, that he will never give out, until nature sinks beneath the complicated ills which press upon him. Then, and then only, will he resign his burden and body to the ground. Nor stripes, nor caresses nor food, nor rest, will make him rise again! His vigor is exhausted, and life ebbs out apace! This the Arabs are very sensible of, and kindly plunge a sword into the breast of the dying beast, to shorten his pangs. Even the Arab feels remorse when he commits this deed: his hardened heart is moved at the loss of a faithful servant.

Eyles Irwin.

In the Monthly Magazine for January 1800, is a letter from professor Heering recommending the introduction of these animals at the Cape, but the Camel is made only for level countries. "This animal is very ill qualified to travel upon the snow or wet ground; the breadth in which they carry their legs, when they slip, often occasions their splitting themselves; so that when they fall with great burdens they seldom rise again."

Jonas Hanway.

The African Arabs say, if one should put the question which is best for you, a Camel, to go up hill or down? he will make answer, God's curse light on 'em both, wheresoever they are to be met with.

Morgan's Hist. of Algiers.

No creature seems so peculiarly fitted to the climate in which it exists. We cannot doubt the nature of the one has been adapted to that of the other by some disposing intelligence. Designing the Camel to dwell in a country where he can find little nourishment, Nature has been sparing of her materials in the whole of his formation, She has not bestowed upon him the plump fleshiness of the ox, horse, or elephant; but limiting herself to what is strictly necessary, she has given him a small head without ears, at the end of a long neck without flesh. She has taken from his legs and thighs every muscle not immediately resquisite for motion; and in short has bestowed on his withered body only the vessels and tendons necessary to connect his frame together. She has furnished him with a strong jaw, that he may grind the hardest aliments; but lest he should consume too much, she has contracted his stomach, and obliged him to chew the cud. She has lined his foot with a lump of flesh, which, sliding in the mud, and being no way adapted for climbing, fits him only for a dry, level, and sandy soil, like that of Arabia. She has evidently destined him likewise to slavery, by refusing him every sort of defence against his enemies. Destitute of the horns of the bull, the hoofs of the horse, the tooth of the elephant, and the swiftness of the stag, how can the camel resist or avoid the attacks of the lion, the tyger, or even the wolf? To preserve the species therefore, Nature has concealed him in the depths of the vast deserts, where the want of vegetables can attract no game, and whence the want of game repels every voracious animal. Tyranny must have expelled man from the habitable parts of the earth, before the Camel could have lost his liberty. Become domestic, he has rendered habitable the most barren soil the world contains. He alone supplies all his master's wants. The milk of the Camel nourishes the family of the Arab, under the various forms of curds, cheese, and butter; and they often feed upon his flesh. Slippers and harness are made of his skin, and tents and clothing of his hair. Heavy burthens are transported by his means, and when the earth denies forage to the horse, so valuable to the Bedouin, the she-camel supplies that deficiency by her milk, at no other cost, for so many advantages, than a few stalks of brambles or wormwood, and pounded date kernels. So great is the importance of the Camel to the desert, that were it deprived of that useful animal, it must infallibly lose every inhabitant.

Volney.

[82] Where any part of these Deserts is sandy and level, the Horizon is as fit for astronomical observations as the sea, and appears at a small distance, to be no less a collection of water. It was likewise equally surprising to observe, in what an extraordinary manner every object appeared to be magified within it; insomuch that a shrub seemed as big as a tree, and a flock of Achbobbas might be mistaken for a caravan of Camels. This seeming collection of water, always advances, about a quarter of a mile before us, whilst the intermediate space appears to be in one continued glow, occasioned by the quivering undulating motion of that quick succession of vapours and exhalations, which are extracted by the powerful influence of the sun.

Shaw.

In the Bahar Danush is a metaphor drawn from this optical deception. "It is the ancient custom of Fortune, and time has long established the habit, that she at first bewilders the thirsty travellers in the path of desire, by the misty vapour of disappointment; but when their distress and misery has reached extremity, suddenly relieving them from the dark windings of confusion and error, she conducts them to the fountains of enjoyment."

"The burning heat of the sun was reflected with double violence from the hot sand, and the distant ridges of the hills, seen thro' the ascending vapour, seemed to wave and fluctuate like the unsettled sea."

Mungo Park.

"I shake the lash over my Camel, and she quickens her pace, while the sultry vapour rolls in waves over the burning cliffs."

Moallakat. Poem of Tarafa.

[83] Perhaps no traveller but Mr. Park ever survived to relate similar sufferings.

"I pushed on as fast as possible, in hopes of reaching some watering-place in the course of the night. My thirst was by this time become insufferable; my mouth was parched and inflamed; a sudden dimness would frequently come over my eyes, with other symptoms of fainting; and my horse being very much fatigued, I began seriously to apprehend that I should perish of thirst. To relieve the burning pain in my mouth and throat, I chewed the leaves of different shrubs, but found them all bitter and of no service to me.

A little before sunset, having reached the top of a gentle rising, I climbed a high tree, from the topmost branches of which I cast a melancholy look over the barren wilderness, but without discovering the most distant trace of a human dwelling. The same dismal uniformity of shrubs and sand every where presents itself, and the horizon, was as level and uninterrupted as that of the sea.

Descending from the tree, I found my horse devouring the stubble and brushwood with great avidity; and as I was now too faint to attempt walking, and my horse too much fatigued to carry me, I thought it but an act of humanity, and perhaps the last I should ever have it in my power to perform, to take off his bridle and let him shift for himself: in doing which I was suddenly affected with sickness and giddiness, and falling upon the sand, felt as if the hour of death was fast approaching. Here then, thought I, after a short but ineffectual struggle, terminate all my hopes of being useful in my day and generation; here must the short span of my life come to an end.—I cast (as I believed) a last look on the surrounding scene, and whilst I reflected on the awful change that was to take place, this world with its enjoyments seemed to vanish from my recollection. Nature however, at length resumed its functions; and on recovering my senses, I found myself stretched upon the sand with the bridle still in my hand, and the sun just sinking behind the trees. I now summoned all my resolution, and determined to make another effort to prolong my existence. And as the evening was somewhat cool, I resolved to travel as far as my limbs would carry me, in hopes of reaching (my only resource) a watering place. With this view I put the bridle on my horse, and driving him before me, went slowly along for about an hour, when I perceived some lightning from the north east, a most delightful sight, for it promised rain. The darkness and lightning increased very rapidly; and in less than an hour I heard the wind roaring among the bushes. I had already opened my mouth to receive the refreshing drops which I expected, but I was instantly covered with a cloud of sand, driven with such force by the wind as to give a very disagreeable sensation to my face and arms, and I was obliged to mount my horse and stop under a bush, to prevent being suffocated. The sand continued to fly in amazing quantities for near an hour, after which I again set forward, and travelled with difficulty, until ten o'clock. About this time I was agreeably surprized by some very vivid flashes of lightning, followed by a few heavy drops of rain. In a little time the sand ceased to fly, and I alighted, and spread out all my clean clothes to collect the rain, which at length I saw would certainly fall.—For more than an hour it rained plentifully, and I quenched my thirst, by wringing and sucking my clothes.

Park's Travels in the Interior of Africa.

[84] All the time I was in Barbary I could never get sight of above three or four Dromedaries. These the Arabs call Mehera, the singular is Meheri. They are of several sorts, and degrees of value, some worth many common Camels, others scarce worth two or three. To look on, they seem little different from the rest of that Species, only I think the Excrescence on a Dromedary's Back is somewhat less than that of a Camel. What is reported of their sleeping, or rather seeming scarce alive, for some Time after coming into this World, is no Fable. The longer they lie so, the more excellent they prove in their Kind, and consequently of higher Price and Esteem. None lie in that Trance more than ten Days and Nights. These that do, are pretty rare, and are called Ashari from Aashara, which signifies ten in Arabick. I saw one such, perfectly white all over, belonging to Lella Oumane Princess of that noble Arab Neja, named Hayl ben Ali, I spoke of, and upon which she put a very great Value, never sending it abroad but upon some extraordinary Occasion, when the greatest Expedition was required; having others, inferior in swiftness, for more ordinary Messages. They say that one of these Aasharies will, in one Night, and thro' a level Country, traverse as much Ground as any single Horse can perform in ten, which is no Exaggeration of the Matter, since many have affirmed to me, that it makes nothing of holding its rapid Pace, which is a most violent Hard Trot, for four and twenty Hours upon a Stretch without shewing the least Sign of Weariness, or Inclination to Bait; and that having then swallowed a Ball or two of Sort of a Paste, made up of Barley-Meal, and may be a little Powder of Dates among it, with a Bowl of Water, or Camel's Milk, if to be had, and which the Courier seldom forgets to be provided with, in Skins, as well for the Sustenance of himself as of his Pegasus, the indefatigable Animal will seem as fresh as at first setting out, and ready to continue running at the same scarce credible Rate, for as many Hours longer, and so on from one Extremity of the African Desarts to the other; provided its Rider could hold out without Sleep, and other Refreshment. This has been averred to me, by, I believe more than a thousand Arabs and Moors, all agreeing in every Particular.

I happened to be, once in particular, at the Tent of that Princess, with Ali ben Mahamoud, the Bey, or Vice-Roy of the Algerine Eastern Province, when he went thither to celebrate his Nuptials with Ambarca, her only Daughter, if I mistake not. Among other Entertainments she gave her Guests, the favourite white Dromedary was brought forth, ready Saddled and Bridled. I say Bridled, because the Thong, which serves instead of a Bridle, was put thro' the Hole purposely made in the Gristle of the Creature's Nose. The Arab appointed to mount, was straightly laced, from the very Loins quite to his Throat, in a strong Leathern Jacket; they never riding these Animals any otherwise accoutred, so impetuously violent are the Concussions the Rider undergoes, during that rapid Motion, that were he to be loose. I much question whether a few Hours such unintermitting Agitation would not endanger the bursting of some of his Entrails: And this the Arabs scruple not to acknowledge. We were to be diverted with seeing this fine Ashari run against some of the swiftest Barbs in the whole Neja, which is famed for having good ones, of the true Libyan Breed, shaped like Greyhounds, and which will sometimes run down an Ostridge; which few of the very best can pretend to do, especially upon a hard Ground, perfectly level. We all started like Racers, and for the first Spurt, most of the best mounted among us kept up pretty well, but our Grass fed Horses soon flagged: Several of the Libyan and Numidian Runners held Pace till we, who still followed upon a good round Hand Gallop, could no longer discern them, and then gave out; as we were told after their Return. When the

Dromedary had been out of our Sight about half an Hour, we again espied it flying towards us with an amazing Volocity, and in a very few Moments was among us, and seemingly nothing concerned; while the Horses and Mares were all on a Foam, and scarce able to breathe, as was, likewise, a fleet, tall Greyhound Bitch, of the young Prince's, who had followed and kept Pace the whole Time, and was no sooner got back to us, but lay down panting as if ready to expire. I cannot tell how many Miles we went; but we were near three Hours in coming leisurely back to the Tents, yet made no Stop in the Way. The young Prince Hamet ben al Guydom ben Sakhari, and his younger Brother Messoud, told their new Brother-in-Law, that they defied all the Potentates of Africa to shew him such an Ashari; and the Arab who rode it, challenged the Bey to lay his Lady a Wager of 1000 Ducats, that he did not bring him an Answer to a Letter from the Prince of Wargala, in less than four Days, tho' Leo Africanus, Marmol, and several others assure us, that it is no less than forty Spanish Leagues, of four Miles each, South of Tuggurt to which Place, upon another Occasion, as I shall observe, we made six tedious Days March from the Neighbourhood of Biscara, North of which we were then, at least thirty Hours riding, if I remember rightly. However the Bey, who was a Native of Biscara, and consequently well acquainted with the Sahara, durst not take him up. By all Circumstances, and the Description given us, besides what I know of the Matter my self, it could not be much less than 400 Miles, and as many back again, the fellow offered to ride, in so short a Time; nay many other Arabs boldly proffered to venture all they were worth in the World, that he would perform it with all the Ease imaginable.

Morgan's History of Algiers.

Chenier says "the Dromedary can travel 60 leagues in a day, his motion is so rapid that the rider is obliged to be girthed to the saddle, and to have a handkerchief before his mouth to break the current of the wind."—These accounts are probably much exaggerated.

"The royal couriers in Persia wear a white sash girded from the shoulders to their waist many times round their bodies, by which means they are enabled to ride for many days without great fatigue."

Hanway.

[85] We were here at once surprised and terrified by a sight surely the most magnificent in the world. In that vast expanse of desert, from W. and to N. W. of us, we saw a number of prodigious pillars of sand at different distances, at times moving with great celerity, at others stalking with a majestic slowness: at intervals we thought they were coming in a very few moments to overwhelm us, and small quantities of sand did actually more than once reach us. Again they would retreat so as to be almost out of sight, their tops reaching to the very clouds. There the tops often separated from the bodies, and these once disjoined, dispersed in the air and did not appear more. Sometimes they were broken near the middle, as if struck with a large cannon shot. About noon they began to advance with considerable swiftness upon us, the wind being very strong at north. Eleven of them ranged alongside of us about the distance of three miles. The greatest diameter of the largest appeared to me at that distance as if it would measure ten feet. They retired from us with a wind at S. E. leaving an impression upon my mind to which I can give no name; though surely one ingredient in it was fear, with a considerable deal of wonder and astonishment. It was in vain to think of flying, the swiftest horse, or fastest sailing ship could be of no use to carry us out of this danger, and the full persuasion of this rivetted me as if to the spot where I stood.

On the 15th the same appearance of moving pillars of sand presented themselves to us, only they seemed to be more in number, and less in size. They came several times in a direction close upon us; that is, I believe, within less than two miles. They began immediately after sun-rise, like a thick wood, and almost darkened the sun. His rays shining through them for near an hour, gave them an appearance of pillars of fire. Our people now became desperate: the Greeks shrieked out, and said it was the day of judgement. Ismael pronounced it to be hell, and the Tucorories that the world was on fire.

Bruce.

[86] The Pelican makes choice of dry and desert places to lay her eggs, when her young are hatched, she is obliged to bring water to them from great distances, to enable her to perform this necessary office Nature has provided her with a large sack which extends from the tip of the under mandible of her bill to the throat, and holds as much water as will supply her brood for several days. This water she pours into the nest to cool her young, to allay their thirst, and to teach them to swim. Lions, Tygers, and other rapacious animals resort to these nests, and drink the water and are said not to injure the young.

Smellie's Philosophy of Natural History.

[87] These prominent features of an Oriental city will be found in all the views of Sir John Chardin.

The mosques, the minarets, and numerous cupolas form a splended spectacle; and the flat roofs of the houses which are situated on the hills, rising one behind another, present a succession of hanging terraces, interspersed with cyprus and poplar trees. Russel's Nat. Hist. of Aleppo. The circuit of Ispahan taking in the suburbs is not less than that of Paris, but Paris contains ten times the number of its inhabitants. It is not however astonishing that this city is so extensive and so thinly peopled, because every family has its own house, and almost every house its garden; so that there is much void ground. From whatever side you arrive you first discover the towers of the Mosques, and then the trees which surround the houses; at a distance Ispahan resembles a forest more than a town.

Tavernier.

Of Alexandria Volney says, "the spreading palm trees, the terraced houses which seem to have no roof, the lofty slender minarets, all announce to the traveller that he is in another world."

[88] Almanzor riding one day with his courtiers along the banks of the Tigris, where Seleucia formerly stood, was so delighted with the beauty of the country, that he resolved there to build his new Capital. Whilst he was conversing with his attendants upon this project, one of them separating from the rest met a hermit whose cell was near, and entered into talk with him and communicated the design of the Caliph. The Hermit replied, he well knew by a tradition of the country that a city would one day be built in that plain, but that its founder would be a man called Moclas, a name very different from both those of the Caliph, Giaffar and Almanzor.

The Officer rejoined Almanzor and repeated his conversation with the Hermit. As soon as the Caliph heard the name of Moclas, he descended from his horse, prostrated himself, and returned thanks to God for that he was chosen to execute his orders. His courtiers waited for an explanation of this conduct with eagerness, and the Caliph told them thus. During the Caliphate of the Ommiades, my brothers and myself being very young and possessing very little, were obliged to live in the country, where each in rotation was to provide sustenance for the whole. On one of my days as I was without money, and had no means of procuring food, I took a bracelet belonging to my nurse and pawned it. This woman made a great outcry, and after much search discovered that I had been the thief. In her anger she abused me plentifully, and among other terms of reproach, she called me Moclas, the name of a famous robber in those days; and during the rest of her life she never called me by any other name. Therefore I know that God has destined me to perform this work.

Marigny.

Almanzor named his new city Dar-al-Salam the City of Peace; but it obtained the name of Bagdat, from that of this Hermit who dwelt upon its site.

Bagdat was founded in consequence of a singular superstition. A sect called Ravendiens conceived that they ought to render those honours to the Caliphs, which the Moslem hold should only be paid to the Deity. They therefore came in great numbers to Haschemia, where the Caliph Almanzor usually resided, and made around his palace the same processions and ceremonies which the Moslem made around the Temple at Mecca. The Caliph prohibited this, commanding them not to profane a religious ceremony which ought to be reserved solely to the Temple at Mecca. The Ravendiens did not regard the prohibition, and continued to act as before.

Almanzor seeing their obstinacy resolved to conquer it, and began by arresting a hundred of these fanatics. This astonished them, but they soon recovered their courage, took arms, marched to the prison, forced the doors, delivered their friends, and then returned to make their processions round the palace in reverence of the Caliph.

Enraged at this insolence the Caliph put himself at the head of his guards, and advanced against the Ravendiens, expecting that his appearance would immediately disperse them. Instead of this they resisted, and repulsed him so vigorously that he had nearly fallen a victim. But timely succours arrived and after a great slaughter these fanatics were expelled the town. This singular rebellion arising from excess of loyalty so disgusted Almanzor that he determined to forsake the town which had witnessed it, and accordingly laid the foundation of Bagdat.

Marigny.

[89] Almanzor signifies the Victorious.

[90] The houses in Persia are not in the same place with their shops, which stand for the most part in long and large arched streets 40 or 50 foot high, which streets are called Basar or the market, and make the heart of the city, the houses being in the out parts, and having almost all gardens belonging to 'em.

Chardin.

At Tauris he says, "there are the fairest Basars that are in any place of Asia, and it is a lovely sight to see their vast extent, their largeness, their beautiful Duomos and the arches over 'em."

At Bagdad the Bazars are all vaulted, otherwise the merchants could not remain in them on account of the heat. They are also watered two or three times a day, and a number of the poor are paid for rendering this service to the public.

Tavernier.

[91] On the other side of the river towards Arabia, over against the city, there is a faire place or towne, and in it a faire Bazario for marchants, with very many lodgings where the greatest part of the marchants strangers which come to Babylon do lie with their marchandize. The passing over

Tygris from Babylon to this Borough is by a long bridge made of boates chained together with great chaines: provided, that when the river waxeth great with the abundance of raine that falleth, then they open the bridge in the middle, where the one halfe of the bridge falleth to the walles of Babylon, and the other to the brinks of this Borough, on the other side of the river; and as long as the bridge is open, they passe the river in small boats with great danger, because of the smallnesse of the boats, and the overlading of them, that with the fiercenesse of the stream they be overthrowen, or els the streame doth cary them away, so that by this meanes, many people are lost and drowned.

Cæsar Frederick, in Hakluyt.

Here are great store of victuals which come from Armenia downe the river of Tygris. They are brought upon raftes made of goate's skinnes blownn full of wind, and bordes layde upon them; which being discharged they open their skinnes, and carry them backe by Camels.

Ralph Fitch in Hakluyt.

[92] In Tavernier's time there were five Mosques at Bagdad, two of them fine, their large Domes covered with varnished tiles of different colours.

[93] At Bagdad are many cranes who build their nests upon the tops of the minarets, and the loftiest houses.

At Adanaqui—cranes are so abundant, that there is scarcely a house which has not several nests upon it. They are very tame, and the inhabitants never molest them. When any thing disturbs these birds, they make a violent clatter with their long beaks, which is sometimes repeated by the others all over the town; and this noise will sometimes continue for several minutes. It is as loud as a watchman's rattle, and not much unlike it in sound.

Jackson.

The cranes were now arrived at their respective quarters, and a couple had made their nest, which is bigger in circumference than a bushel, on a dome close by our chamber. This pair stood, side by side, with great gravity, shewing no concern at what was transacting beneath them, but at intervals twisting about their long necks, and cluttering with their beaks, turned behind them upon their backs, as it were in concert. This was continued the whole night. An Owl, a bird also unmolested, was perched hard by, and as frequently hooted. The crane is tall, like a heron, but much larger; the body white, with black pinions, the neck and legs very long, the head small, and the bill thick. The Turks call it friend and brother, believing it has an affection for their nation, and will accompany them into the countries they shall conquer. In the course of our journey we saw one hopping on a wall with a single leg, the maimed stump wrapped in linen.

Chandler's Travels in Asia Minor.

[94] I will rise up against them, saith the Lord of Hosts, and cut off from Babylon the name and remnant, and son and nephew saith the Lord. I will also make it a possession for the Bittern and pools of water.

Isaiah. XIV. 22. 23.

[95] —Walls, within

Whose large inclosure the rude hind, or guides
His plough, or binds his sheaves, while shepherds guard
Their flocks, secure of ill: on the broad top
Six chariots rattle in extended front.
Each side in length, in height, in solid bulk,
Reflects its opposite a perfect square;
Scarce sixty thousand paces can mete out
The vast circumference. An hundred gates
Of polished brass lead to that central point
Where thro' the midst, bridged o'er with wondrous art
Euphrates leads a navigable stream,
Branch'd from the current of his roaring flood.
Roberts's Judah Restored.

[96] Within the walls
Of Babylon was rais'd a lofty mound
Where flowers and aromatic shrubs adorn'd
The pensile garden. For Nebassar's queen,
Fatigued with Babylonia's level plains,
Sigh'd for her Median home, where nature's hand
Had scoop'd the vale, and cloath'd the mountain's side
With many a verdant wood; nor long she pin'd
Till that uxorious monarch called on art
To rival nature's sweet variety.
Forthwith two hundred thousand slaves uprear'd
This hill, egregious work; rich fruits o'er hang
The sloping walks and odorous shrubs entwine
Their undulating branches.
Roberts's Judah Restored.

[97] Our early Travellers have given us strange and circumstantial accounts of what they conceive to have been the Temple of Belus.

The Tower of Nimrod or Babel is situate on that side of Tygris that Arabia is, and in a very great plaine distant from Babylon seven or eight miles; which tower is ruinated on every side, and with the falling of it there is made a great mountaine; so that it hath no forme at all, yet there is a great part of it standing, which is compassed and almost covered with the aforesayd fallings: this Tower was builded and made of foure-square brickes, which brickes were made of earth, and dried in the Sunne in maner and forme following: first they layed a lay of brickes, then a mat made of canes, square as the brickes, and instead of lime, they daubed it with earth: these mats of canes are at this time so strong, that it is a thing woonderfull to beholde, being of such great antiquity: I have gone round about it, and have not found any place where there hath bene any doore or entrance: it may be in my judgement in circuit about a mile, and rather lesse than more.

This Tower in effect is contrary to all other things which are seene afar off, for they seeme small and the more nere a man commeth to them the bigger they be: but this tower afar off seemeth a very great thing, and the nerer you come to it the lesser. My judgement and reason of this is, that because the Tower is set in a very great plaine, and hath nothing more about to make any shew saving the ruines of it which it hath made round about, and for this respect descrying it afarre off, that piece of the Tower which yet standeth with the mountaine that is made of the substance that hath fallen from it, maketh a greater shew than you shall finde comming neere to it.

Cæsar Frederick.

John Eldred mentions the same deception. "Being upon a plaine grounde it seemeth afarre off very great, but the nerer you come to it, the lesser and lesser it appeareth. Sundry times I have gone thither to see it, and found the remnants yet standing about a quarter of a mile in compasse, and almost as high as the stone worke of St. Paul's steeple in London, but it sheweth much bigger."

Hakluyt.

In the middle of a vast and level plain, about a quarter of a league from Euphrates, which in that place runs westward, appears a heap of ruined buildings, like a huge mountain, the materials of which are so confounded together that one knows not what to make of it. Its figure is square, and rises in form of a tower or pyramid with four fronts which answer to the four quarters of the compass; but it seems longer from north to S. than from E. to W. and is, as far as I could judge by my pacing it, a large quarter of a league. Its situation and form correspond with that pyramid which Strabo calls the tower of Belus; and is in all likelihood the tower of Nimrod in Babylon or Babel, as that place is still called. In that author's time it had nothing remaining of the stairs and other ornaments mentioned by Herodotus, the greatest part of it having been ruined by Xerxes; and Alexander who designed to have restored it to its former lustre, was prevented by death. There appear no marks of ruins without the compass of that huge mass, to convince one that so great a city as Babylon had ever stood there; all one discovers within 50 or 60 paces of it, being only the remains here and there of some foundations of buildings; and the country round about it so flat and level, that one can hardly believe it should be chosen for the situation of so great and noble a city as Babylon, or that there were ever any remarkable buildings on it. But for my part I am astonished there appears so much as there does, considering it is at least 4000 years since that city was built; and that Diodorus Siculus tells us, it was reduced almost to nothing in his time. The height of this mountain of ruins is not in every part equal, but exceeds the highest palace in Naples: it is a mishapen mass, wherein there is no appearance of regularity; in some places it rises in points, is craggy and inaccessible; in others it is smoother and is of easier ascent; there are also tracks of torrents from the top to the bottom caused by the rains, and both withinside and upon it, one sees parts, some higher and some lower. It is not to be discovered whether ever there were any steps to ascend it, or any doors to enter into it; whence one may easily judge that the stairs ran winding about on the outside; and that being the less solid parts, they were soonest demolished, so that not the least sign of any appears at present.

Withinside one finds some grottos, but so ruined that one can make nothing of them, whether they were built at the same time with that work, or made since by the peasants for shelter, which last seems to be the most likely. The Mohammedans believe that these caverns were appointed by God as places of punishment for Harut and Marut, two angels, who they suppose were sent from heaven to judge the armies of men, but did not execute their commissions as they ought. It is evident from these ruins, that the tower of Nimrod was built with great and thick bricks, as I carefully observed, causing holes to be dug in several places for the purpose; but they do not appear to have been burnt, but dried in the sun, which is extreme hot in those parts. In laying these bricks neither lime nor sand was employed, but only earth tempered and petrified, and in those parts which made the floors, there had been mingled with that earth which served instead of lime, bruised reeds, or hard straw, such as large mats are made of to strengthen the work. Afterwards one perceives at certain distances in divers places, especially where the strongest buttresses were to be, several other bricks of the same size, but more solid and burnt in a kiln, and set in good lime, or bitumen, nevertheless the greatest number consists of those which are only dried in the sun.

I make no doubt but this ruin was the ancient Babel, and the tower of Nimrod; for besides the evidence of its situation, it is acknowledged to be such by the people of the country, being vulgarly called Babil by the Arabs.

Pietro delle Valle. Universal Hist.

Eight towers arise,
Each above each, immeasurable height,
A monument at once of eastern pride
And slavish superstition. Round, a scale
Of circling steps entwines the conic pile;
And at the bottom on vast hinges grates
Four brazen gates, towards the four winds of heaven
Placed in the solid square.
Roberts's Judah Restored.

[98] And Babylon the glory of kingdoms, the beauty of the Chaldees excellency shall be as when God overthrew Sodom and Gomorrah.

It shall never be inhabited, neither shall it be dwelt in from generation to generation; neither shall the Arabian pitch tent there, neither shall the Shepherds make their fold there.

Isaiah. XIII. 19. 20.

[99] The stupid superstition of the Turks with regard to hidden treasures is well known, it is difficult or even dangerous for a traveller to copy an inscription in sight of those barbarians.

"On a rising ground, at a league's distance from the river Shelliff, is Memoun-turroy, as they call an old square tower, formerly a sepulchral monument of the Romans. This, like many more ancient edifices, is supposed by the Arabs, to have been built over a treasure. Agreeably to which account, they tell us, these mystical lines were inscribed upon it. Prince Maimoun Tizai wrote this upon his tower.

My Treasure is in my Shade,
And my Shade is in my Treasure.
Search for it; despair not:
Nay despair; do not search.
Shaw.

So of the ruines of ancient Tubuna.

The Treasure of Tubnah lyeth under the shade of what is shaded. Dig for it? alas! it is not there.

Shaw.

[100] The springs of bitumen called Oyun Hit, the fountains of Hit, are much celebrated by the Arabs and Persians; the latter call it Cheshmeh kir, the fountain of pitch. This liquid bitumen they call Nafta; and the Turks, to distinguish it from pitch, give it the name of hara sakiz, or black mastich. A Persian geographer says, that Nafta issues out of the springs of the earth as ambergrise issues out of those of the sea. All the modern travellers, except Rauwolf, who went to Persia and the Indies by the way of the Euphrates before the discovery of the Cape of Good Hope, mention this fountain of liquid

bitumen as a strange thing. Some of them take notice of the river mentioned by Herodotus; and assure us, that the people of the country have a tradition, that, when the tower of Babel was building, they brought the bitumen from hence; which is confirmed by the Arab and Persian historians.

Hit, Heit, Eit, Ait, or Idt, as it is variously written by travellers, is a great Turkish town situate upon the right or west side of the Euphrates; and has a castle; to the south-west of which and three miles from the town, in a valley, are many springs of this black substance; each of which makes a noise like a smith's forge, incessantly puffing and blowing out the matter so loud, that it may be heard a mile off: wherefore the Moors and Arabs call it Bab al Jehennam; that is hell gate. It swallows up all heavy things; and many camels from time to time fall into the pits, and are irrecoverably lost. It issues from a certain lake, sending forth a filthy smoke, and continually boiling over with the pitch; which spreads itself over a great field, that is always full of it. It is free for every one to take: they use it to chaulk or pitch their boats, laying it on two or three inches thick; which keeps out the water: with it also they pitch their houses, made of palm-tree branches. If it was not that the inundations of the Euphrates carry away the pitch, which covers all the sands from the place where it rises to the river, there would have been mountains of it long since. The very ground and stones thereabouts afford bitumen; and the fields abundance of salt petre.

Universal History.

[101] The Mussulmanns use, like the Roman Catholics, a rosary of beads called Tusbah, or implement of praise. It consists, if I recollect aright, of ninety nine beads; in dropping which through the fingers, they repeat the attributes of God, as "O Creator, O Merciful, O Forgiving, O Omnipotent, O Omniscient, &c. &c." This act of devotion is called Taleel, from the repetition of the letter L, or Laum, which occurs in the word Allah, (God), always joined to the epithet or attribute, as Ya Allah Khalick, O God, the Creator; Ya Allah Kerreem, O God, the Merciful, &c. &c. The devotees may be seen muttering their beads as they walk the streets, and in the interval of conversation in company. The rosaries of persons of fortune and rank have the beads of diamonds, pearls, rubies and emeralds. Those of the humble are strung with berries, coral, or glass beads.

Note to the Bahar Danush.

The ninety nine beads of the Mohammedan rosary are divided into three equal lengths, by a little string, at the end of which hang a long piece of coral and a large bead of the same. The more devout, or hypocritical Turks, like the Catholics have usually their bead string in their hands.

Tavernier.

[102] "The Mahummedans believe that the decreed events of every man's life are impressed in divine characters on his forehead, tho' not to be seen by mortal eye. Hence they use the word Nusseeb, anglicé stamped, for destiny. Most probably the idea was taken up by Mahummud from the sealing of the Elect, mentioned in the Revelations."

Note to the Bahar-Danush.

"The scribe of decree chose to ornament the edicts on my forehead with these flourishes of disgrace."

Bahar-Danush.

The Spanish physiognomical phrase, traérlo escrito en la frente, to have it written on the forehead, is perhaps of Arabian origin.

[103] Zohak was the fifth King of the Pischdadian dynasty, lineally descended from Shedâd who perished with the tribe of Ad. Zohak murdered his predecessor, and invented the punishments of the cross, and of fleaing alive. The Devil who had long served him, requested at last as a recompence, permission to kiss his shoulders, immediately two serpents grew there, who fed upon his flesh and endeavoured to get at his brain. The Devil now suggested a remedy, which was to quiet them by giving them every day the brains of two men, killed for that purpose: this tyranny lasted long, till a blacksmith of Ispahan whose children had been nearly all slain to feed the King's serpents, raised his leathern apron as the standard of revolt, and deposed Zohak. Zohak, say the Persians, is still living in the cave of his punishment, a sulphureous vapour issues from the place, and if a stone be flung in there comes out a voice and cries, why dost thou fling stones at me? this cavern is in the mountain of Demawend, which reaches from that of Elwend, towards Teheran.

D'Herbelot. Olearius.

[104] "I shall transcribe a foreign piece of Superstition, firmly believed in many parts of France, Germany and Spain. The account of it, and the mode of preparation, appears to have been given by a judge: in the latter there is a striking resemblance to the charm in Macbeth.

Of the Hand of Glory, which is made use of by housebreakers, to enter into houses at night, without fear of opposition.

I acknowledge that I never tried the secret of the Hand of Glory, but I have thrice assisted at the definitive judgment of certain criminals, who, under the torture, confessed having used it. Being asked what it was, how they procured it, and what were its uses and properties? they answered, first, that the use of the Hand of Glory was to stupify those to whom it was presented, and to render them motionless, insomuch that they could not stir, any more than if they were dead; secondly, that it was the hand of a hanged man; and thirdly, that it must be prepared in the manner following.

Take the hand, left or right, of a person hanged and exposed on the highway; wrap it up in a piece of a shroud or winding sheet, in which let it be well squeezed, to get out any small quantity of blood that may have remained in it; then put it into an earthen vessel with Zimat saltpetre, salt, and long pepper, the whole well powdered; leave it fifteen days in that vessel; afterwards take it out, and expose it to the noontide sun in the dog days, till it is thoroughly dry, and if the Sun is not sufficient, put it into an oven heated with fern and vervain. Then compose a kind of candle with the fat of a hanged man, virgin wax, and sisame of Lapland. The Hand of Glory is used as a candlestick to hold this candle, when lighted. Its properties are, that wheresoever any one goes with this dreadful instrument, the persons to whom it is presented will be deprived of all power of motion. On being asked if there was no remedy or antidote, to counteract this charm, they said the Hand of Glory would cease to take effect, and thieves could not make use of it, if the threshold of the door of the house, and other places by which they might enter, were anointed with an unguent composed of the gall of a black cat, the fat of a white hen, and the blood of a screech owl, which mixture must necessarily be prepared during the dog days.

Grose. Provincial Glossary and Popular Superstitions.

[105] The habitations of the Saints are always beside the sanctuary, or tomb, of their ancestors, which they take care to adorn. Some of them possess, close to their houses, gardens, trees, or cultivated grounds, and particularly some spring or well of water. I was once travelling in the south

in the beginning of October, when the season happened to be exceedingly hot, and the wells and rivulets of the country were all dried up. We had neither water, for ourselves, nor for our horses; and after having taken much fruitless trouble to obtain some, we went and paid homage to a Saint, who at first pretended a variety of scruples before he would suffer infidels to approach; but on promising to give him ten or 12 shillings, he became exceedingly humane, and supplied us with as much water as we wanted; still however vaunting highly of his charity, and particularly of his disinterestedness.

Chenier.

[106] No nation in the world is so much given to superstition as the Arabs, or even as the Mahometans in general. They hung about their children's necks the figure of an open hand, which the Turks and Moors paint upon their ships and houses, as an antidote and counter-charm to an evil eye: For five is with them an unlucky number and five (fingers perhaps) in your eyes, is their proverb of cursing and defiance. Those who are grown up, carry always about with them some paragraph or other of their Koran, which, like as the Jews did their phylacteries, they place upon their breast, or sow under their caps, to prevent fascination and witchcraft, and to secure themselves from sickness and misfortunes. The virtue of these charms and scrolls is supposed likewise to be so far universal, that they suspend them upon the necks of their cattle, horses and other beasts of burthen.

Shaw.

The hand-spell is still common in Portugal, it is called the figa, and thus probably our vulgar phrase "a fig for him" is derived from a Moorish amulet.

[107] In the Vision of Thurcillus Adam is described as beholding the events of the world with mingled grief and joy; his original garment of glory gradually recovering its lustre, as the number of the elect increases, till it be fulfilled.

Matthew Paris.

[108] The arabian horses are divided into two great branches; the Kadischi whose descent is unknown, and the Kochlani, of whom a written genealogy has been kept for 2000 years. These last are reserved for riding solely, they are highly esteemed and consequently very dear, they are said to derive their origin from King Solomon's studs, however this may be they are fit to bear the greatest fatigues, and can pass whole days without food, they are also said to show uncommon courage against an enemy, it is even asserted, that when a horse of this race finds himself wounded and unable to bear his rider much longer, he retires from the fray and conveys him to a place of security. If the rider falls upon the ground his horse remains beside him, and neighs till assistance is brought: the Kochlani are neither large nor handsome but amazingly swift, the whole race is divided into several families, each of which has its proper name. Some of these have a higher reputation than others, on account of their more ancient and uncontaminated nobility.

Niebuhr.

[109] In travelling by night thro' the vallies of Mount Ephraim, we were attended, for above the space of an hour, with an Ignis Fatuus, that displayed itself in a variety of extraordinary appearances. For it was sometimes globular, or like the flame of a candle; immediately after it would spread itself and involve our whole company in its pale inoffensive light, then at once contract itself and disappear. But in less than a minute it would again exert itself as at other times, or else, running along from one place to another with a swift progressive motion, would expand itself, at certain

intervals over more than two or three acres of the adjacent mountains. The atmosphere from the beginning of the evening, had been remarkably thick and hazy, and the dew, as we felt it upon our bridles, was unusually clammy and unctuous. In the like disposition of the weather, I have observed those luminous bodies, which at sea skip about the masts and yards of ships, and are called Corpusánse[i] by the mariners.

Shaw.

[i] A corruption of Cuerpo Santo as this meteor is called by the Spaniards.

[110] The Hammam Meskouteen, the Silent or Inchanted Baths, are situated on a low ground, surrounded with mountains. There are several fountains that furnish the water, which is of an intense heat, and falls afterwards into the Ze-nati. At a small distance from these hot fountains, we have others, which upon comparison are of as an intense a coldness; and a little below them, somewhat nearer the banks of the Ze-nati, there are the ruins of a few houses, built perhaps for the conveniency of such persons, who came hither for the benefit of the waters.

Besides the strong sulphureous steams of the Hammam[j] Meskouteen, we are to observe farther of them, that their water is of so intense a heat, that the rocky ground it runs over, to the distance sometimes of a hundred foot, is dissolved, or rather calcined by it. When the substance of these rocks is soft and uniform, then the water by making every way equal impressions, leaveth them in the shape of cones or hemispheres; which being six foot high and a little more or less of the same diameter, the Arabs maintain to be so many tents of their predecessors turned into stone. But when these rocks, besides their usual soft chalky substance, contain likewise some layers of harder matter, not so easy to be dissolved, then, in proportion to the resistance the water is thereby to meet with, we are entertained with a confusion of traces and channels, distinguished by the Arabs into Sheep, Camels, Horses, nay into Men, Women and Children, whom they suppose to have undergone the like fate with their habitations. I observed that the fountains which afforded this water, had been frequently stopped up: or rather ceasing to run at one place, broke out immediately in another, which circumstance seems not only to account for the number of cones, but for that variety likewise of traces, that are continued from one or other of these cones or fountains, quite down to the river Zenati.

[j] They call the Thermæ of this country Hammams, from whence our Hummums.

This place, in riding over it, giveth back such a hollow sound, that we were afraid every moment of sinking thro' it. It is probable therefore that the ground below us was hollow: and may not the air then, which is pent up within these caverns, afford, as we may suppose, in escaping continually thro' these fountains, that mixture of shrill, murmuring and deep sounds, which, according to the direction of the winds and the motion of the external air, issue out along with the water? the Arabs, to quote their strength of imagination once more, affirm these sounds to be the music of the Jenoune, Fairies, who are supposed, in a particular manner, to make their abodes at this place, and to be the grand agents in all these extraordinary appearances.

There are other natural curiosities likewise at this place. For the chalky stone being dissolved into a fine impalpable powder and carried down afterwards with the stream, lodgeth itself upon the sides of the channel, nay sometimes upon the lips of the fountains themselves; or else embracing twigs, straws and other bodies in its way, immediately hardeneth and shoots into a bright fibrous substance, like the Asbestos, forming itself at the same time, into a variety of glittering figures and beautiful christalizations.

Shaw.

[111] In the place where the Whang-ho rises, there are more than an hundred springs which sparkle like stars, whence it is called Hotun Nor, the Sea of Stars. These sources form two great lakes called Hala Nor, the black sea or lake; afterwards there appear 3 or 4 little rivers, which join'd form the Whang-ho, which has 8 or 9 branches. These sources of the river are called also Oton-tala. It is in Thibet.

Gaubil. Astley's Collect. of Voy. and Travels.

The Whang ho, or as the Portugueze call it Hoam-ho, i. e. the yellow River, rises not far from the source of the Ganges in the Tartarian mountains west of China, and having run thro' it with a course of more than six hundred leagues, discharges itself into the eastern sea. It hath its name from a yellow mud which always stains its water, and which after rains composes a third part of its quantity. The watermen clear it for use by throwing in alum. The Chinese say its waters cannot become clear in a thousand years; whence it is a common proverb among them for any thing which is never likely to happen, when the yellow river shall run clear.

Note to the Chinese Tale Hau Kiou Choann.

[112] Among the mountains of the Beni Abbess, four leagues to the S. E. of the Welled Mansoure, we pass thro' a narrow winding defile, which, for the space of near half a mile, lyeth on each side under an exceeding high precipice, at every winding, the Rock or Stratum, that originally went across it and thereby separated one valley from another, is cut into the fashion of a door case six or seven feet wide, giving thereby the Arabs an occasion to call them Beeban, the Gates; whilst the Turks in consideration of their strength and ruggedness, know them by the additional appellation of Dammer Cappy, the Gates of Iron. Few persons pass them without horror, a handful of men being able to dispute the passage with a whole Army. The rivulet of salt water which glides thro' this valley, might possibly first point out the way which art and necessity would afterwards improve.

Shaw.

[113] In 1568 the Persian Sultan gave the Grand Seigneur two most stately pavilions made of one piece, the curtains being interlaced with gold and the supporters imbroidred with the same, also nine fair conopies to hang over the ports of their pavilions, things not used among the Christians.

Knolles.

[114] The expences the Persians are at in their gardens is that wherein they make greatest ostentation of their wealth. Not that they much mind furnishing of them with delightful flowers as we do in Europe; but these they slight as an excessive liberality of Nature by whom their common fields are strewed with an infinite number of tulips and other flowers; but they are rather desirous to have their gardens full of all sorts of fruit trees, and especially to dispose them into pleasant walks of a kind of plane or poplar, a tree not known in Europe, which the Persians call Tzinnar. These trees grow up to the height of the Pine, and have very broad leaves not much unlike those of the vine. Their fruit hath some resemblance to the chesnut, while the outer coat is about it, but there is no kernel within it, so that it is not to be eaten. The wood thereof is very brown and full of veins, and the Persians use it in doors and shutters for windows, which being rubbed with oil, look incomparably better than any thing made of wallnut tree, nay indeed than the root of it which is now[k] so very much esteemed.

Amb. Travels.

[k] 1637.

[115] Major Scott informs us that scars and wounds by Persian writers are compared to the streaky tints of the tulip. The simile here employed is equally obvious and more suited to its place.

[116] "We pitched our tents among some little hills where there was a prodigious number of lillies of many colours, with which the ground was quite covered. None were white, they were mostly either of a rich violet with a red spot in the midst of each leaf, or of a fine black and these were the most esteemed. In form they were like our lillies, but much larger."

Tavernier.

[117] This was an expression of Ariosto in one of his smaller poems, I believe in a Madrigal. I cannot now quote the line.

[118] The Thracians say that the nightingales which build their nests about the Sepulchre of Orpheus sing sweeter and louder than other nightingales.

Pausanias.

Gongora has addressed this Bird with somewhat more than his usual extravagance of absurdity,

Con diferencia tal, con gracia tanta
Aquel Ruiseñor llora, que sospecho,
Que tiene otros cien mil dentro del pecho,
Que alternan su dolor por su garganta.

With such a grace that Nightingale bewails
That I suspect, so exquisite his note,
An hundred thousand other Nightingales
Within him, warble sorrow thro' his throat.

[119] In the Caherman Nameh, the Dives having taken in war some of the Peris, imprisoned them in iron cages, which they hung from the highest trees they could find. There from time to time their companions visited them, with the most precious odours. These odours were the usual food of the Peris, and procured them also another advantage, for they prevented the Dives from approaching or molesting them. The Dives could not bear the perfumes, which rendered them gloomy and melancholy whenever they drew near the cage in which a Peri was suspended.

D'Herbelot.

[120] Nuptials of Mohammed and Cadijah.—Dum autem ad nuptias celebrandas solemnissimum convivium pararetur, concussus est Angelis admirantibus, thronus Dei: atque ipse Deus majestate plenus præcepit Custodi Paradisi, ut puellas, & pueros ejus cum festivis ornamentis educeret, & calices ad bibendum ordinatim disponeret: grandiores item puellas, & jam sororiantibus mammis præditas, & juvenes illis coævos, pretiosis vestibus indueret. Jussit proeterea Gabrielem vexillum laudis supra Meccanum Templum explicare. Tunc vero valles omnes & montes proe loetitiâ gestire cæperunt, & tota Mecca nocte illa velut olla super ignem imposita efferbuit.—Eodem tempore proecepit Deus Gabrieli, ut super omnes mortales unguenta pretiosissima dispergeret, admirantibus

omnibus subitum illum atque insolitum odorem, quem in gratiam novorum conjugum divinitus exhalasse universi cognovere.

Maracci.

[121] Sclymus 2. received the Embassadors sitting upon a pallat which the Turks call Mastabe used by them in their chambers to sleep and to feed upon, covered with carpets of silk, as was the whole floor of the chamber also.

Knolles.

Among the presents that were exchanged between the Persian and Ottoman Sovereigns in 1568, were carpets of silk, of camel's hair, lesser ones of silk and gold, and some called Teftich; made of the finest lawn, and so large that seven men could scarcely carry one of them.

Knolles.

In the beautiful story of Ali Beg it is said Cha Sefi when he examined the house of his father's favourite was much surprized at seeing it so badly furnished with plain skins and coarse carpets, whereas the other Nobles in their houses trod only upon carpets of silk and gold.

Tavernier.

[122] On the way from Macao to Canton in the rivers and channels there is taken a vast quantity of oysters, of whose shells they make glass for the windows.

Gemelli Careri.

In the Chinese Novel Hau Kiou Choaan, we read Shueyping-sin ordered her servants to hang up a curtain of mother of pearl across the hall. She commanded the first table to be set for her guest without the curtain and two lighted tapers to be placed upon it. Afterwards she ordered a second table, but without any light, to be set for herself within the curtain, so that she could see every thing thro' it, unseen herself.

Master George Turbervile in his letters form Muscovy 1568, describes the Russian windows

They have no English glasse; of slices of a rocke Hight Sluda they their windows make, that English glasse doth mocke. They cut it very thinne, and sow it with a thred In pretie order like to panes, to serve their present need. No other glasse, good faith, doth give a better light, And sure the rock is nothing rich, the cost is very slight.

Hakluyt.

The Indians of Malabar use mother of pearl for window panes.

Fra Paolino da San Batolomeo.

[123] The King and the great Lords have a sort of cellar for magnificence, where they sometimes drink with persons whom they wish to regale. These cellars are square rooms, to which you descend by only two or three steps. In the middle is a small cistern of water, and a rich carpet covers the ground from the walls to the cistern. At the four corners of the cistern are four large glass bottles,

each containing about twenty quarts of wine, one white, another red. From one to the other of these, smaller bottles are ranged of the same material and form, that is, round with a long neck, holding about four or five quarts, white and red alternately. Round the cellar are several rows of niches in the wall, and in each nich is a bottle also of red and white alternately.—Some niches are made to hold two. Some windows give light to the apartment, and all these bottles so well ranged with their various colours have a very fine effect to the eye. They are always kept full, the wine preserving better, and therefore are replenished as fast as they are emptied.

Tavernier.

[124] The Cuptzi, or King of Persia's merchant, treated us with a collation, which was served in, in plate vermilion-gilt.

The Persians having left us, the Ambassadors sent to the Chief Weywode a present, which was a large drinking cup, vermilion-gilt.

Ambassador's Travels.

At Ispahan the King's horses were watered with silver pails thus coloured.

The Turks and Persians seem wonderfully fond of gilding, we read of their gilt stirrups, gilt bridles, gilt maces, gilt scymetars, &c. &c.

[125] Mohammedes vinum appellabat Matrem peccatorum; cui sententiæ
Hafez, Anacreon ille Persarum, minime ascribit suam; dicit autem

"Acre illud (vinum) quod vir religiosus matrem peccatorum vocitat,
Optabilius nobis ac dulcius videtur, quam virginis suavium."
Poeseos Asiat. Com.

Illide ignem illum nobis liquidum,
Hoc est, ignem illum aquæ similem affer.

Hafez.

[126] They export from Com earthen ware both white and varnished, and this is peculiar to the white ware which is thence transported, that in the summer it cools the water wonderfully and very suddenly, by reason of continual transpiration. So that they who desire to drink cool and deliciously, never drink in the same pot above five or six days at most. They wash it with rose water the first time, to take away the ill smell of the earth, and they hang it in the air full of water, wrapped up in a moist linen cloth. A fourth part of the water transpires in six hours the first time; after that still less from day to day, till at last the pores are closed up by the thick matter contained in the water which stops in the pores. But so soon as the pores are stopt, the water stinks in the pots, and you must take new ones.

Chardin.

In Egypt people of fortune burn Scio mastic in their cups, the penetrating odour of which pervades the porous substance, which remains impregnated with it a long time, and imparts to the water a perfume which requires the aid of habit to render it pleasing.

Sonnini.

[127] Casbin produces the fairest grape in Persia, which they call Shahoni, or the royal grape, being of a gold colour, transparent, and as big as a small olive. These grapes are dried and transported all over the kingdom. They also make the strongest wine in the world and the most luscious, but very thick as all strong and sweet wines usually are. This incomparable Grape grows only upon the young branches, which they never water. So that for five months together they grow in the heat of summer and under a scorching sun, without receiving a drop of water, either from the sky or otherwise. When the vintage is over, they let in their cattle to browze in the vineyards, afterwards they cut off all the great wood, and leave only the young stocks about three foot high, which need no propping up with poles as in other places, and therefore they never make use of any such supporters.

Chardin.

[128] Dr. Fryer received a present from the Caun of Bunder-Abassæ of Apples candied in snow.

When Tavernier made his first visit to the Kan at Erivan, he found him with several of his Officers regaling in the Chambers of the Bridge. They had wine which they cooled with ice, and all kinds of fruit and melons in large plates, under each of which was a plate of ice.

A great number of camels were laden with snow to cool the liquors and fruit of the Caliph Mahadi, when he made the pilgrimage to Mecca.

[129] Of the Indian dancing women who danced before the Ambassadors at Ispahan, "some were shod after a very strange manner, they had above the instep of the foot a string tied, with little bells fastened thereto, whereby they discovered the exactness of their cadence, and sometimes corrected the music itself; as they did also by the Tzarpanes or Castagnets, which they had in their hands, in the managing whereof they were very expert."

At Koojar Mungo Park saw a dance "in which many performers assisted, all of whom were provided with little bells, which were fastened to their legs and arms."

[130] At Seronge a sort of cloth is made so fine, that the skin may be seen thro' it, as tho' it were naked. Merchants are not permitted to export this, the Governor sending all that is made to the Seraglio of the Great Mogul and the chief Lords of his court. C'est de quoy les Sultanes & les femmes des Grands Seigneurs, se font des chemises, & des robes pour la chaleur, & le Roy & les Grands se plaisent a les voir au travers de ces chemises fines, & a les faire danser.

Tavernier.

[131] I came to a Village called Cupri-Kent, or the Village of the bridge, because there is a very fair bridge that stands not far from it, built upon a river called Tabadi. This bridge is placed between two mountains separated only by the river, and supported by four arches, unequal both in their height and breadth. They are built after an irregular form, in regard of two great heaps of a rock that stand in the river, upon which they laid so many arches. Those at the two ends are hollowed on both sides and serve to lodge passengers, wherein they have made to that purpose little chambers and porticos, with every one a chimney. The Arch in the middle of the river is hollowed quite thro' from one part to the other with two chambers at the ends, and two large balconies covered, where they take the cool air in the summer with great delight, and to which there is a descent of two pair of stairs hewn out of the rock, there is not a fairer bridge in all Georgia.

Chardin.

Over the river Isperuth "there is a very fair bridge, built on six arches, each whereof hath a spacious room, a kitchen and several other conveniences, lying even with water, the going down into it is by a stone pair of stairs, so that this bridge is able to find entertainment for a whole caravanne."

Amb. Tr.

The most magnificent of these bridges is the Bridge of Zulpha at Ispahan.

[132] The dust which overspreads these beds of sand is so fine, that the lightest animal, the smallest insect, leaves there as on snow, the vestiges of its track. The varieties of these impressions produce a pleasing effect, in spots where the saddened soul expects to meet with nothing but symptoms of the proscriptions of nature. It is impossible to see any thing more beautiful than the traces of the passage of a species of very small lizards extremely common in these desarts. The extremity of their tail forms regular sinuosities, in the middle of two rows of delineations, also regularly imprinted by their four feet, with their five slender toes. These traces are multiplied and interwoven near the subterranean retreats of these little animals, and present a singular assemblage which is not void of beauty.

Sonnini.

[133] These lines are feebly adapted from a passage in Burnet's Theory of the Earth.

Hæc autem dicta vellem de genuinis & majoribus terræ montibus; non gratos Bacchi colles hîc intelligimus, aut amoenos illos monticulos, qui viridi herbâ & vicino fonte & arboribus, vim æstivi solis repellunt: hisce non deest sua qualiscunque elegantia, & jucunditas. Sed longe aliud hic respicimus, nempe longæva illa, tristia & squalentia corpora, telluris pondera, quæ duro capiti rigent inter nubes, infixisque in terram saxeis pedibus, ab innumeris seculis steterunt immobilia, atque nudo pectore pertulerunt tot annorum ardentes soles, fulmina & procellas. Hi sunt primævi & immortales illi montes, qui non aliunde, quam ex fractâ mundi compage ortum suum ducere potuerunt, nec nisi cum eâdem perituri sunt.

The whole chapter de montibus is written with the eloquence of a Poet. Indeed Gibbon bestowed no exaggerated praise on Burnet in saying that he had "blended scripture, history, and tradition into one magnificent system, with a sublimity of imagination scarcely inferior to Milton himself." This work should be read in Latin, the Author's own translation is miserably inferior. He lived in the worst age of English prose.

[134] The Zaccoum is a tree which issueth from the bottom of Hell: the fruit thereof resembleth the heads of Devils; and the damned shall eat of the same, and shall fill their bellies therewith; and there shall be given them thereon a mixture of boiling water to drink; afterwards shall they return to Hell.

Koran. Chap. 37.

This hellish Zaccoum has its name from a thorny tree in Tehâma, which bears fruit like an almond, but extremely bitter; therefore the same name is given to the infernal tree.

Sale.

[135] When the sister of the famous Derar was made prisoner before Damascus with many other Arabian women, she excited them to mutiny, they seized the poles of the tents and attacked their captors. This bold resolution, says Marigny, was not inspired by impotent anger. Most of these women had military inclinations already; particularly those who were of the tribe of Hemiar or of the Homerites, where they are early exercised in riding the horse, and in using the bow, the lance, and the javelin. The revolt was successful, for during the engagement Derar came up to their assistance.

Marigny.

[136] In the N. E. parts of Persia there was an old man named Aloadin, a Mahumetan, which had inclosed a goodly vally, situate between two hilles, and furnished it with all variety which Nature and Art could yield, as fruits, pictures, rilles of milk, wine, honey, water, pallaces, and beautifull damosells, richly attired, and called it Paradise. To this was no passage but by an impregnable castle, and daily preaching the pleasures of this Paradise to the youth which he kept in his court, sometimes would minister a sleepy drinke to some of them, and then conveigh them thither, where being entertained with these pleasures 4 or 5 days they supposed themselves rapt into Paradise, and then being again cast into a trance by the said drink, he caused them to be carried forth, and then would examine them of what they had seene, and by this delusion would make them resolute for any enterprize which he should appoint them, as to murther any Prince his enemy, for they feared not death in hope of their Mahumetical Paradise. But Haslor or Ulan after 3 years siege destroyed him and this his fools Paradise.

Purchas.

In another place Purchas tells the same tale, but calls the Impostor Aladeules, and says that Selim the Ottoman Emperor, destroyed his Paradise.

The story is told by so many writers and with such difference of time and place, as wholly to invalidate its truth, even were the circumstances more probable.

Travelling on further towards the south, I arrived at a certaine countrey called Melistorte, which is a very pleasant and fertile place. And in this countrey there was a certeine aged man called Senex de monte, who round about two mountaines had built a wall to inclose the sayd mountaines. Within this wall there were the fairest and most chrystall fountaines in the whole world: and about the sayd fountaines there were most beautiful virgins in great number, and goodly horses also, and in a word every thing that could be devised for bodily solace and delight, and therefore the inhabitants of the countrey call the same place by the name of Paradise.

The sayd olde Senex, when he saw any proper and valiant young man, he would admit him into his paradise. Moreover by certaine conducts he makes wine and milke to flow abundantly. This Senex, when he hath a minde to revenge himselfe, or to slay any king or baron, commandeth him that is governor of the sayd paradise, to bring thereunto some of the acquaintance of the sayd king or baron, permitting him awhile to take his pleasure therein, and then to give him a certeine potion being of force to cast him into such a slumber as should make him quite voide of all sense, and so being in a profound sleepe to convey him out of his paradise: who being awaked, and seeing himselfe thrust out of the paradise, would become so sorrowfull, that he could not in the world devise what to do, or whither to turne him. Then would he go unto the foresaide old man, beseeching him that he might be admitted againe into his paradise: who saith unto him, you cannot be admitted thither, unlesse you will slay such or such a man for my sake, and if you will give the attempt onely whether you kill him or no, I wil place you againe in paradise, that there you may remaine alwayes: then would the party without faile put the same in execution, indevouring to murther all those against whom the sayd olde man had conceived any hatred. And therefore all the kings of the east stood in awe of the sayd olde man, and gave unto him great tribute.

And when the Tartars had subdued a great part of the world, they came unto the sayd olde man, and tooke from him the custody of his paradise: who being incensed thereat, sent abroad divers desperate and resolute persons out of his forenamed paradise, and caused many of the Tartarian nobles to be slaine. The Tartars seeing this, went and besieged the city wherein the sayd olde man was, tooke him, and put him to a most cruell and ignominious death.

Odoricus.

The most particular account is given by that undaunted liar Sir John Maundevile.

"Beside the Yle of Pentexoire, that is the Lond of Prestre John, is a gret Yle long and brode, that men clepen Milsterak; and it is in the Lordschipe of Prestre John. In that Yle is gret plentee of godes. There was dwellinge somtyme a ryche man; and it is not long sithen, and men clept him Gatholonabes; and he was full of cauteles and of sotylle disceytes: and had a fulle fair Castelle and a strong, in a mountayne, so strong and so noble that no man cowde devise a fairere ne a strengere. And he had let muren all the mountayne aboute with a strong walle and a fair. And with inne the walles he had the fairest gardyn that ony man might behold; and therein were trees beryinge all maner of frutes that ony man cowde devyse, and therein were also alle maner vertuous herbes of gode smelle, and alle other herbes also that beren faire floures, and he had also in that gardyn many faire welles, and beside the welles he had lete make faire halles and faire chambres, depeynted alle with gold and azure. And there weren in that place many dyverse thinges, and many dyverse stories: and of bestes and of bryddes that songen fulle delectabely, and moveden be craft that it semede that thei weren quyke. And he had also in his gardyn all maner of fowles and of bestes, that ony man myghte thinke on, for to have pley or desport to beholde hem. And he had also in that place, the faireste Damyseles that myghte ben founde under the age of 15 Zere, and the fairest zonge striplynges that men myghte gete of that same age: and all thei weren clothed in clothes of Gold fully rychely, and he seyde that tho weren Angeles. And he had also let make 3 welles faire and noble and all envyround with ston of Jaspre, of cristalle, dyapred with gold and sett with precious stones and grete orient Perles. And he had made a conduyt under erthe, so that the 3 Welles, at his list, on scholde renne milk, another wyn, and another hony and that place he clept Paradys. And whan that ony gode Knyght, that was hardy and noble, cam to see this Rialtee, he would lede him into his Paradys, and schewen him theise wondirfulle thinges to his desport, and the marveyllous and delicious song of dyverse Bryddes, and the faire Damyseles and the faire welles of mylk, wyn, and honey plentevous rennynge. And he woulde let make dyverse instrumentes of musick to sownen in an high Tour, so merily that it was joye for to here, and no man scholde see the craft thereof: and tho, he sayde, weren Aungeles of God, and that place was Paradys that God had behyghte to his friendes, saying Dabo vobis terram fluentem lacte & melle. And thanne wolde he maken hem to drynken of certeyn drynk, whereof anon thei sholden be dronken, and thanne wolde hem thinken gretter delyt than thei hadden before. And then wolde he seye to hem that zif thei wolde dyen for him and for his love, that after hire dethe thei scholde come to his Paradys, and their scholde ben of the age of the Damyseles, and thei scholde pleyen with hem and zit ben Maydenes. And after that zit scholde he putten hem in a fayrere Paradys, where that thei scholde see God of nature visibely in his Magestee and in his blisse. And than wolde he schewe hem his entent and seye hem, that zif thei wolde go sle such a Lord, or such a man, that was his Enemye or contrarious to his list, that thei scholde not drede to don it, and for to be sleyn therefore hemself: for aftir hire dethe he wolde putten hem into another Paradys, that was an 100 fold fairere than ony of the tothere: and there scholde thei dwellen with the most fairest Damyseles that myghte be, and pley with hem ever more. And thus wenten many dyverse lusty Bacheleres for to sle grete Lords, in dyverse Countrees, that weren his enemyes, and maden hemself to ben slayn in hope to have that Paradys. And thus often tyme he was revenged of his enemyes by his sotylle disceytes and false cauteles. And whan the worthe men of the Contree hadden perceyved this sotylle falshod of this Gatholonabes, thei assembled hem with force, and assayleden his Castelle, and slowen him, and destroyden all the faire places, and alle the nobletees of that Paradys. The place of the welles and of the walles and of many other thinges bene zit apertly sene, but the richesse is voyded clene, and it is not long gon sithen that place was destroyed."

Sir John Maundeville.

[137] Let the royal apparel be brought which the King useth to wear, and the horse that the King rideth upon, and the crown royal which is set upon his head:

And let this apparel and horse be delivered to the hand of one of the King's most noble princes, that they may array the man withal whom the King delighteth to honour, and bring him on horseback thro' the street of the city, and proclaim before him, Thus shall it be done to the man whom the King delighteth to honour.

Esther.. VI. 8. 9.

[138] As the celestial Apostle, at his retreat from Medina, did not perform always the five canonical prayers at the precise time, his disciples, who often neglected to join with him in the Namaz, assembled one day to fix upon some method of announcing to the public those moments of the day and night when their master discharged this first of religious duties. Flags, bells, trumpets, and fire were successively proposed as signals. None of these, however, were admitted. The flags were rejected as unsuited to the sanctity of the object; the bells, on account of their being used by Christians; the trumpets, as appropriated to the Hebrew worship; the fire, as having too near an analogy to the religion of the pyrolators. From this contrariety of opinions the disciples separated without any determination. But one of them, Abdullah ibn Zeid Abderiyé, saw the night following, in a dream, a celestial being clothed in green: he immediately requested his advice, with the most zealous earnestness, respecting the object in dispute. I am come to inform you, replied the heavenly visitor, how to discharge this important duty of your religion. He then ascended to the roof of the house, and declared the Ezann with a loud voice, and in the same words which have been ever since used to declare the canonical periods. When he awoke, Abdullah ran to declare his vision to the prophet, who loaded him with blessings, and authorized that moment Bilal Habeschy, another of his disciples, to discharge, on the top of his house, that august office, by the title of Muzzinn.

These are the words of the Ezann: Most high God! most high God! most high God! I acknowledge that there is no other except God; I acknowledge that there is no other except God! I acknowledge that Mohammed is the Prophet of God! come to prayer! come to prayer! come to the temple of salvation! Great God! great God! there is no God except God.

This declaration must be the same for each of the five canonical periods, except that of the morning, when the Muezzinn ought to add, after the words, come to the temple of salvation, the following: prayer is to be preferred to sleep, prayer is to be preferred to sleep.

This addition was produced by the zeal and piety of Bilal Habeschy: as he announced one day the Ezann of the dawn in the prophet's antichamber, Aische in a whisper informed him, that the celestial envoy was still asleep; this first of the Muezzinns then added these words, prayer is to be preferred to sleep: when he awoke the prophet applauded him, and commanded Bilal to insert them in all the morning Ezanns.

The words must be chanted, but with deliberation and gravity, those particularly which constitute the profession of the faith. The Muezzinn must pronounce them distinctly; he must pay more attention to the articulation of the words than to the melody of his voice; he must make proper intervals and pauses, and not precipitate his words, but let them be clearly understood by the people. He must be interrupted by no other object whatever. During the whole Ezann he must stand, with a finger in each ear, and his face turned, as in prayer, towards the Keabe of Mecca. As he utters these words, come to prayer, come to the temple of salvation, he must turn his face to the right and left, because he is supposed to address all the nations of the world, the whole expanded universe. At this time the auditors must recite with a low voice the Tehhlil. There is no strength, there is no power, but what is in God, in that supreme Being, in that powerful Being.

D'Ohsson.

[139] In the Meidan, or Great Place of the city of Tauris, there are people appointed every evening when the sun sets, and every morning when he rises, to make during half an hour a terrible concert of trumpets and drums. They are placed on one side of the Square, in a gallery somewhat elevated; and the same practice is established in every city in Persia.

Tavernier.

[140] If we except a few persons, who are buried within the precincts of some sanctuary, the rest are carried out at a distance from their cities and villages, where a great extent of ground is allotted for that purpose. Each family hath a particular portion of it, walled in like a garden, where the bones of their ancestors have remained undisturbed for many generations. For in these enclosures[l] the graves are all distinct and separate; having each of them a stone, placed upright, both at the head and feet, inscribed with the name of the person who lieth there interred; whilst the intermediate space is either planted with flowers, bordered round with stone or paved all over with tiles. The graves of the principal citizens are further distinguished by some square chambers or Cupolas[m] that are built over them.

[l] These seem to be the same with the [Greek: Periboloi] of the Antients. Thus Euripides. Troad. l. 1141.

[Greek: All' anti kedrou peribolôn telainôn
En têde thapsai paida.]

[m] Such places probably as these are to be understood, when the Demoniack is said to have his dwelling among the tombs.

Now as all these different sorts of tombs and sepulchres, with the very walls likewise of the enclosures, are constantly kept clean, white-washed and beautified, they continue, to this day, to be an excellent comment upon that expression of our Saviour's, where he mentions the garnishing of the sepulchres, and again where he compares the scribes, pharisees and hypocrites, to whited sepulchres, which indeed appear beautiful outward, but are within full of dead men's bones and all uncleanness. For the space of two or three months after any person is interred, the female relations go once a week to weep over the grave and perform their parentalia upon it.

Shaw.

About a quarter of a mile from the town of Mylasa, is a sepulchre of the species called by the antients, Distoeya or Double-roofed. It consisted of two square rooms. In the lower, which has a door way, were deposited the urns with the ashes of the deceased. In the upper, the relations and friends solemnized the anniversary of the funeral, and performed stated rites. A hole made through the floor was designed for pouring libations of honey, milk, or wine, with which it was usual to gratify the manes or spirits.

Chandler's Travels in Asia Minor.

[141] In the Lettres Juives is the following extract from the Mercure Historique et Politique. Octob. 1736.

We have had in this country a new scene of Vampirism, which is duly attested by two officers of the Tribunal of Belgrade, who took cognizance of the affair on the spot, and by an officer in his Imperial Majesty's troops at Gradisch (in Sclavonia) who was an eye-witness of the proceedings.

In the beginning of September there died at the village of Kisilova, three leagues from Gradisch, an old man of above threescore and two: three days after he was buried he appeared in the night to his son, and desired he would give him somewhat to eat, and then disappeared. The next day the son told his neighbours these particulars. That night the Father did not come, but the next evening he made him another visit, and desired something to eat. It is not known whether his son gave him any thing or not, but the next morning the young man was found dead in his bed. The Magistrate or Bailiff of the place had notice of this, as also that the same day five or six persons fell sick in the village, and died one after the other. He sent an exact account of this to the tribunal of Belgrade, and thereupon two commissioners were dispatched to the village attended by an executioner, with instructions to examine closely into the affair. An officer in the Imperial service, from whom we have this relation, went also from Gradiseh, in order to examine personally an affair of which he had heard so much. They opened in the first place the graves of all who had been buried in six weeks. When they came to that of the old man, they found his eyes open, his colour fresh, his respiration quick and strong, yet he appeared to be stiff and insensible. From these signs they concluded him to be a notorious Vampire. The executioner thereupon, by the command of the commissioners, struck a stake thro' his heart; and when he had so done, they made a bonfire, and therein consumed the carcase to ashes. There was no marks of Vampirism found on his son, or on the bodies of the other persons who died so suddenly.

Thanks be to God, we are as far as any people can be from giving into credulity, we acknowledge that all the lights of physick do not enable us to give any account of this fact, nor do we pretend to enter into its causes. However, we cannot avoid giving credit to a matter of fact juridically attested by competent and unsuspected witnesses, especially since it is far from being the only one of the kind. We shall here annex an instance of the same sort in 1732, already inserted in the Gleaner, No. 18.

In a certain town of Hungary, which is called in Latin Oppida Heidonum, on the other side Tibiscus, vulgarly called the Teysse; that is to say, the river which washes the celebrated territory of Tokay as also a part of Transilvania. The people known by the name of Heydukes believe that certain dead persons, whom they call Vampires, suck the blood of the living, insomuch that these people appear like skeletons, while the dead bodies of the suckers are so full of blood, that it runs out at all the passages of their bodies, and even at their very pores. This odd opinion of theirs they support by a multitude of facts attested in such a manner, that they leave no room for doubt. We shall here mention some of the most considerable.

It is now about five years ago, that a certain Heyduke, an inhabitant of the village of Medreiga, whose name was Arnold Paul, was bruised to death by a hay-cart, which ran over him. Thirty days after his death, no less than four persons died suddenly, in that manner, wherein, according to the tradition of the country, those people generally die who are sucked by Vampires. Upon this a story was called to mind, that this Arnold Paul had told in his life-time, viz: that at Cossova on the Frontiers of the Turkish Servia, he had been tormented by a Vampire; (now the established opinion is that a person sucked by a Vampire, becomes a Vampire himself, and sucks in his turn.) But that he had found a way to rid himself of this evil, by eating some of the earth out of the Vampire's grave, and rubbing himself with his blood. This precaution however did not hinder his becoming a Vampire; insomuch that his body being taken up forty days after his death, all the marks of a notorious Vampire were found thereon. His complexion was fresh, his hair, nails and beard were grown; he was full of fluid blood, which ran from all parts of his body upon his shroud. The Hadnagy or Bailiff of the place, who was a person well acquainted with Vampirism, caused a sharp stake to be thrust, as the custom is, through the heart of Arnold Paul, and also quite through his body; whereupon he cried out dreadfully as if he had been alive. This done, they cut off his head, burnt his body, and threw the ashes thereof into Saave. They took the same measures with the bodies of those persons who had died of Vampirism, for fear that they should fall to sucking in their turns.

All these prudent steps did not hinder the same mischief from breaking out again about five years afterwards, when several people in the same village died in a very odd manner. In the space of three months, seventeen persons of all ages and sexes died of Vampirism, some suddenly, and some after two or three days suffering. Amongst others there was one Stanoska, the daughter of a Heyduke whose name was Jovitzo who going to bed in perfect health, waked in the middle of the night, and making a terrible outcry, affirmed that the son of a certain Heyduke whose name was Millo, and who had been dead about three weeks, had attempted to strangle her in her sleep. She continued from that time in a languishing condition, and in the space of three days died. What this girl had said discovered the son of Millo to be a Vampire. They took up the body and found him so in effect. The principal persons of the place, particularly the Physician and Surgeons, began to examine very narrowly, how, in spite of all their precautions, Vampirism had again broke out in so terrible a manner. After a strict inquisition, they found that the deceased Arnold Paul had not only sucked the four persons before mentioned, but likewise several beasts, of whom the new Vampires had eaten, particularly the son of Millo. Induced by these circumstances, they took a resolution, of digging up the bodies of all persons who had died within a certain time. They did so, and amongst forty bodies, there were found seventeen evidently Vampires. Through the hearts of these they drove stakes, cut off their heads, burnt the bodies, and threw the ashes into the river. All the informations we have been speaking of were taken in a legal way, and all the executions were so performed, as appears by certificates drawn up in full form, attested by several officers in the neighbouring garrisons, by the surgeons of several Regiments, and the principal inhabitants of the place. The verbal process was sent towards the latter end of last January to the council of war at Vienna, who thereupon established a special commission to examine into these facts. Those just now mentioned were attested by the Hadnagi Barriarer, the principal Heyduke of the village, as also by Battuer, first Lieutenant of Prince Alexander of Wirtemberg, Flickstenger, surgeon major of the regiment of Furstemberg, three other surgeons of the same regiment, and several other persons.

A similar superstition prevails in Greece. The man whose story we are going to relate, was a Peasant of Mycone, naturally ill natured and quarrelsome, this is a circumstance to be taken notice of in such cases. He was murdered in the fields, nobody knew how, or by whom. Two days after his being buried in a Chapel in the town, it was noised about that he was seen to walk in the night with great haste, that he tumbled about people's goods, put out their lamps, griped them behind, and a thousand other monkey tricks. At first the story was received with laughter; but the thing was looked upon to be serious when the better sort of people began to complain of it; the Papas themselves gave credit to the fact, and no doubt had their reasons for so doing; masses must be said, to be sure: but for all this, the Peasant drove his old trade and heeded nothing they could do. After divers meetings of the chief people of the city, of priests, and monks, it was gravely concluded, that 'twas necessary in consequence of some musty ceremonial to wait till nine days after the interment should be expired.

On the tenth day they said one mass in the chapel where the body was laid, in order to drive out the Demon which they imagined was got into it. After mass they took up the body, and got every thing ready for pulling out its heart. The butcher of the town, an old clumsy fellow, first opens the belly instead of the breast, he groped a long while among the entrails, but could not find what he looked for; at last somebody told him he should cut up the Diaphragm. The heart was then pulled out, to the admiration of all the spectators. In the mean time the Corpse stunk so abominably that they were obliged to burn frankincense; but the smoke mixing with the exhalations from the carcass increased the stink, and began to muddle the poor people's pericranies. Their imagination, struck with the spectacle before them, grew full of visions. It came into their noddles, that a thick smoke came out of the body; we durst not say 'twas the smoke of the incense. They were incessantly bawling out Vroucolacas in the chapel and place before it; this is the name they give to these pretended Redivivi. The noise bellowed thro' the streets, and it seemed to be a name invented on purpose to rend the roof of the chapel. Several there present averr'd that the wretches blood was extremely red; the Butcher swore the body was still warm, whence they concluded that the Deceas'd was a very ill man for not being thoroughly dead, or in plain terms for suffering himself to be re-animated by Old Nick; which is the notion they have of Vroucolacas. They then roar'd out that name in a stupendous manner. Just at this time came in a flock of people loudly protesting they plainly perceived the Body was not grown stiff when it was carried from the fields to Church to be buried, and that consequently it was a true Vroucolacas; which word was still the burden of the song.

I don't doubt they would have sworn it did not stink, had not we been there; so mazed were the poor people with this disaster, and so infatuated with their notion of the Dead being re-animated. As for us, who were got as close to the corpse as we could, that we might be more exact in our observations, we were almost poisoned with the intolerable stink that issued from it. When they asked us what we thought of this body, we told them we believed it to be very thoroughly dead: but as we were willing to cure, or at least not to exasperate their prejudiced imaginations, we represented to them, that it was no wonder the butcher should feel a little warmth when he groped among Entrails that were then rotting, that it was no extraordinary thing for it to emit fumes, since dung turned up will do the same; that as for the pretended redness of the blood, it still appeared by the butcher's hands to be nothing but a very stinking nasty smear.

After all our reasons they were of opinion it would be their wisest course to burn the dead man's heart on the sea-shore: but this execution did not make him a bit more tractable; he went on with his racket more furiously than ever; he was accused of beating folks in the night, breaking down doors, and even roofs of houses, clattering windows, tearing clothes, emptying bottles and vessels. 'Twas the most thirsty Devil! I believe he did not spare any body but the Consul in whose house we lodged. Nothing could be more miserable than the condition of this island; all the inhabitants seemed frighted out of their senses: the wisest among them were stricken like the rest; 'twas an epidemical disease of the brain, as dangerous and infectious as the madness of dogs. Whole families quitted their houses, and brought their tent beds from the farthest parts of the town into the public place, there to spend the night. They were every instant complaining of some new insult; nothing was to be heard but sighs and groans at the approach of night: the better sort of people retired into the country.

When the prepossession was so general, we thought it our best way to hold our tongues. Had we opposed it, we had not only been accounted ridiculous blockheads, but Atheists and Infidels, how was it possible to stand against the madness of a whole people? Those that believed we doubted the truth of the fact, came and upbraided us with our incredulity, and strove to prove that there were such things as Vroucolacasses, by citations out of the Buckler of Faith, written by F. Richard a Jesuit Missionary. He was a Latin, say they, and consequently you ought to give him credit. We should have got nothing by denying the justness of the consequence: it was as good as a Comedy to us every morning to hear the new follies committed by this night bird; they charged him with being guilty of the most abominable sins.

Some Citizens, that were most zealous for the good of the public, fancied they had been deficient in the most material part of the ceremony. They were of opinion that they had been wrong in saying mass before they had pulled out the wretches heart: had we taken this precaution, quoth they, we had bit the Devil as sure as a gun; he would have been hanged before he would ever have come there again: whereas saying mass first, the cunning Dog fled for it awhile and came back again when the danger was over.

Notwithstanding these wise reflections, they remained in as much perplexity as they were the first day: they meet night and morning, they debate, they make professions three days and three nights, they oblige the Papas to fast; you might see them running from house to house, holy-water-brush in hand sprinkling it all about, and washing the doors with it; nay they poured it into the mouth of the poor Vroucolacas.

We so often repeated it to the Magistrates of the town, that in Xtendom we should keep the strictest watch a nights upon such an occasion, to observe what was done; that at last they caught a few vagabonds, who undoubtedly had a hand in these disorders: but either they were not the chief ringleaders, or else they were released too soon. For two days afterwards, to make themselves amends for the Lent they had kept in prison, they fell foul again upon the wine tubs of those who were such fools as to leave their houses empty in the night: so that the people were forced to betake themselves again to their prayers.

One day as they were hard at this work, after having stuck I know not how many naked swords over the grave of this corpse, which they took up three or four times a day, for any man's whim; an Albaneze that happened to be at Mycone, took upon him to say with a voice of authority, that it was to the last degree ridiculous to make use of the swords of Xtians in a case like this. Can you not conceive, blind as ye are, says he, that the handles of these swords being made like a cross, hinders the Devil from coming out of the body? Why do you not rather take the Turkish sabres? The advice of this learned man had no effect: the Vroucolacas was incorrigible, and all the inhabitants were in a strange consternation; they knew not now what Saint to call upon, when of a sudden with one voice, as if they had given each other the hint, they fell to bawling out all thro' the city, that it was intolerable to wait any longer; that the only way left was to burn the Vroucolacas intire; that after so doing, let the Devil lurk in it if he could; that 'twas better to have recourse to this extremity than to have the island totally deserted, and indeed whole families began to pack up, in order to retire to Syre or Tinos. The magistrates therefore ordered the Vroucolacas to be carryed to the point of the island St. George, where they prepared a great pile with pitch and tar, for fear the wood, as dry as it was, should not burn fast enough of itself. What they had before left of this miserable carcass was thrown into this fire and consumed presently: 'twas on the first of January, 1701. We saw the flame as we returned from Delos; it might justly be called a bonfire of joy, since after this no more complaints were heard against the Vroucolacas; they said that the Devil had now met with his match, and some ballads were made to turn him into ridicule.

Tournefort.

[142] In these lines I have versified a passage in Bishop Taylor's Sermons, altering as little as possible, his unimproveable language.

"For so have I known a luxuriant Vine swell into irregular twigs and bold excrescencies, and spend itself in leaves and little rings, and afford but trifling clusters to the wine-press, and a faint return to his heart which longed to be refreshed with a full vintage: but when the Lord of the vine had caused the dressers to cut the wilder plant and made it bleed, it grew temperate in its vain expence of useless leaves, and knotted into fair and juicy branches, and made accounts of that loss of blood by the return of fruit."

[143] My readers will recollect the Lenora. The unwilling resemblance has been forced upon me by the subject. I could not turn aside from the road because Burger had travelled it before. The "Old Woman of Berkely" has been foolishly called an imitation of that inimitable Ballad: the likeness is of the same kind as between Macedon and Monmouth. Both are Ballads, and there is a Horse in both.

[144] How came Mohareb to be Sultan of this Island? Every one who has read Don Quixote knows that there are always Islands to be had by Adventurers. He killed the former Sultan and reigned in his stead. What could not a Domdanielite perform? The narration would have interrupted the flow of the main story.

[145] In this valley, we found plenty of provender for our cattle: rosemary bushes, and other shrubs of uncommon fragance, which, being natives of the desert, are still perhaps without a name. Though these scented plants are the usual food of the camel, it is remarkable that his breath is insufferably nauseous. But when he is pushed by hunger, he devours thistles and prickles indiscriminately, without the least damage to his mouth, which seems proof to the sharpest thorns.

Eyles Irwin.

[146] The hawk is used at Aleppo in taking the hare. "As soon as the hare is put up, one, or a brace of the nearest greyhounds are slipped, and the Falconer galloping after them, throws off his hawk. The hare cannot run long where the hawk behaves properly, but sometimes getting the start of the dogs, she gains the next hill and escapes. It now and then happens when the hawk is fierce and voracious in an unusual degree, that the hare is struck dead at the first stroke, but that is very uncommon; for the hawks preferred for hare hunting are taught to pounce and buffet the game, not to seize it, and they rise a little between each attack, to descend again with fresh force. In this manner the game is confused and retarded, till the greyhounds come in.

Russell.

The Shaheen or Falcon Gentle, flies at a more dangerous game. Were there not, says the elder Russell, several gentlemen now in England to bear witness to the truth of what I am going to relate, I should hardly venture to assert that with this bird, which is about the size of a pigeon, they sometimes take large Eagles. The Hawk in former times was taught to seize the Eagle under his pinion, and thus depriving him of the use of one wing, both birds fell to the ground together: but I am informed the present mode is to teach the Hawk to fix on the back between the wings, which has the same effect, only that the bird tumbling down more slowly, the Falconer has more time to come in to his Hawk's assistance; but in either case, if he be not very expeditious, the Falcon is inevitably destroyed.

Dr. Patrick Russell says, this sport was disused in his time, probably from its ending more frequently in the death of the Falcon than of the Eagle. But he had often seen the Shaheen take Herons and Storks. "The hawk when thrown off flies for some time in a horizontal line not six feet from the ground, then mounting perpendicularly with astonishing swiftness, he seizes his prey under the wing, and both together come tumbling to the ground. If the Falconer is not expeditious the game soon disengages itself.

We saw about twenty antelopes, which, however, were so very shy, that we could not get near enough to have a shot, nor do I think it possible to take them without hawks, the mode usually practised in those countries. The swiftest greyhounds would be of no use, for the antelopes are much swifter of foot than any animal I ever saw before.

Jackson's Journey over Land.

The Persians train their hawks thus. They take the whole skin of a stag, of the head, body, and legs, and stuff it with straw to the shape of the animal. After fixing it in the place where they usually train the bird, they place his food upon the head of the stuffed stag, and chiefly in the two cavities of the eyes, that the Bird may strike there. Having accustomed him for several days to eat in this manner, they fasten the feet of the stag to a plank which runs upon wheels, which is drawn by cords from a distance; and from day to day they draw it faster, insensibly to accustom the Bird not to quit his prey; and at last they draw the stag by a horse at full speed. They do the same with the wild boar, the ass, the fox, the hare, and other beasts of chase.—They are even taught to stop a horseman at full speed, nor will they quit him till the Falconer recalls them and shows them their food.

Tavernier.

As the Persians are very patient and not deterred by difficulty, they delight in training the Crow in the same manner as the Hawk.

Tavernier.

I do not recollect in what history or romance there is a tale of two dogs trained in this manner to destroy a Tyrant. But I believe it is an historical fiction. The farmers in Norway believe that the Eagle will sometimes attack a deer, in this enterprize he makes use of this stratagem; he soaks his wings in water, and then covers them with sand and gravel, with which he flies against the deer's face, and blinds him for a time; the pain of this sets him running about like a distracted creature, and frequently he tumbles down a rock or some steep place, and breaks his neck; thus he becomes a prey to the eagle.

Pontoppidan.

[147] I saw this appearance of death at a bull-fight—the detestable amusement of the Spaniards and Portugueze. To the honour of our country, few Englishmen visit these spectacles a second time.

[148] They have a beast called an Ounce, spotted like a Tyger, but very gentle and tame. A horseman carries it, and on perceiving the Gazelle lets it loose: and tho' the Gazelle is incredibly swift, it is so nimble that in three bounds it leaps upon the neck of its prey. The Gazelle is a sort of small antelope, of which the country is full. The Ounce immediately strangles it with its sharp talons, but if unluckily it misses its blow and the Gazelle escapes, it remains upon the spot ashamed and confused, and at that moment a child might take or kill it without its attempting to defend itself.

Tavernier.

The Kings of Persia are very fond of the chase, and it is principally in that, that they display their magnificence. It happened one day that Cha-Sefi wished to entertain all the Ambassadors who were at his court, and there were then ministers there from Tartary, Muscovy and India. He led them to the chase, and having taken in their presence a great number of large animals, stags, does, hinds and wild boars, he had them all dressed and eat the same day, and while they were eating an Architect was ordered to erect a tower in the middle of Ispahan, only with the heads of these animals: the remains of it are yet to be seen. When the Tower was raised to its proper height, the Architect came exultingly to the King who was then at the banquet with the Ambassadors, and informed him that nothing was wanting to finish the work well, but the head of some large beast for the point. The Prince in his drunkenness, and with a design of showing the Ambassadors how absolute he was over his subjects, turned sternly to the Architect—You are right, said he, and I do not know where to find a better head than your own. The unhappy man was obliged to lose his head, and the royal order was immediately executed.

Tavernier.

[149] A serpent which that aspidis
Is cleped, of his kinde hath this,
That he the stone noblest of all
The whiche that men carbuncle call,
Bereth in his head above on high.
For whiche whan that a man by slight
The stone to wynne, and him to dante,
With his carecte him wolde enchante,
Anone as he perceiveth that
He leyth downe his one ear all plat
Unto the ground, and halt it fast,
And eke that other eare als faste
He shoppeth with his taille so sore,
That he the wordes, lasse or more
Of his enchantement ne hereth.
And in this wise himself he skiereth,
So that he hath the wordes wayved,
And thus his eare is nought deceived.
Gower.

Does not "the deaf adder, that heareth not the voice of the charmer, charm he never so wisely," allude to some snake that cannot be enticed by music, as they catch them in Egypt?

[150] As for the wax it is the finest and whitest that may be had tho' of bees: and there is such plenty as serves the whole empire. Several provinces produce it, but that of Huquam exceeds all the others, as well in quantity as whiteness. It is gathered in the province of Xantung upon little trees; but in that of Huquam upon large ones, as big as those of the Indian Pagods, or chesnut-trees in Europe. The way nature has found to produce it, to us appears strange enough. There is in this province a creature, or insect of the bigness of a flea, so sharp at stinging, that it not only pierces the skins of men and beasts, but the boughs and bodies of the trees. Those of the province of Xantung are much valued; where the inhabitants gather their eggs from the trees, and carry them to sell in the province of Huquam. In the spring, there come from these eggs certain worms, which about the beginning of the summer they place at the foot of the tree, whence they creep up, spreading themselves

wonderfully over all the branches. Having placed themselves there, they gnaw, pierce, and bore to the very pith, and their nourishment they convert into wax as white as snow, which they drive out to the mouth of the hole they have made, where it remains congealed in drops by the wind, and cold. Then the owners of the trees gather it, and make it into cakes as we do, which are sold about China.

Gemelli Careri.

Du Halde's account is somewhat different from this, the worms, he says, fasten on the leaves of the tree, and in a short time form combs of wax, much smaller than the Honey Combs.

[151] It being notorious that fire enters into the composition of a Devil, because he breathes smoke and flames, there is an obvious propriety in supposing every Witch her own tinder-box, as they approximate to diabolic nature. I am sorry that I have not the Hierarchie of the Blessed Angels to refer to, otherwise by the best authorities, I could show that is the trick of Beelzebub to parody the costume of religion, the inflammability of Saints may be abundantly exampled.

It happened upon a time, before St. Elfled was chosen Abbesse, that being in the Church at mattins, before day, with the rest of her sisters, and going into the middest according to the custome, to read a lesson, the candle wherewith she saw to read, chanced to be put out, and thereupon wanting light, there came from the fingers of her right hand such an exceeding brightnesse upon the suddaine, that not only herselfe, but all the rest of the Quire also might read by it.

English Martyrologe. 1608.

Dead Saints have frequently possessed this phosphoric quality like rotten wood or dead fish. "St. Bridget was interred at the towne of Dunne in the province of Ulster, in the tombe, togeather with the venerable bodyes of S. Patricke and S. Columbe, which was afterward miraculously reveyled to the Bishop of that place, as he was praying one night late in the church, about the yeare of Christ 1176, over which, there shined a great light."

English Martyrologe.

So when the nurse of Mohammed first entered the chamber of Amena his mother, she saw a coruscating splendour, which was the light of the infant prophet, so that Amena never kindled her lamp at night.

Maracci.

Another Mohammedan miracle of the same genus is no ways improbable. When the head of Hosein was brought to Couffah, the Governor's gates were closed, and Haula the bearer took it to his own house. He awoke his wife and told her what had so speedily brought him home. I bring with me, said he, the most valuable present that could possibly be made to the Caliph, and the woman asking earnestly what it could be, the head of Hosein, here it is, I am sent with it to the Governor. Immediately she sprung from the bed, not that she was shocked or terrified at the sight, for the Arabian women were accustomed to follow the army, and habituated to the sight of blood and massacre. But Hosein by Fatima his mother was grandson of the prophet, and this produced an astonishing effect upon the mind of the woman. By the Apostle of God, she exclaimed, I will never again lie down with a man who has brought me the head of his grandson. The Moslem who according to the custom of his nation had many wives sent for another who was not so conscientious. Yet the presence of the head which was placed upon a table prevented her from sleeping, because she said she saw a great glory playing around if all the night.

Marigny.

After Affonso de Castro had been martyred in one of the Molucca Islands his body was thrown into the sea. But it was in a few days brought back by Providence to the spot where he had suffered, the wounds fresh as if just opened, and so strange and beautiful a splendour flowing from them, that it was evident the fountain of such a light must be that body, whose spirit was in the enjoyment of eternal happiness.

The Moors interpreted one of these phosphoric miracles with equal ingenuity to favour their own creed, a light was seen every night over the tomb of a Maronite whom they had martyred, and they said the Priest was not only tortured with fire in hell, but his very body burnt in the grave.

Vasconcellos.

[152] A well known ceremony of witchcraft, old as classical superstition, and probably not yet wholly disbelieved.

[153] On mount Ararat, which is called Lubar, or the descending place, is an Abbey of St. Gregorie's Monks. These Monkes if any list to believe them, say that there remaineth yet some part of the Arke, kept by Angels; which, if any seeke to ascend, carrie them backe as farre in the night as they have climbed in the day.

Purchas.

[154] A thicket of balm trees is said to have sprung up from the blood of the Moslem slain at Beder.

Ælianus avoucheth, that those vipers which breed in the provinces of Arabia, altho' they do bite, yet their biting is not venomous, because they doe feede on the baulme tree, and sleepe under the shadow thereof.

Treasury of ancient and modern Times.

The balsam tree is nearly of the same size as a sprig of myrtle, and its leaves are like those of the herb sweet-marjoram. Vipers take up their residence about these plants, and are in some places more numerous than in others; for the juice of the balsam tree is their sweetest food, and they are delighted with the shade produced by its leaves. When the time therefore arrives for gathering the juice of this Tree, the Arabians come into the sacred grove, each of them holding two twigs, by shaking these, they put to flight the Vipers; for they are unwilling to kill them, because they consider them as the sacred inhabitants of the balsam. And if it happens that any one is wounded by a Viper, the wound resembles that which is made by iron, but is not attended with any dangerous consequences; for these animals being fed with the juice of the balsam tree, which is the most odoriferous of all trees, their poison becomes changed from a deadly quality into one which produces a milder effect.

Pausanias.

The inhabitants of Helicon say that none of the herbs or roots which are produced in this mountain are destructive to mankind, they add that the pastures here even debilitate the venom of serpents; so that those who are frequently bit by serpents in this part, escape the danger with greater ease than if they were of the nation of the Psylli, or had discovered an antidote against poison.

Pausanias.

[155] The common people of England have long been acquainted with this change which muscular fibre undergoes. Before the circumstance was known to philosophers, I have heard them express a dislike and loathing to spermaceti.—"because it was dead-men's fat."

[156] The Persians are strangely superstitious about the burial of their Kings. For fearing lest by some magical art any enchantments should be practised upon their bodies to the prejudice of their children, they conceal, as much as in them lies, the real place of interment.

To this end they send to several places several coffins of lead, with others of wood, which they call Taboat, and bury all alike with the same magnificence. In this manner they delude the curiosity of the people, who cannot discern by the outside in which of the coffins the real body should be. Not but it might be discovered by such as would put themselves to the expence and trouble of doing it. And thus it shall be related in the life of Habas the great, that twelve of these coffins were conveyed to twelve of the principal Mosques, not for the sake of their riches, but of the person which they enclosed; and yet nobody knew in which of the twelve the King's body was laid, tho' the common belief is, that it was deposited at Ardevil.

It is also said in the life of Sefie I. that there were three coffins carried to three several places, as if there had been a triple production from one body, tho' it were a thing almost certainly known, that the coffin where the body was laid, was carried to this same city of Kom, and to the same place where the deceased King commanded the body of his deceased father to be carried.

Chardin.

They imagine the dead are capable of pain, a Portugueze gentleman had one day ignorantly strayed among the tombs, and a Moor, after much wrangling obliged him to go before the Cadi. The gentleman complained of violence and asserted he had committed no crime, but the judge informed him he was mistaken, for that the poor dead suffered when trodden on by Christian feet. Muley Ishmael once had occasion to bring one of his wives thro' a burial ground, and the people removed the bones of their relations, and murmuring said he would neither suffer the living nor the dead to rest in peace.

Chenier. additional chapt. by the Translator.

Were this Moorish superstition true, there would have been some monkish merit in the last request of St. Swithin, "when he was ready to depart out of this world, he commanded (for humilityes sake) his body to be buried in the Church-yard, whereon every one might tread with their feet.

English Martyrologe.

There is a story recorded, how that St. Frithstane was wont every day to say masse and office for the dead; and one evening as he walked in the Church-yard reciting the said office, when he came to requiescant in pace, the voyces in the graves round about made answere aloud, and said Amen.

English Martyrologe.

[157] The Mohammedan tradition is even more horrible than this: The corpse of the wicked is gnawed and stung till the resurrection of ninety-nine Dragons, with seven heads each, or as others

say, their sins will become venomous Beasts, the grievous ones stinging like Dragons, the smaller like Scorpions, and the others like Serpents; circumstances which some understand in a figurative sense.

Sale's preliminary discourse.

This Mohammedan tale may be traced to the Scripture; "whose worm dieth not."

[158] The night Léïleth-ul-cadr is considered as being particularly consecrated to eneffable mysteries. There is a prevailing opinion, that a thousand secret and invisible prodigies are performed on this night; that all the inanimate beings then pay their adoration to God; that all the waters of the sea lose their saltness and become fresh at these mysterious moments; that such in fine, is its sanctity, that prayers said during this night are equal in value to all those which can be said in a thousand successive months. It has not however pleased God, says the author of the celebrated theological work entitled Ferkann, to reveal it to the faithful: no prophet, no saint has been able to discover it: hence this night, so august, so mysterious, so favoured by Heaven, has hitherto remained undiscovered.

D'Ohsson.

[159] In Persia, when the King is in his Megeler, that is in his Council Chamber, with the Lords whose right it is to be present, there is a sort of half-curtain suspended from a plank, which certain officers wave backward and forward with cords, as a fan, to freshen the air. This is called Badzen, wind for the women.

Tavernier.

[160] A Physician of Ragusa was deputed by that little Republic to negotiate with the Emperor of the Turks. Before he embarked on this voyage he took into his service a boy of a red complection, the only son of a widow, a poor woman, but a woman of honour and virtuous. This Envoy on his arrival at Constantinople immediately addressed himself to the first Physician of his imperial highness, that thro' his favour he might have more access to negociate for his country. The Mahometan had no sooner set eyes on the young Ragusan, than he employed every artifice to induce his master to leave him. The boy himself, at last, wishing to remain at Constantinople, flattered by the fair prospects that were held out to him, and touched with a tender and heroic compassion for her who had given him birth, prayed his protector to leave him with the Barbarian, and carry to his mother the money which on that account he would receive: So that the Ragusan physician left his servant to the Byzantian, and received from him a purse of a thousand sequins. After some days the Italian went to take leave of the Mohammedan Physician, and to thank him for his favours; and he requested earnestly to see the red-headed boy before his departure. The Turk was obliged to own he had made poison of him, and led him into a chamber where the naked body of the boy was still suspended by the feet. The first master of the red-headed boy was greatly surprized at the sight and still more so when he heard that the boy had been beaten upon the belly for six hours, by slaves who relieved one another, till he died: and that a poison was made of the last foam that came from his mouth, so penetrating, that if the stirrup of a horse were touched with the point of a pin that had been dipt in it, he who should mount would immediately die.

Plaidoyers Historiques par M. Tristan. 1650.

In this volume the pleadings of the Mother against the Ragusan physician, and his defence are given. The Mother says, it is impossible that he, being a Physician himself, should not have known for what the Infidel Physician wanted to purchase a red-headed boy, as he himself would have made the same use of him had he not been afraid of the laws, the rest is in the usual stile of Tristan's rhetoric.

As the Moslem employed a red-headed Christian in this manufactory, it should seem that a Turk ought to be used in Christendom. But as Turks are not easily caught, a Jew might do.

In the Islands of Barlovento and in all the country of Brazil, in Santa Marta and in the new kingdom, and in other countries, where a cruel sort of Indians inhabited, they used another sort of poison; for they would take the leg of an Indian whom they had killed, and hang it up in the air against the sun, and fill it with many barbs of poisoned arrows, which were taken out of the flesh of an Indian, which after some days they took out, and without cleansing of them, they dried them in the air where the sun did not come, and then they headed their arrows with them; and that became the most malevolent poison, and the most hard to be cured in the world. After the Spaniards came into that country and waged war upon the Indians, they then made it with the flesh of Spaniards, whom they killed or took; but more particularly they desired the flesh of some red-headed Spaniard, whose hairs were of a deep saffron colour; for they were of opinion that there was more heat in that flesh, and consequently more virulency in the poison which it produced: but perhaps they may have heard it often said amongst the Spaniards themselves, that red-headed men are fit to make a composition of poison.

Garcilasso's Royal Commentaries of Peru.

"Three ounces of a red-haired wench" were among the ingredients of the witch-caldron in Macbeth. Why red-hair was supposed to be a symptom of leprosy, was one of the questions proposed by Michaelis to Niebuhr and his fellow-travellers for investigation. It is singular that at the time when these opinions prevailed universally, golden locks should enter into almost every description of female beauty. If the word of a poet may he taken (and the rhymer now quoted cannot be suspected of invention enough for a lie,) the ladies even wore red wigs, for he says of Absalom

Hasta los hombros pende su cabello
Mas que el oro de Arabia roxo y bello.

Cada año qual renuevo lo cortava
A damas se vendia para ornato.
David, del Doctor Jacobo Uziel.

Adown his shoulders his long tresses roll'd,
More beautiful and red than Eastern gold,
And annual as he cropt, the envied hair
Was yearly sold to ornament the fair.

The Javanese had a method of procuring poison similar to the Turkish receipt which I have employed.

The Cameleon, or Indian Salamander, otherwise called Gekko.

This creature, which is not only found in Brasil, but also in the Isle of Java, belonging to the East Indies, and which by our people is called Gekko, from its constant cry, (like among us that of the Cuckoe) is properly an Indian Salamander. It is about a foot long, its skin of of a pale or sea green colour, with red spots. The head is not unlike that of a tortoise, with a streight mouth. The eyes are very large, starting out of the head, with long and small eye-apples. The tail is distinguished by several white rings; its teeth are so sharp as to make an impression even upon steel. Each of its four legs had five crooked claws aimed on the end with nails. Its gait is very slow, but wherever it fastens it is not easily removed. It dwells commonly upon rotten trees, or among the ruins of old houses and churches; it oftentimes settles near the bedsteads, which makes sometimes the moors pull down their huts.

Its constant cry is gekko, but before it begins it makes a kind of hissing noise. The sting of this creature is so venomous, that the wound proves mortal, unless it be immediately burnt with a red hot iron, or cut off. The blood is of a palish colour, resembling poison itself.

The Javanese use to dip their arrows in the blood of this creature; and those who deal in poisons among them, (an art much esteemed in the island of Java, by both sexes) hang it up with a string tied to the tail on the cieling, by which means it being exasperated to the highest pitch sends forth a yellow liquor out of its mouth, which they gather in small pots set underneath, and afterwards coagulate into a body in the sun. This they continue for several months together, by giving daily food to the creature. It is unquestionably the strongest poison in the world; its urine being of so corrosive a quality, that it not only raises blisters, wherever it touches the skin, but turns the flesh black, and causes a gangrene.

Nieuhoff.

Is there any analogy between a foam thus procured and the saliva of a mad dog?

[161] The fiction of the Upas is too well known from the Botanic Garden, to need repetition. Suffice it here to remark that the Tree is said to have sprung up as a punishment to the guilty Islanders.

None of our early travellers mention this Tree, and they were too fond of wonders to omit so monstrous a tale, had it been true. It is curious that such a story should have been invented by a Dutchman.

Perhaps the seed of the Upas is contained in the following passage.

Neere unto the said Iland (Java) is another countrey called Panten, or Tathalamasin. In this land there are trees yeelding meale, hony and wine, and the most deadly poison in all the whole world: for against it there is but one onely remedy; and that is this; if a man hath taken of the poyson, and would be delivered from the danger thereof, let him temper the dung of aman in water, and so drinke a good quantity thereof and it expels the poyson immediately.

Odoricus the Minorite Frier. In Hakluyt.

[162] When any person is to be buried, it is usual to bring the corpse at mid-day or afternoon prayers, to one or other of these Mosques, from whence it is accompanied by the greatest part of the congregation, to the grave. Their processions, at these times, are not so slow and solemn as in most parts of Christendom: for the whole company make what haste they can, singing as they go along, some select verses of their Coran. That absolute submission which they pay to the will of God, allows them not to use any consolatory words upon these occasions: no loss or misfortune is to be hereupon regretted or complained of: instead likewise of such expressions of sorrow and condolence, as may regard the deceased, the compliments turn upon the person, who is the nearest concerned, a blessing (say his friends) be upon your head.

Shaw.

All Mahometans inter the dead at the hour set apart for prayer; the defunct is not kept in the house, except he expires after sunset, but the Body is transported to the Mosque, whither it is carried by those who are going to prayer; each from a spirit of devotion is desirous to carry in his turn. Women regularly go on Friday to weep over, and pray at the sepulchres of the dead, whose memory they hold dear.

Chenier.

This custom of crowding about a funeral contributes to spread the plague in Turkey.—It is not many years since, in some parts of Worcestershire, the mourners were accustomed to kneel with their heads upon the coffin during the burial service.

The fullest account of a Mohammedan funeral is in the Lettres sur la Grece, of M. Guys. Chance made him the spectator of a ceremony which the Moslem will not suffer an Infidel to prophane by his presence.

"About ten in the morning I saw the grave-digger at work; the slaves and the women of the family were seated in the burial ground, many other women arrived, and then they all began to lament. After this prelude they one after the other embraced one of the little pillars which are placed upon the graves, crying out Ogloum, ogloum, soena Mussaphir gueldi, My Son, my Son, a guest is coming to see thee. At these words their tears and sobs began anew; but the storm did not continue long; they all seated themselves, and entered into conversation.

At noon I heard a confused noise, and cries of lamentation, it was the funeral which arrived. A Turk preceded it, bearing upon his head a small chest; four other Turks carried the bier upon their shoulders, then came the father, the relations and the friends of the dead in great numbers. Their cries ceased at the entrance of the burial ground, but then they quarrelled—and for this. The man who bore the chest opened it, it was filled with copies of the Koran, a croud of Turks, young and old, threw themselves upon the books and scrambled for them. Those who succeeded ranged themselves around the Iman, and all at once began to recite the Koran, almost as Boys say their lesson. Each of the readers received ten parats, about fifteen sols, wrapt in paper. It was then for these fifteen pence that these pious assistants had quarrelled, and in our own country you might have seen them fight for less.

The bier was placed by the grave, in which the grave-digger was still working, and perfumes were burnt by it. After the reading of the Koran the Iman chanted some Arabic prayers, and his full-chant would, no doubt, have appeared to you, as it did to me, very ridiculous. All the Turks were standing; they held their hands open over the grave, and answered Amen to all the prayers which the Iman addressed to God for the deceased.

The prayers finished, a large chest was brought about six feet long and three broad; its boards were very thick. The coffin is usually made of cypress; thus literally is verified the phrase of Horace that the cypress is our last possession.

Neque harum, quas colis, arborum,
Te, præter invisas cupressus,
Ulla brevem dominum sequetur.

The cemeteries of the Turks are usually planted with these trees, to which they have a religious attachment. The chest which was in loose pieces, having been placed in the grave, the coffin was laid in it, and above planks, with other pieces of wood. Then all the Turks, taking spades, cast earth upon the grave to cover it. This is a part of the ceremony at which all the bystanders assisted in their turn.

Before the corpse is buried it is carried to the Mosque. Then after having recited the Fatka (a prayer very similar to our Lord's prayer, which is repeated by all present) the Iman asks the congregation what they have to testify concerning the life and morals of the deceased. Each then in his turn relates those good actions with which he was acquainted. The body is then washed, and wrapped up like a mummy, so that it cannot be seen. Drugs and spices are placed in the bier with it, and it is carried to interment. Before it is lowered into the grave, the Iman commands silence, saying, "Cease your lamentations for a moment, and let me instruct this Moslem how to act, when he arrives in the other world." Then in the ear of the corpse, he directs him how to answer the Evil Spirit who will not fail to question him respecting his religion, &c. This lesson finished, he repeats the Fatka with all the assistants, and the body is let down into the grave. After they have thrown earth three times upon the grave, as the Romans used, they retire. The Iman only remains, he approaches the grave, stoops down, inclines his ear, and listens to hear if the Dead disputes when the Angel of Death comes to take him: then he bids him farewell, and in order to be well paid, never fails to report to the family the best news of the dead.

[163] The Turks bury not at all within the walls of the city, but the great Turkish Emperors themselves, with their wives and children about them, and some few other of their great Bassaes, and those only in chappels by themselves built for that purpose. All the rest of the Turks are buried in the fields; some of the better sort in tombs of marble, but the rest with tomb-stones laid upon them, or with two great stones, one set up at the head and the other at the feet of every grave; the greatest part of them being of white marble, brought from the Isle of Marmora.

They will not bury any man where another hath been buried, accounting it impiety to dig up another man's bones: by reason whereof they cover all the best ground about the city with such great white stones: which, for the infinite number of them, are thought sufficient to make another wall about the city.

Knolles.

The Turks bury by the way-side, believing that the passengers will pray for the souls of the dead.

Tavernier.

[164] All that day we travelled over plains all covered with snow as the day before, and indeed it is not only troublesome but very dangerous to travel thro' these deep snows. The mischief is that the beams of the sun which lie all day long upon it, molest the eyes and face with such a scorching beat as very much weakens the sight, whatever remedy a man can apply, by wearing as the people of the country do, a thin handkerchief of green or black silk, which no way abates the annoyance.

Chardin.

When they have to travel many days thro' a country covered with snow, Travellers to preserve their sight, cover the face with a silk kerchief made on purpose, like a sort of black crape. Others have large furred bonnets, bordered with goat skin, and the long goat-hair hanging over the face is as serviceable as the crape.

Tavernier.

An Abyssinian historian says, that the village, called Zinzenam, rain upon rain, has its name from an extraordinary circumstance that once happened in these parts, for a shower of rain fell, which was not properly of the nature of rain, as it did not run upon the ground, but remained very light, having scarce the weight of feathers, of a beautiful white colour like flower; it fell in showers, and occasioned a darkness in the air more than rain, and liker to mist. It covered the face of the whole country for several days, retaining its whiteness the whole time, then went away like dew, without leaving any smell, or unwholsome effect behind it.

So the Dutch were formerly expelled from an East Indian Settlement, because their Consul, in narrating to the Prince of the Country the wonders of Europe, chanced to say that in his own Country, Water became a solid body once a year, for some time: when Men or even Horses might pass over it without sinking.—The prince in a rage said that he had hitherto listened to his tales with patience, but this was so palpable a Lie, that he would never more be connected with Europeans, who only could assert such monstrous falshoods.

[165] A strange account of the Cedars of Lebanon is given by De la Roque. Voyage de Syrie & du Mont Liban. 1722.

"This little forest is composed of twenty Cedars of a prodigious size, so large indeed that the finest Planes, Sycamores, and other large trees which we had seen could not be compared with them. Besides these principal Cedars, there were a great number of lesser ones, and some very small, mingled with the large trees, or in little clumps near them. They differed not in their foliage, which resembles the Juniper, and is green throughout the year: but the great Cedars spread at their summit and form a perfect round, whereas the small ones rise in a pyramidal form like the Cypress. Both diffuse the same pleasant odour; the large ones only yield fruit, a large cone in shape almost like that of the Pine, but of a browner colour, and compacter shell. It gives a very pleasant odour, and contains a sort of thick and transparent balm, which oozes out thro' small apertures, and falls drop by drop. This fruit which it is difficult to separate from the stalk, contains a nut like that of the Cypress; it grows at the end of the boughs, and turns its point upwards.

The nature of this tree is not to elevate its trunk, or the part between the root and the first branches; for the largest Cedars which we saw did not in the height of their trunks exceed six or seven feet. From this low but enormously thick body, prodigious branches rise, spreading as they rise, and forming by the disposition of their boughs and leaves which point upward, a sort of wheel which appears to be the work of art. The bark of the cedar, except at the trunk, is smooth and shining, of a brown colour. Its wood white and soft immediately under the bark, but hard and red within, and very bitter, which renders it incorruptible and almost immortal. A fragrant gum issues from the tree.

The largest Cedar which we measured was seven feet in circumference, wanting two inches, and the whole extent of its branches, which it was easy to measure from their perfect roundness, formed a circumference of about 120 feet.

The Patriarch of the Maronites, fully persuaded of the rarity of these Trees, and wishing by the preservation of those that remain to shew his respect for a forest so celebrated in Scripture has pronounced canonical pains, and even excommunication against any Christians who shall dare to cut them; scarcely will he permit a little to be sometimes taken for Crucifixes and little tabernacles in the chapels of our Missionaries.

The Maronites themselves have such a veneration for these Cedars, that on the day of Transfiguration they celebrate the festival under them with great solemnity, the Patriarch officiates and says Mass pontifically, and among other exercises of devotion they particularly honour the Virgin Mary there, and sing her praises, because she is compared to the Cedars of Lebanon, and Lebanon itself used as a metaphor for the mother of Christ.

The Maronites say that the snows have no sooner begun to fall than these Cedars, whose boughs in their infinite number are all so equal in height that they appear to have been shorn, and form, as we have said, a sort of wheel or parasol,—than these Cedars, I say, never fail at that time to change their figure. The branches which before spread themselves rise insensibly, gathering together it may be said, and turn their points upward towards Heaven, forming altogether a pyramid. It is Nature, they say, who inspires this movement, and makes them assume a new shape, without which these Trees never could sustain the immense weight of snow, remaining for so long a time.

I have procured more particular information of this fact, and it has been confirmed by the testimony of many persons, who have often witnessed it. This is what the Secretary of the Maronite Patriarch wrote to me in one of his letters, which I think it right to give in his own words. Cedri Libani quas plantavit Deus, ut Psalmist: loquitur, sitae sunt in planitie quâdam, aliquantulum infra altissimum Montis-Libani cacumen, ubi tempore hyemali maxima nivium quantitas descendit, tribusque & ultra, mensibus mordaciter dominatur. Cedri in altum ascendunt extensis tamen ramis in gyrum solo parallelis, confioientibus suo gyro fere umbellam solarem. Sed superveniente nive, quia coacervaretur in magnâ quantitate eos desuper, neque possent pati tantum pondus tanto tempore premens, sine certo fractionis discrimine, Natura, rerum omnium provida mater, ipsis concessit, ut adveniente hyeme & descendente nive, statim rami in altum assurgant, & secum invicem uniti constituant quasi conum, ut melius sese ab adveniente hoste tueantur. Naturá enim ipsâ verum est, virtutem quamlebet unitam simul reddi fortiorem.

The Cedars of Lebanon, which, as the Psalmist says, God himself planted, are situated in a little plain, somewhat below the loftiest summit of mount Lebanon, where in the winter a great quantity of snow falls, and continues for three months, or longer. The Cedars are high, but their boughs spread out parallel with the ground into a circle, forming almost a shield against the sun. But when the snow falls, which would be heaped upon them in so great a quantity, that they could not endure such a weight so long a time, without the certain danger of breaking, Nature, the provident mother of all, has endued them with power, that when the winter comes and the snow descends, their boughs immediately rise, and uniting together form a cone, that they may be the better defended from the coming Enemy. For in Nature itself it is true, that virtue as it is united, becomes stronger.

[166] The Coffee plant is about the size of the orange tree, the flower in colour, size, and smell, resembles the white jessamine, the berry is first green, then red, in which ripe state it is gathered.

Olearius's description of Coffee is amusing. "They drink a certain black water which they call Cahwa, made of a fruit brought out of Egypt, and which is in colour like ordinary wheat, and in taste like Turkish wheat, and is of the bigness of a little bean. They fry, or rather burn it in an iron pan without any liquor, beat it to powder, and boyling it with fair water, they make this drink thereof, which hath as it were the taste of a burnt crust, and is not pleasant to the palate.

Amb. Travels.

[167] It is well known how much the Orientalists are addicted to this pretended science. There is a curious instance of public folly in Sir John Chardin's travels.

"Sephie-Mirza was born in the year of the Egire 1057. For the superstition of the Persians will not let us know the month or the day. Their addiction to Astrology is such that they carefully conceal the moments of their Princes birth, to prevent the casting their nativities, where they might meet perhaps with something which they should be unwilling to know."

At the coronation of this Prince two Astrologers were to be present, with an Astrolabe in their hands, to take the fortunate hour, as they term it, and observe the lucky moments that a happy constellation should point out for proceedings of that importance.

Sephie-Mirza having by debauchery materially injured his health, the Chief Physician was greatly alarmed, "in regard his life depended upon the King's, or if his life were spared yet he was sure to lose his estate and his liberty, as happens to all those who attend the Asiatic Sovereigns, when they die under their care. The Queen Mother too accused him of treason or ignorance, believing that since he was her Son's Physician he was obliged to cure him. This made the Physician at his wits end, so that all his receipts failing him, he bethought himself of one that was peculiarly his own invention, and which few physicians would ever have found out, as not being to be met with neither in Galen nor Hippocrates. What does he then do, but out of an extraordinary fetch of his wit, he begins to lay the fault upon the stars and the King's Astrologers, crying out that they were altogether in the wrong, that if the King lay in a languishing condition and could not recover his health it was because they had failed to observe the happy hour, or the Aspect of a fortunate constellation at the time of his coronation." The stratagem succeeded, the King was recrowned and by the new name of Solyman!

Chardin.

[168] We have now to refute their errour who are persuaded that Brazen Heads made under certain constellations may give answers, and be as it were guides and counsellors, upon all occasions, to those that had them in their possession. Among these is one Yepes who affirms that Henry de Villeine made such a one at Madrid, broken to pieces afterwards by order of John 2. King of Castile. The same thing is affirmed by Bartholomew Sibillus, and the Author of the Image of the World, of Virgil; by William of Malmsbury of Sylvester; by John Gower of Robert of Lincoln; by the common people of England of Roger Bacon; and by Tostatus Bishop of Avilla, George of Venice, Delrio, Sibillus, Raguseus, Delancre and others, too many to mention, of Albertus Magnus; who as the most expert, had made an entire man of the same metal, and had spent thirty years without any interruption in forming him under several aspects and constellations. For example, he formed the eyes, according to the said Tostatus in his commentaries upon Exodus, when the Sun was in a sign of the Zodiac correspondent to that part, casting them out of divers metals mixt together and mark'd with the characters of the same signs and planets, and their several and necessary aspects. The same method he observed in the head, neck, shoulders, thighs, and legs, all which were fashioned at several times, and being put and fastened together in the form of a man, had the faculty to reveal to the said Albertus the solutions of all his principal difficulties. To which they add (that nothing be lost of the story of the statue) that it was battered to pieces by St. Thomas, meerely because he could not endure its excesse of prating.

But to give a more rational account of this Androides of Albertus, as also of all these miraculous heads, I conceive the original of this fable may well be deduced from the Teraph of the Hebrews, by which as Mr. Selden affirms, many are of opinion, that we must understand what is said in Genesis concerning Laban's Gods, and in the first book of Kings concerning the image which Michol put into the bed in David's place. For R. Eleazar holds that it was made of the head of a male child, the first born and that dead-born, under whose tongue they applyed a lamen of Gold, whereon were engraved the characters and inscriptions of certain planets, which the Jews superstitiously wandered up and down with, instead of the Urim and Thummim, or the Ephod of the High Priest. And that this original is true and well deduced, there is a manifest indicium, in that Henry D'Assia, and

Bartholomæus Sibillus affirm, that the Androides of Albertus, and the Head made by Virgil, were composed of flesh and bone, yet not by nature, but by art. But this being judged impossible by modern Authors, and the vertue of Images, Annulets, and planetary Sigills being in great reputation, men have thought ever since (taking their opinion from Trismegistus affirming in his Asclepion, that of the Gods, some were made by the Sovereign God, and others by men, who, by some art, had the power to unite the invisible Spirits to things visible and corporeal, as is explained at large by St. Augustine) that such figures were made of copper or some other metal, whereon men had wrought under some favourable Aspects of Heaven and the planets.

My design is not absolutely to deny that he might compose some head or statue of man, like that of Memnon, from which proceeded a small sound and pleasant noise, when the rising Sun came by his heat to rarify and force out, by certain small conduits, the air which in the cold of the night was condensed within it. Or haply they might be like those statues of Boetius, whereof Cassiodorus speaking said, Metalla mugiunt, Diomedis in ære grues buccinant, ænus anguis insibilat, aves simulatæ fritinniunt, et quæ propriam vocem nesciunt, ab ære dulcedinem probantur emittere cantilenæ; for such I doubt not but may be made by the help of that part of Natural Magic which depends on the Mathematics.

History of Magic.

The title page to this book is wanting;, but the Epistle Dedicatory is signed J. Davies. By the stile, spelling, and extensive reading of the author, it appears to be a work of the last century.

[169] This Table is suspended in the Seventh Heaven, and guarded from the Demons, lest they should change or corrupt any thing thereon. Its length is so great as is the space between Heaven and Earth, its breadth equal to the distance from the East to the West, and it is made of one pearl. The divine Pen was created by the finger of God: that also is of pearls, and of such length and breadth that a swift horse could scarcely gallop round it in five hundred years. It is so endowed, that self-moved it writes all things, past, present, and to come. Light, is its ink, and the language which it uses, only the Angel Seraphael understands.

Maracci.

[170] They celebrate the night Léïleth-ul-beraeth on the 15th of the month of Schabann, with great apprehension and terror, because they consider it as the tremendous night on which the angels Kiramenn-keatibinn, placed on each side of mankind to write down their good and bad actions, deliver up their books and receive fresh ones for the continuance of the same employment. It is believed also, that on that night the archangel Azrail, the angel of death, gives up also his records and receives another book in which are written the names of all those destined to die in the following year.

D'Ohsson.

[171] The Balance of the Dead is an article in almost every creed. Mohammed borrowed it from the Persians. I know not from whence the Monks introduced it; probably they were ignorant enough to have invented the obvious fiction.

In the Vision of Thurcillus the ceremony is accurately described. "At the end of the north wall, within the church, sate St. Paul, and opposite him, without, was the Devil and his Angels. At the feet of the Devil a burning pit flamed up, which was the mouth of the Pit of Hell. A Balance equally poised, was fixed upon the wall between the Devil and the Apostle, one scale hanging before each. The Apostle had two weights, a greater and a less, all shining and like gold, and the Devil also had two smoky and black ones. Therefore the Souls that were all black came one after another, with great fear and trembling, to behold the weighing of their good and evil works: for these weights weighed the works of all the souls, according to the good or evil which they had done. When the scale inclined to the Apostle, he took the Soul, and introduced it thro' the Eastern gate, into the fire of Purgatory, that there it might expiate its crimes. But when the scale inclined and sunk towards the Devil, then he and his Angels snatched the soul miserably howling and cursing the father and mother that begot it to eternal torments, and cast it with laughter and grinning into the deep and fiery pit which was at the feet of the Devil. Of this Balance of good and evil much may be found in the writings of the holy Fathers."

Matthew Paris.

"Concerning the salvation of Charlemagne, Archbishop Turpin, a man of holy life, wrote thus. "I, Turpin, Archbishop of Rheims, being in my chamber, in the city of Vienna, saying my prayers, saw a legion of Devils in the air, who were making a great noise. I adjured one of them to tell me from whence they came, and wherefore they made so great an uproar. And he replied that they came from Aix la Chapelle, where a great Lord had died, and that they were returning in anger because they had not been able to carry away his soul. I asked him who the great Lord was, and why they had not been able to carry away his soul. He replied that it was Charlemagne, and that Saint Jago had been greatly against them. And I asked him how St. Jago had been against them; and he replied, we were weighing the good and the evil which he had done in this world, and Saint Jago brought so much timber and so many stones from the churches which he had founded in his name, that they greatly over-balanced all his evil works; and so we had no power over his soul. And having said this the Devil disappeared."

We must understand from this vision of Archbishop Turpin, that they who build or repair churches in this world, erect resting places and inns for their salvation.

Historia do Imperador Carlos Magno, & dos Doze Pares de França.

Two other corollaries follow from the vision. The Devil's way home from Aix la Chapelle lay thro' Vienna;—and as churches go by weight, an architect of Sir John Vanbrugh's school should always be employed."

This Balance of the Dead was an easy and apt metaphor, but clumsily imagined as an actual mode of trial.

"For take thy Ballaunce, if thou be so wise,
"And weigh the winde that under heaven doth blow;
"Or weigh the light that in the East doth rise:
"Or weigh the thought that from man's mind doth flow
"But if the weight of these thou canst not show,
"Weigh but one word which from thy lips doth fall."

Spenser.

[172] This double meaning is in the spirit of oracular prediction. The classical reader will remember the equivocations of Apollo, the fable of the young man and the Lion in the tapestry will be more generally recollected: we have many buildings in England to which this story has been applied,— Cook's Folly near Bristol derives its name from a similar tradition.

The History of the Buccaneers affords a remarkable instance of prophecy occasioning its own accomplishment.

"Before my first going over into the South-Seas with Captain Sharp (and indeed before any Privateers, at least since Drake and Oxenham) had gone that way which we afterwards went, except La Sound, a French Captain, who by Capt. Wright's instructions had ventured as far as Cheapo town with a body of men, but was driven back again, I being then on board Capt. Coxon, in company with three or four more Privateers, about four leagues to the East of Portobel, we took the packets bound thither from Carthagena. We opened a great quantity of the Merchant's letters, and found the contents of many of them to be very surprizing, the Merchants of several parts of Old-Spain thereby informing their correspondents of Panama, and elsewhere, of a certain prophecy that went about Spain that year, the tenor of which was, that there would be English privateers that year in the West-Indies, who would make such great discoveries, as to open a door into the South-Seas; which they supposed was fastest shut: and the letters were accordingly full of cautions to their friends to be very watchful and careful of their coasts.

This door they spake of we all concluded must be the passage over land through the country of the Indians of Darien, who were a little before this become our friends, and had lately fallen out with the Spaniards, breaking off the intercourse which for some time they had with them: And upon calling also to mind the frequent invitations we had from those Indians a little before this time, to pass through their Country, and fall upon the Spaniards in the South-Seas, we from henceforward began to entertain such thoughts in earnest, and soon came to a resolution to make those attempts which we afterwards did with Capt. Sharp, Coxon, &c. So that the taking these letters gave the first life to those bold undertakings: And we took the advantage of the fears the Spaniards were in from that prophecy, or probable conjecture, or whatever it were; for we sealed up most of the letters again, and sent them ashore to Portobel.

Dampier.

[173] The Souls of the Blessed are supposed by some of the Mohammedans to animate green Birds in the Groves of Paradise. Was this opinion invented to conciliate the Pagan Arabs, who believed, that of the Blood near the dead person's brain was formed a Bird named Hamah, which once in a hundred years visited the sepulchre?

To this there is an allusion in the Moallakat. "Then I knew with certainty, that, in so fierce a contest with them, many a heavy blow would make the Perched Birds of the Brain fly quickly from every Skull."

Poem of Antara.

In the Bahar-Danush, Parrots are called the green-vested resemblers of Heaven's dwellers. The following passages in the same work may perhaps allude to the same superstition, or perhaps are merely metaphorical, in the usual stile of its true Oriental bombast. "The Bird of Understanding fled from the nest of my brain." "My joints and members seemed as if they would separate from each other, and the Bird of Life would quit the nest of my Body." "The Bird of my Soul became a captive in the net of her glossy ringlets."

I remember in a European Magazine two similar lines by the Author of the Lives of the Admirals.

My beating Bosom is a well-wrought cage,

Whence that sweet Gold-finch Hope shall ne'er elope!

The Grave of Francisco Jorge, the Maronite Martyr, was visited by two strange Birds of unusual size. No one knew whence they came. They emblemed, says Vasconcellos, the purity and the indefatigable activity of his soul.

The inhabitants of Otaheite have assigned a less respectable part of the Body, as the Seat of the Soul.

The disembowelling of the body there, is always performed in great secrecy, and with much religious superstition. The bowels are, by these people, considered as the immediate organs of sensation, where the first impressions are received, and by which all the operations of the mind are carried on: it is therefore natural to conclude, that they may esteem, and venerate the intestines, as bearing the greatest affinity to the immortal part. I have frequently held conversations on this subject, with a view to convince them, that all intellectual operations were carried on in the head; at which they would generally smile, and intimate, that they had frequently seen men recover whose skulls had been fractured, and whose heads had otherways been much injured; but that, in all cases in which the intestines had been wounded, the persons on a certainty died. Other arguments they would also advance in favour of their belief; such as the effect of fear, and other passions, which caused great agitation and uneasiness, and would sometimes produce sickness at the stomach, which they attributed intirely to the action of the bowels.

Vancouver.

[174] When Hosein the son of Ali was sick of a grievous disorder, he longed for a pomegranate, tho' that fruit was not then in season. Ali went out, and diligently enquiring found a single one in the possession of a Jew. As he returned with it, a sick man met him and begged half the pomegranate, saying it would restore his health. Ali gave him half, and when he had eaten it, the man requested he would give him the other half, the sooner to complete his recovery. Ali benignantly complied, returned to his son and told him what had happened, and Hosein approved what his father had done.

Immediately behold a miracle! as they were talking together the door was gently knocked at. He ordered the woman servant to go there, and she found a man, of all men the most beautiful, who had a plate in his hand covered with green silk, in which were ten pomegranates. The woman was astonished at the beauty of the man and of the pomegranates, and she took one of them and hid it, and carried the other nine to Aly, who kissed the present. When he had counted them he found that one was wanting, and said so to the servant, she confessed that she had taken it on account of its excellence, and Ali gave her her liberty. The Pomegranates were from Paradise, Hosein was cured of his disease only by their odour, and rose up immediately, recovered, and in full strength.

Maracci.

I suspect, says Maracci, that this is a true miracle wrought by some Christian Saint, and falsely attributed to Ali. However this may be, it does not appear absurd that God should by some especial favour reward an act of remarkable charity even in an Infidel, as he has sometimes by a striking chastisement punished enormous crimes. But the assertion that the Pomegranates were sent from Paradise, exposes the fable.

Maracci after detailing and ridiculing the Mohammedan miracles, contrasts with them in an appendix a few of the real and permanent miracles of Christianity which are proved by the testimony of the whole world. He selects five as examples. 1. The Chapel of Loretto, brought by angels from Nazareth to Illyricum, and from Illyricum to Italy; faithful messengers having been sent to both places, and finding in both its old foundations, in dimensions and materials, exactly corresponding.

2. The cross of St. Thomas in Urbe Malipuritana (Masulipatan) in the E. Indies. A Bramin, as the Saint was extended upon his cross in prayer, slew him. On the anniversary of his martyrdom, during the celebration of Mass, the cross gradually becomes luminous, till it shines one white glory. At elevating the host it resumes its natural colour, and sweats blood profusely, in which the faithful dip their clothes, by which many miracles are wrought.

3. Certissimum quia evidentissimum—at Barii (Bari on the Adriatic) in Apulia a liquor flows from the bones of St. Nicholas, they call it St. Nicholas's manna, which being preserved in bottles never corrupts or breeds worms—except the possessor be corrupt himself—and daily it works miracles.

4. At Tolentinum (Tolentino in the Marche of Anconia) the arms of St. Nicholas swell with blood, and pour out copious streams—when any great calamity impends over Christendom.

5. The blood of St. Jaunarius at Naples.

These, says Maracci, are miracula perseverantia, permanent miracles—and it cannot be said as of the Mohammedan ones, that they are tricks of the Devil.

[175] In the Bahar-Danush the Simorg is mentioned as a genus—not an individual, this is heresy,—the unity of the Simorg being expressed in all the books of canonical Romance.

The Simorg is a monstrous Bird like a Griffin; in the History of Caherman, he is made to say, That he had existed through all the revolutions of ages and of created things, which passed before the time of Adam. These created things were reasonable beings, but had not human shape. They were governed by the various Solomons mentioned in the note Vol. I. Page 214.

[176] Araf is a place between the Paradise and the Hell of the Mohammedans, some deem it a veil of separation, some a strong wall; others hold it to be a Purgatory in which those believers will remain, whose good and evil works have been so equal that they were neither virtuous enough to enter Paradise, nor guilty enough to be condemned to the fire of Hell. From thence they see the glory of the Blessed, and are near enough to congratulate them; but their ardent desire to partake the same happiness becomes a great pain. At length at the Day of Judgement, when all men before they are judged, shall be cited to render homage to their Creator, those who are here confined shall prostrate themselves before the face of the Lord, in adoration: and by this act of religion which shall be accounted a merit, the number of their good works will exceed their evil ones, and they will enter into glory.

Saadi says that Araf appears a hell to the happy, and a Paradise to the damned.

D'Herbelot.

The Fall of Robespierre (1794)

Joan of Arc (1796)
Icelandic Poetry, or The Edda of Sæmund (1797)
Poems (1797–1799)
Letters Written During a Short Residence in Spain and Portugal (1797)
St. Patrick's Purgatory (1798)
After Blenheim (1798)
The Devil's Thoughts (1799). Revised edition published in 1827 as "The Devil's Walk".
English Eclogues (1799)
The Old Man's Comforts and How He Gained Them (1799)
Thalaba the Destroyer (1801)
The Inchcape Rock (1802)
Madoc (1805)
Letters from England: By Don Manuel Alvarez Espriella (1807), the observations of a fictitious Spaniard.
Chronicle of the Cid. Translated from the Spanish (1808)
The Curse of Kehama (1810)
History of Brazil (3 volumes) (1810–1819)
The Life of Horatio, Lord Viscount Nelson (1813)
Roderick the Last of the Goths (1814)
Sir Thomas Malory's Le Morte D'Arthur (1817)
Wat Tyler: A Dramatic Poem (1817)
Cataract of Lodore (1820)
The Life of Wesley; and Rise and Progress of Methodism (2 volumes) (1820)
What Are Little Boys Made Of? (1820)
The Vision of Judgement (1821)
History of the Peninsular War, 1807-1814 (3 volumes) (1823-1832)
Sir Thomas More; or, Colloquies on the Progress and Prospects of Society (1829)
The Works of William Cowper (15 vols.) (Editor) (1833-1837)
Lives of the British Admirals, with an Introductory View of the Naval History of England (5 volumes) (1833-40); republished as "English Seamen" in 1895.
The Doctor (7 volumes) (1834-1847). Includes The Story of the Three Bears (1837).
The Poetical Works of Robert Southey, Collected by Himself (1837)

Printed in Great Britain
by Amazon

25436684R10126